Fine WoodWorking
on Making and Modifying Machines

Fine WoodWorking on Making and Modifying Machines

29 articles selected by
the editors of
Fine Woodworking
magazine

The Taunton Press

Cover photo by Jerry D. Martini

© 1986 by The Taunton Press, Inc.

First printing: January 1986
International Standard Book Number: 0-918804-43-4
Library of Congress Catalog Card Number: 85-51880
Printed in the United States of America

A FINE WOODWORKING Book

FINE WOODWORKING® is a trademark of The Taunton Press, Inc.,
registered in the U.S. Patent and Trademark Office.

The Taunton Press, Inc.
63 South Main Street
Box 355
Newtown, Connecticut 06470

Contents

Introduction

There's a heavy solidity about factory-made woodworking machines, all engineered cast iron and machined aluminum. They gleam with an evolved completeness, and they do not seem subject to change.

This book defies the finality of manufactured machinery for woodworking. You can modify your machinery, and you can build your own woodworking machines.

The very idea of making your own machinery may seem daringly audacious, but why not? The keys are the modern electric motor, readily available in any size, the ball-bearing pillow-block, and the common bolt. We can use the motor to whirl any kind of cutter. Then we devise auxiliary mechanisms for managing the cutter's movement into the workpiece, like a boring machine, or for controlling the work's movement into the cutter, like a tablesaw with fences. And then there is the lathe which, uniquely, rotates the workpiece into a stationary cutter.

In 29 articles reprinted from the first ten years of *Fine Woodworking* magazine, authors who are also craftsmen show how the ordinary woodworker can modify machinery to suit his own purposes, and can build machinery to suit his own tastes and needs. There are tablesaws and panel saws, router thicknessers and thickness sanders, shapers, lathes and sharpening machines, even a wooden-bed jointer.

A companion volume in this series, *Fine Woodworking on Woodworking Machines,* discusses how to purchase, maintain and use conventional, factory-made machinery. This book is for those who would go further.

John Kelsey, editor

Making Your Own Machines
Learn what you need to know, then experiment

by Giles Gilson

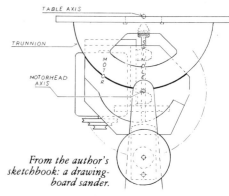

From the author's sketchbook: a drawing-board sander.

If you need a machine you can't afford or are frustrated by back ordering, poor design or malfunction caused by poor quality control, you should consider building the machine yourself. It will test your creativity, ingenuity and ability to scrounge. It will require time and possibly study, but the result can be a machine custom-built to meet your needs.

Don't be discouraged by someone else's reservations. A good way to start is first to find out what you need to know, second, to get that information and third, to practice applying it. Machines are generally simple. They have a basic function and accessories that support that function. Most woodworking machines simply rotate a cutting tool into the work. Different structures control the speed or orientation of the cutter; hold, move or guide the work; protect the operator; and generally hold the whole thing together. By studying its separate parts, you can uncover a machine's principles.

I have built a number of machines and modified several more; these illustrate what experimentation and makeshift applications can yield. Combining performance, accuracy, safety and convenience is a creative task. If your materials are properly chosen and your construction is sound, your home-built machine can be better than a store-bought one.

In design work, decisions are most easily made through drawings. Some people prefer a detailed technical drawing in which most of the problems can be worked out; others draw only enough to establish reference points or to determine shapes. It is not necessary to use conventional symbols or elaborate instruments. If you plan to show your drawing to designers or suppliers, however, you must be sure they understand your terminology. The basic tool is the standard foot ruler, with which several scale sizes can be read directly; at ¼ size, for example, 3 in. = 1 ft., and ¹⁄₁₆ in. = ¼ in. You'll also need a compass, a 30°-60° triangle, and a protractor. The edges of precut paper are usually square and can be used as references from which to measure.

It may help to make a model in conjunction with the drawing. This is educational and entertaining, and when you get frustrated, you can smash it. Models help you visualize. They point out problems that may not show on the drawing, so there are fewer bugs to be worked out of the final product.

Average auto-maintenance tools will do in most cases. In addition, you should have a set of taps and dies, calipers, some metal snips, spare hacksaw blades, a dial indicator and a surface gauge. For operations that you are not equipped to handle, you can either get the tools as you need them, rent them or farm out that part of the work.

One advantage the woodworker has is that some of his machines need not be as rigid as those used for metal; therefore machine bodies and stands can be made of non-ferrous materials. Wood, including plywood and composition board, is convenient; aluminum and fiberglass might work in some applications. A new material, used in conjunction with fiberglass, is almost as strong as steel, but can be worked with carbide cutters. It's a single-component epoxy called Arnox. I have band-sawn and lathe-turned sample sheets, tubes, and rods, and it has possibilities for many machine parts, including shafts, gears, plates and pulleys. General Electric (Plastics Div., 1 Plastics Ave., Pittsfield, Mass. 01201) was developing Arnox; they have since decided it doesn't suit their needs, and are looking for a buyer for the technology, so it may become available later. In any case, don't ignore new products as you work out your own plans and designs.

One of my favorite materials for models and light-duty machinery structures is MD-44. It is produced by Masonite Corp. and comes in the same sizes as plywood, but is cheaper. It has about the same strength as fir ply, has a smooth finish and holds a clean edge when machined. It can be sculpted, but because the surfaces are tempered, it may chip a little near the faces. If you paint MD-44 or laminate it with plastic or sheet metal, you must do both faces to prevent warping.

Don't get locked into buying only new parts and materials. Wood and composition boards are often in the shop as leftovers from jobs. Metal can be obtained in small quantities and odd shapes from scrapyards. Machine parts can be found in scrapyards and repair shops, or adapted from other applications. An inventory of hardware should be kept in categories: nuts and bolts, handwheels, pulleys and belts. These can be collected over a period of time the same way you collect wood. You do not have to seal and sticker hardware; it is usually dry.

Some design considerations are evident right away, and some may not be. Often convenience to the operator is overlooked. Avoid putting adjustment controls underneath or behind the machine where they are awkward and dangerous to reach for. On some machines, there is no choice, but if there is an alternative, use the most convenient location. This also applies to accessory storage. How often have you had to use a machine whose table was too low or too high? In general, tables, lathe spindles (not ways) and the like should be the same height as your elbows. Make tables large enough for the work you plan to do, or provide for extensions.

Versatility is important as long as it does not require too much time to change from one mode to another and does not compromise performance. Adjustments should be fast and easy. Movable parts should be clamped with devices that are quickly released without additional tools.

When designing a machine, be aware of industry standards. Find out what sizes and methods are most commonly used for attachments. If you are building a disc sander and want to buy the backing disc instead of making it, what size is its centerhole? How is it fastened? These things determine shaft size. If you are building a lathe, what is the most com-

Giles Gilson, a designer/sculptor, lives in Schenectady, N.Y.

From *Fine Woodworking* magazine (March 1980) 21:43-46

mon spindle thread for faceplates? Machinery catalogs usually mention spindle diameters, thread pitches, belt sizes, etc.

The choice of bearings is important. Think about how the workloads will be distributed from the shaft through the bearings to the structure of the machine. Which way will the work push against the spindle? What pressure is the drive belt putting on the shaft? What is the maximum speed? Consider the environment of the machine. What kind of foreign material will be present? Normal sawing produces fine chips as well as dust, turning produces curls and dust, and sanding produces abrasive grit and dust. What will these substances do to machinery?

Oil-impregnated bronze (Oilite) inserts are made as a single piece and called sleeves, or as two halves usually called clamshells. They are good for many applications, and also inexpensive and quiet. However, they should be used only on precision-ground shafts and often must be align-bored or reamed to size after installation. This can be done by a machine shop if you do not have the facilities.

Anti-friction bearings are generally noisier than sliding types. They are more efficient, however, and sometimes require much less power to run. The most common type of anti-friction bearing is a ball bearing. These withstand side-loading well. Needle or roller bearings are simply a series of cylindrical rollers that replace the balls in a bearing. They sometimes use the shaft as an inner race, and often have no retainer, which means the rollers must be individually placed between the shaft and the outer race. This type of bearing is used where thickness is a problem. A variation on the ball and needle bearing is the thrust bearing, used to handle pressure along the centerline of a shaft. An example is the guide wheel behind the blade on most bandsaws. Thrust bearings use balls, tapered rollers arranged radially, or are simply a Babbitt bearing or bronze shoulder.

Tapered roller bearings handle both axial thrust and side loads. They are quiet, but require preloading. This means they must have a specified amount of pressure holding them in place. A shoulder or snap ring supports one race while the adjustable support for the other is set to apply the preload and locked in place. The most common method of installing bearings designed for a press fit is to freeze the shaft and heat the bearing in oil to about 200°—do not heat the bearing directly.

For mounting bearings, a pillow block is convenient. A self-aligning pillow block with a sealed ball bearing is shown in the photo at center on page 4. The grease fitting in the housing allows lubrication without having to take things apart. The advantage of a self-aligning pillow block is that if the block can't be mounted exactly perpendicular to the shaft, the bearing will line up properly anyway. The outside of the bearing fits inside a spherical casing, allowing the bearing to be oriented to the shaft even if the block is not. Pillow blocks are made with almost any kind of bearing. You must specify rigid or self-aligning, and bearing type. Bearing distributors and their catalogs are helpful. Check the Yellow Pages under "Bearings."

The best operating speed for most cutting tools has been established and can be found in owner's manuals, from manufacturers, repair shops or in reference books. There are cases, though, where experimentation will show that higher or lower speeds are more effective. Variable speed may be important. A pair of step pulleys can allow three or four speeds

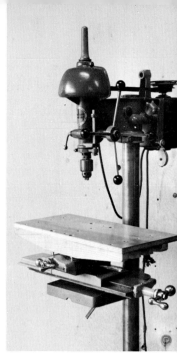

Band-saw accessories, left, include plywood cover latched with Volkswagen convertible-roof holddown and blade guide from roller bearings, angle iron, nuts and bolts. Right, cross-slide and compound-angle jig cannibalized from metal lathe are mounted on drill press.

and, if necessary, a jack shaft can be added to increase the speed choices.

To find the pulley or gear sizes needed to attain a desired spindle RPM, you must know the motor speed. This is most often either 1725 or 3450 RPM. Divide the higher speed by the lower—this gives the ratio. Then use a pair of pulleys whose diameters establish this ratio. For example, if the motor speed is 1725 RPM and the desired spindle speed is 431 RPM, 1725 ÷ 431 = 4.0023, or for practical purposes, 4. The ratio is 4:1. One pulley diameter must be four times the other. Since the spindle is to turn more slowly than the motor, the smaller pulley goes on the motor. Usually the speeds need not be exact. If you want 1200 RPM and it's easy to get 1050 RPM, 1050 RPM will probably do. Many gadgets and accessories have maximum speed ratings. Don't exceed them.

Align the pulleys with a straightedge to be sure they are in the same plane and neither is tilted in relation to the other. Bear in mind that V-belts will not bend around very small pulleys. If your calculations call for a small pulley, either find a belt that will make the bend, or enlarge both pulleys.

You will have to decide how to fasten the parts of your contraption. Welding is strong and can save space, if you are equipped to do it or can have it done, but it is difficult to disassemble welded parts. Be sure to allow for changes you may want to make later. Rivets do the same thing as nuts and bolts, but also require special equipment and are difficult to remove. They do not vibrate loose though, and look better. Pop rivets are good for some applications because they are easy to use and readily available.

Threaded fasteners are the most common choice for assembly of parts. They are sturdy and they allow disassembly. They could be inconvenient, however, if used to hold often-moved accessories. Loosening nuts and bolts to remove a guard or change a sanding belt takes time. If a threaded fastener is needed, some convenience can be added by using handwheels, knobs or thumbscrews. Handwheels may be purchased, but they are easily made by burying a nut between two or three layers of plywood, then turning, using the nut (or a bolt threaded into it) as the center. A handwheel should be large enough for leverage and feel comfortable to hold. If the finish is too slick. . . well, you'll see.

Nonthreaded quick-release fasteners are excellent for holding accessories, but be sure they are strong enough for the application. Latches, buckles, lever and cam devices and Dzus fasteners are listed in industrial hardware catalogs, usually with their measurements and sometimes a technical drawing of their parts. An ideal application for these is guards for band saws and belt sanders, where quick removal can facilitate blade and belt changes. Lever-and-cam clamps are good for holding fences, trunnions, belt tensioners and stops. Dzus fasteners, a form of bayonet plug used primarily in the aircraft industry, hold sheet metal in place. A dime or quarter fits into the slotted, round head to release them. If you use them, keep your pockets full of change. Spring-loaded clamps serve well as depth gauges, such as the ones found on drill presses, and movable stops along fences. Refined adjustments could be built into stops with an added miniature fence and thumbscrew arrangement.

Don't neglect safety. Keep in mind that the structure of the machine must be able to withstand heavy impact, vibration and misuse. Think about what could happen if the cutter or blade suddenly flew off and hit someone. This becomes more important as the speeds get higher. Consult machine designers or mechanical engineers who are familiar with the type of machine you are building, especially if you are not certain the material will hold up.

Remember such things as inherent movement in materials. Wood shrinks and swells; bolts through wood may come loose. Check all materials for faults. Round sharp edges and corners—brackets sticking out or sheet-metal edges can easily cut you. Moving parts like to be covered whenever possible.

No vibration should be transmitted to the machine operator. If there is vibration caused by a malfunctioning part, it should be repaired or replaced. Vibration inherent in the machine can be damped with rubber mounting devices, or where applicable by counterbalancing. Noise should also be kept to a minimum. One way is to construct with wood, which will dampen sound, unless it is a thin panel walling a hollow. Cover resonating panels with sound-deadening material, or fix them with stiffeners.

Most of the time, you can use standard electrical parts. National and local codes show procedures and required precautions. Be certain to use wiring and parts that are rated for the current that the motor calls for. The open-frame motor shown below at right was used for experimental purposes only and has since been changed to a totally enclosed fan-cooled motor in accordance with national electrical codes.

Switches and connections should be mounted in containers, usually metal conduit boxes designed for this purpose. These should be enclosed to keep out dust and chips. Wood is an insulator, so extra shockproofing is an added feature of a wooden machine.

A drawing-board sander — Now let's look at an example of a homebuilt machine. I call this sander "drawing board" because with its table tilted, that's what it looks like. I designed it for light to medium duty, but made allowances for changes to heavier components. I had two functions in mind: light spindle-sanding and foamback-disc and drum finish-sanding. (For more on home-built disc and small drum sanders, see the articles on pages 42 through 45.) In the spindle-sanding mode, the motorhead and table can be tilted separately for beveling, or as a unit for comfort. The machine has two speeds, 2000 RPM for spindle-sanding and 550 RPM for finishing. I used both modes to make the sculpted boxes shown at the top of the opposite page, first the spindle to shape and sand the inside walls, then the disc to finish the outside contours to 320 grit.

I did the rough design in my spare time by sketching ideas and forming a basic concept of the major parts. I made re-

The drawing-board sander in spindle mode, left. The table, of aluminum-laminated MD-44, measures 24 in. by 24 in., and is 48 in. high when not tilted. The base consists of 2x6s covered with plywood, and the trunnions, fixed in position by tightening the handwheel, are birch ply. Center, the table is removed, the large birch-ply handwheel loosened and the spindle positioned horizontally to receive foam-backed discs or drums. Self-aligning pillow blocks bear the shaft. Right, the ⅛-HP motor fitted with pulleys yields 2000 RPM and 550 RPM at the spindle.

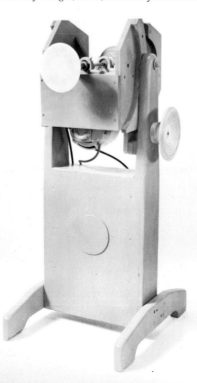

Left to right, boxes finished on the drawing-board sander: 'Geyser of Light,' 13½ in. by 9 in. by 5 in., birch ply, lauan, curly maple, East Indian rosewood; 'Antigravity Box #1: Dumping Karo Syrup on the Enemy,' 14½ in. by 13 in. by 7½ in., padauk, walnut, maple, lucite; and two views of 'Big Brother and Little Joe,' 20 in. by 13 in. by 4½ in., walnut, figured maple, rosewood.

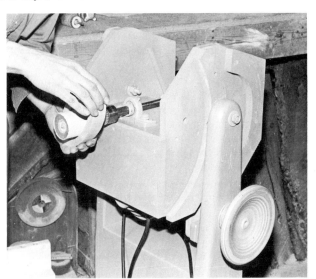

Left, drawing-board sander spindle tilts independently of table. Right, foam-backed drum finishes the inside of a piece.

finements during construction. Because it was necessary to find certain reference points, I made a more technical drawing at the workbench. Lines that didn't provide measurements I sketched freehand to save time. I built the motorhead and table without a preliminary model, although I made a mockup of the base. This proved valuable because it demonstrated where the machine would be unstable, showed some clearance problems and indicated just how comfortable the machine would be at the planned height.

The base is made of 2x6s with plywood covers rabbeted into the frame. The motorhead and table are made from MD-44 with gussets for rigidity. The trunnions are solid birch ply because it will wear well where the parts slide. The table top is aluminum laminated to the MD-44 and finished with a low-speed sanding disc, 320 grit. The large handwheel for the motorhead clamp is made from birch plywood scraps that were on their way to the woodstove. I used self-aligning, ball-bearing pillow blocks simply because they were easiest.

A homebuilt machine is often a prototype, especially if it incorporates new ideas, and therefore will have to be "field tested" to find out what the necessary improvements are. The drawing-board sander is in this stage now. I'm compiling notes evaluating the tool for durability and actual usefulness. Already there is a need for a taller spindle. This will require heavier mountings, which can be installed because of the allowances I made earlier. The machine serves its original pur-

pose well, but it can be changed to do more.

A valuable test is to have people experienced with similar machinery use and evaluate it. (Be sure they know it is experimental and that you know it is safe to use.) Others will spot things you might overlook. You may not want to bother making a change because you've already done a lot of work, and have become used to the tool the way it is—"it does the job," and "that can be done later." But will it? If you're taking the trouble to build a machine, why not build the best? □

Further Reading

Fundamentals of Tool Design, American Society of Tool and Mfg. Engineers, Prentice-Hall (out of print; check libraries). Principles and techniques of tool design: cutters, dies, jigs and fixtures. Recommended because the better you understand what the cutter is doing, the better you can design the machine to power it.

Mechanical Design of Machines, Siegel, Maleev and Hartman, Int'l Textbook Co., Scranton, Pa. (out of print). Highly technical. Has charts on shaft loading and describes forces on machine members.

Mechanical Engineering Design, Joseph E. Shigley, McGraw-Hill, New York, 1963; 4th ed. 1983. Starts with fundamentals, and though it becomes very technical, is easy to follow. Includes drawings of welded joints and a fine section on bearings.

Pictorial Handbook of Technical Devices, Otto B. Schwarz and Paul Grafstein, Chemical Publishing Co., New York, 1971. Valuable technical drawings of mechanical devices used in machinery; also includes structures, industrial processes and electrical parts.

Chainsaw Lumbermaking
Good-bye to vibration and fumes

by Will Malloff

Anyone can make lumber. All you need is a chainsaw attached to a mill, a straight board, a hammer and three nails. The board, positioned and nailed to a log, is a guide for the mill, which is adjusted to the depth of cut plus board thickness. The mill is pushed along the board and the sawbar pivoted out of the log at the end of the cut. That's all there is to it. But for efficient lumbermaking and the best results, there are a number of other considerations. Over the years I've developed and refined milling equipment and techniques, and now I feel I have the most effective, simplest system for ecological lumber production. To my surprise, a lot of people agree with me.

With a chainsaw, the logger decides what to harvest—trees that are mature, damaged or crowding other trees. A tree is felled and milled where it falls. Only usable lumber is removed, leaving the by-products to feed the land. Once you start to make your own lumber, you begin to notice usable wood everywhere you go. You're not restricted to milling only standing trees and you're not limited to working with the sizes and species available at the lumberyard.

EDITOR'S NOTE: This article is adapted from Will Malloff's *Chainsaw Lumbermaking,* The Taunton Press, Newtown, Conn. (hardcover, 224 pp.). Malloff, of Alert Bay, B.C., is a professional logger and lumbermaker. Besides describing and illustrating the milling process in great detail, Malloff's book explains how to choose and modify ripping chains and mills, and how to make milling gear for timber joinery, natural boat knees, and more.

Ripping chain—The most important factor in successful lumbermaking is properly prepared and maintained saw chain. Although you can use standard crosscutting chain, this will result in inefficient milling. You really need ripping chain, which you can make by modifying crosscut chain, using either a grinder or a hand file (figure 1). It's better to modify regular chain than skip-tooth chain or safety chain. I use a Stihl 090 saw for most of my milling, and I usually start with Oregon square-edge chisel chain (model 52L) made by Omark (Oregon Saw Chain Division, 9701 S.E. McLoughlin Blvd., Portland, Ore. 97222).

You'll find that a good disc-wheel chain grinder will soon pay for itself by its accuracy and speed in modifying and sharpening ripping chain. And one properly shaped grinding stone will do the work of several dozen hand files.

Chain modification—I grind my ripping chain cutters straight across the fronts with the round-edged grinding stone

Minimum milling: a chainsaw mill, a plank to guide the first cut, and a few nails to hold the plank on the log. Malloff, a chainsaw logger by profession, has improved every aspect of this setup, developing the rig shown on the following pages.

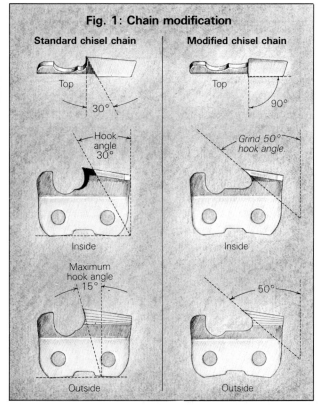

Fig. 1: Chain modification

Standard chisel chain

Top

30°

Hook angle 30°

Inside

Maximum hook angle 15°

Outside

Modified chisel chain

Top

90°

Grind 50° hook angle.

Inside

50°

Outside

Photos: Beth Erickson; drawings: Lee Hov

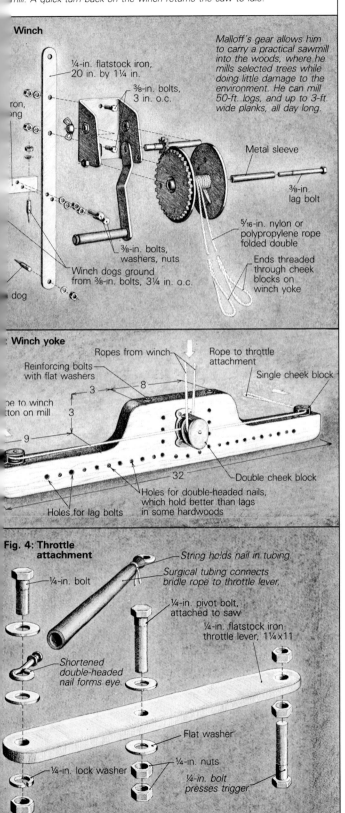

The winch ropes, fig. 2, pass through the cheek blocks on the yoke, fig. 3. One rope hooks to the nosebar end of the mill, the other to a short bridle rope, attached between the saw itself and the surgical tubing on the throttle attachment, fig. 4. As the winch ropes tighten, the attachment pivots, and the ¼-in. bolt on the end of the lever depresses the chainsaw's trigger switch to bring the saw to full throttle before forward pull is applied to the mill. A quick turn back on the winch returns the saw to idle.

Winch

¼-in. flatstock iron, 20 in. by 1¼ in.

⅜-in. bolts, 3 in. o.c.

Malloff's gear allows him to carry a practical sawmill into the woods, where he mills selected trees while doing little damage to the environment. He can mill 50-ft. logs, and up to 3-ft. wide planks, all day long.

Metal sleeve

⅜-in. lag bolt

5/16-in. nylon or polypropylene rope folded double

⅜-in. bolts, washers, nuts

Winch dogs ground from ⅜-in. bolts, 3¼ in. o.c.

Ends threaded through cheek blocks on winch yoke

dog

Winch yoke

Ropes from winch

Rope to throttle attachment

Reinforcing bolts with flat washers

Single cheek block

pe to winch ton on mill

3   8

3

9

32

Double cheek block

Holes for double-headed nails, which hold better than lags in some hardwoods

Holes for lag bolts

Fig. 4: Throttle attachment

String holds nail in tubing.

¼-in. bolt

Surgical tubing connects bridle rope to throttle lever.

¼-in. pivot bolt, attached to saw

¼-in. flatstock iron throttle lever, 1¼ x 11

Shortened double-headed nail forms eye.

Flat washer

¼-in. lock washer

¼-in. nuts

¼-in. bolt presses trigger.

---

adjusted 50° from vertical (40° from horizontal). Commercial sawmills grind their blades for circular saws, gangsaws and bandsaws this way for a smooth, fast cut. Adjust the grinder so the stone is 90° to the chain, then tilt the stone to a 50° hook angle. Mount your chain in the chain track and adjust the stone to grind off the entire angled edge of the cutter—no more and no less. It is critical that the teeth be the same length and that the depth gauges be filed evenly.

Hand-filing—Chain modification with a file guide and round file is essentially the same as with a grinder; but file a 45° hook angle on each cutter instead of a 50° hook. The round file leaves a hollow-ground edge; if the hook were filed to 50°, the cutting edge would be weakened. Because guides are normally set by the factory to cut a 5° hook angle, you have to shim the file under both clamps to lower it so it will make the 45° hook. Start off with the file diameter recommended for your chain, but switch to the next smaller size (1/32 in. less) when the chain's cutters are about half-worn.

Keep filing until the hook angle on the side of the cutter is 45° and the top plate is 90° across. The bottom of the cutter gullet should be just above the top of the drive link. At least two files will usually be necessary to modify one chain.

The winch and yoke—In lumbermaking, you normally have to push the mill and roaring chainsaw through a cut, breathing exhaust fumes and spitting out sawdust all the while. But with my setup (photo, next page), you can stand back from the noise and vibration, and move the saw through the cut with minimum labor—all you have to do is crank a winch handle. Besides the winch, you'll need a remote throttle attachment for your saw, winch buttons to hold the ropes, and a winch yoke to pull the mill straight. The yoke also helps keep the guide rails of the mill level on the top plank.

I use a small boat-trailer winch as the base mechanism (figure 2). Make winch dogs (spikes that attach the winch unit to the log) by tapering ⅜-in. bolts. Hold each bolt in the chuck of an electric hand drill and, with the drill switched on, grind the taper on a bench grinder.

Assemble the winch and mount the winch rope. Cut a length of ¼-in. or 5/16-in. nylon or polypropylene rope a little longer than double the length of the log you'll be milling, then splice or tie an eye to each end. Fold the rope in half and attach the fold to the winch drum. Later you'll thread the rope ends through the cheek blocks on the winch yoke (figure 3).

Throttle attachment—Because the operator is at one end of the log and the saw at the other when milling with my system, you need to build a remote throttle attachment to work the saw trigger (figure 4). This one is designed for a Stihl 090, so if you're using a different engine, you might have to adapt a little. The surgical tubing should be long enough (about 6 in. to 8 in.) to provide proper tension in both the open-throttle and closed-throttle positions. Through the saw handle, drill and tap a ¼-in. thread and mount the attachment by screwing the bolt into the hole and locking it with a nut and washer. I'll explain how to use this remote throttle attachment when we get to setting up.

Saw bridle button—I use a modified Granberg Mark III mill, but any mill should work. The winching rope is attached at one end to the mill and at the other end to the

---

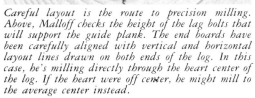

Careful layout is the route to precision milling. Above, Malloff checks the height of the lag bolts that will support the guide plank. The end boards have been carefully aligned with vertical and horizontal layout lines drawn on both ends of the log. In this case, he's milling directly through the heart center of the log. If the heart were off center, he might mill to the average center instead.

A yoke, fastened just below the line of cut, keeps the cut straight as Malloff cranks the winch, above. One rope is attached to the modified Granberg mill; the other rope is connected, by means of an adjustable bridle rope, to the saw itself and to a lever that controls its throttle. The mill, with its log-section counterweight, will be pulled to the end of the guide plank. Then the plank will be slid forward on the supporting lag bolts until it rests on the end board. The winch is attached to the plank itself, and the cut continues. Subsequent cuts don't require the plank and lags because the mill can ride directly on the flat-cut surface of the log. At left, with steel end dogs in place to control twisting, milling is well under way.

middle of a length of rope I call the bridle rope. One end of the bridle rope goes to the remote throttle attachment; the other end must attach to the saw. But since there's no place on the saw to accept a rope, you have to make a holding button. I call this the bridle button. On the Stihl 090, I substitute a $\frac{5}{16}$-in. by $1\frac{1}{2}$-in. bolt for the original shorter metric bolt in the handle to make this bridle button. This is the logical place for it, as the bolt is in a strong position on the saw and in the line of pull when winching through a cut.

End dogs—The inner tensions that have grown into a tree often make boards twist or bend while they're being sawn. This distortion can throw off a properly aligned milling system. So I've designed end dogs to help keep boards straight until the cut is complete—the dogs tack the board and log together, so the board can't deform during the cut (bottom photo, facing page).

The best end dogs can be forged from short pieces of automobile leaf spring, though other hardened steel would probably do as well. To make them, first round the ends of the spring stock. Then heat and bend the ends so that they are at right angles to the flat stock. Reheat the dog to a dull red, and allow it to cool slowly in the air. Grind the upturned ends from the outside to a sharp edge and then grind the edge straight across so that it is about $\frac{1}{32}$ in. to $\frac{1}{16}$ in. wide. End dogs with edges that are too sharp eventually deform and become difficult to drive.

I insert wooden kerf wedges every few feet in the cut. The wedges support the piece being milled and keep the kerf open, allowing the bar to travel freely. I also insert wedges behind the saw just before the end of the cut. This allows the mill to exit easily and eliminates end run-off. Six or eight wedges are enough for most jobs.

Setting up—Before you can begin to mill any lumber, you must establish a level surface on each log to guide the first cut. My system consists of a straight guide plank resting on end boards and pairs of leveled lag bolts placed along the length of the log. The wider the plank, the more support for the mill. The plank should also be thick enough to support the weight of the mill with minimum help from the lag bolts. The guide plank needn't be as long as the log, because you can mill in stages by sliding the plank off the end board and along the lag bolts as you go.

To stiffen the plank and help keep it straight, and to allow the plank to slide along the lag bolts without damage, attach two $\frac{3}{16}$-in., $1\frac{1}{2}$-in. by $1\frac{1}{2}$-in. angle irons to the plank edges, using countersunk screws about every 12 in.

The guide plank is supported at both ends of the log by end boards nailed or lag-bolted into the log end. The top edges of the end boards must be the same distance above horizontal index lines, reference points drawn on the ends of the logs, from which you calculate your milling patterns (upper left photo, facing page). I usually make pairs of end boards from common, 2-in. thick, dressed lumber. Heights of 4 in., 6 in., 8 in. and 10 in., cut to the width of the guide plank being used, cover most milling situations.

Measure and mark the log for the supporting lag bolts. When using a 10-ft. guide plank, I usually place a pair of lags every 4 ft. Remember to make sure the lags don't go so deep that they're in the path of the cut.

Position the guide plank, looking under it to make sure the angle irons rest securely on the lags and end boards. You'll need an overhang of at least 12 in. to support the mill as it begins the cut, so pull the plank out that far.

If you're milling with a winch, you'll need a weight to counterbalance the saw engine and to hold the guide rails of the mill flat on the plank. Make this from a block of log that is slightly larger in diameter than the space between the mill guide rails. Notch the log to fit over the mill handle.

The first cut—Determine how high to set the mill for the first cut by measuring on a vertical index line drawn on the end of the log. Mount the mill on the guide plank. Keep the thrust skid against the log and begin the cut with the nose end of the sawbar. Come to full throttle and cut until the back guide rail of the mill just passes the end board. Pause, and drive in both end dogs, spacing them as far apart as possible without splitting the slab.

Now position the winch yoke. Center it on the butt end of the log so that the outside pulleys are 1 in. or 2 in. below the mark on the vertical index line, and thread the winch ropes through the cheek blocks. Now slip one end of the bridle rope over the bridle button on the saw engine, and hook the other end of the bridle rope to the eye on the remote throttle attachment's surgical tubing. Gently take up the slack in the winch rope, and thread it through the bridle rope so that it will pull the throttle wide open before it begins to pull the mill forward.

When the winch is set up, start the saw engine and position the counterweight. As you start cranking the winch, the engine should open up to full throttle. To stop milling, or if the saw sticks in the cut, quickly crank the winch handle several turns backward. This will stop the pull and allow the engine to return to idle. Keep an eye on the guide rails of the mill to be sure they remain flat on the guide plank, and mill up to the last set of lag bolts. Crank the winch backward quickly to stop milling, allow the engine to idle and then turn the engine off. Leave the mill in the cut.

Pull the guide plank forward to the next cutting position. In the last position, the plank will just cover the end board. So set the winch dogs into the end of the guide plank and continue milling, adding kerf wedges as necessary. When the mill comes close to the end of the cut, remove the counterweight, winch ropes and yoke. Pull the guide plank forward so it projects beyond the end board to support the mill as it finishes the cut. Complete the cut by hand, keeping a firm downward as well as forward pressure on the mill.

You can mill a board or two off the top slab if you invert it in place on top of the log. Estimate the center of weight of the slab and drive a wedge on either side to provide a pivot. Absolute balance is not necessary, but the closer you guess, the easier it will be to move the slab. Swing the slab with a peavey, so that it crosses the log. Use a peavey or jack to flip the slab over. Swing the slab back into place, then lift it to near level and block it with wedges.

I don't normally use the winch yoke on shallow cuts. I attach the winch rope to the bridle rope at the engine end as when using the yoke, but attach the nose-end rope by slipping the loop over the mill's riser post. Once the counterweight is in position, you can start milling. The winch system is more complicated than hand-milling, but certainly less tedious. I often hand-mill short and narrow cuts, but find a day's work much easier with a winch. □

Expensive Tools Do Not a Craftsman Make
Making Do in Mexico

by William J. Taylor

Moving to Mexico last year was a difficult time in our lives. Thousands of decisions came up in our packing, since neither my wife nor I wanted to part with our "treasures." For me the worst was what to do with my 30-year accumulation of tools. The final decision was that I could pack some hand tools if she could take her sewing machine. A handsaw, smoothing plane, four wood chisels, several rasps, a square, a ⅜-in. electric drill, a brace and a set of bits—I ended up with two boxes of miscellaneous tools, plus a portable circular saw and a router. Sadly, I turned my back on my radial-arm saw, 10-in. table saw and lathe. Oh well, I said to myself, maybe I can get by.

We arrived without incident and finally found a house that had two extra rooms I could use for a shop and storage. The house was unfurnished and we had brought no furniture. First things being first, I made a simple platform bed and bought a foam mattress—no problem with the tools I had with me. While building the bed, I could hear

from down the street the unmistakable whine of a table saw. At the first chance I followed the sound, like a bird dog after a covey of quail. Soon I was standing in the open doorway of a Mexican cabinet shop. The two men looked up, and I spoke one of the few Spanish phrases I knew, *"Buenos días."* One of the men said *"Pase, señor,"* which sounded like "pass," so I walked in. The shop was poorly lit and the workbench primitive, with little equipment beyond hand tools in evidence. Near one wall I saw the source of the saw noise—an unpainted, roughly made wooden frame with a 12-in. circular sawblade projecting through a slit in the wood top. It seemed unbelievable that they actually expected to turn out work on this thing. The two cabinetmakers and I became friends when they found out that woodworking was my hobby. Watching what they could do with that saw soon opened my eyes. In addition to the usual saw functions, a drill chuck stuck out the side of the table frame with an adjustable shelf under it. With

this arrangement they would drill and clean out mortises by sliding the work back and forth on the shelf. I had to have one of these saws.

I bought some pine lumber, arbitrarily decided on a table of 28 in. by 30 in., then built the frame to fit. The tabletop hinges at the far end, so to lower the sawblade you raise the table's near end. I acquired a ¾-HP, 3450-RPM electric motor and felt like a child at Christmas. I bought two ball-bearing mandrels from Sears, mounting one for the sawblade and the other alongside the first with its threaded shaft sticking out a hole in the side of the frame. I put step pulleys on both mandrel shafts and another on the motor, using a mounting device that I had discovered 30 years earlier when my only power source was a salvaged washing-machine motor that drove several tools. I put a wood base on the motor into which I placed two eye bolts, with two more eye bolts on the tool I wished to power. I then could connect the motor to the tool by putting a ½-in. rod through the eye bolts, so the

Taylor's homemade table saw. The top is hinged at the far end and raised to adjust depth of cut, by means of the slotted board and wing nut attached to the frame. The mortising spindle and an adjustable table are mounted on the right.

The crosscutting fixture consists of two crossed boards, glued and screwed at 90°. One board rides the edge of the table, the other pushes the work. A similar device permits 45° miter cuts.

Horizontal mortising: Workpiece is pushed into bit and moved from side to side to clean out waste.

Mounting the mandrel vertically makes the machine into a shaper. The same arrangement can accept drum sanders, or a chuck for router bits.

Once you've come this far, a tenoning jig is easy.

From *Fine Woodworking* magazine (January 1980) 20:36-37

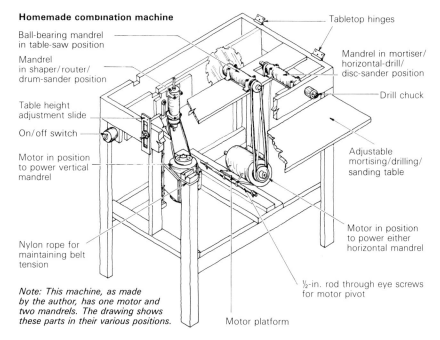

Homemade combination machine

Ball-bearing mandrel
in table-saw position

Mandrel
in shaper/router/
drum-sander position

Table height
adjustment slide

On/off switch

Motor in position
to power vertical
mandrel

Nylon rope for
maintaining belt
tension

Tabletop hinges

Mandrel in mortiser/
horizontal-drill/
disc-sander position

Drill chuck

Adjustable
mortising/drilling/
sanding table

Motor in position
to power either
horizontal mandrel

½-in. rod through eye screws
for motor pivot

Motor platform

*Note: This machine, as made
by the author, has one motor and
two mandrels. The drawing shows
these parts in their various positions.*

motor could slide sideways to accommodate the pulley steps. By taking the V-belt off the saw mandrel and putting it on the drill mandrel, I had a horizontal drill and could also attach a sanding disc. Now, I thought, we are getting somewhere, and what else could I do with it? As I still had some inside space to work with, I decided to rig up a vertical motor mount so I could have a shaper as well. Working this out took a few days—no use overdoing it in the tropics. When I finally got it all together, the ugly thing worked, and I gleefully dragged my wife out to the shop for a demonstration.

By this time our furniture consisted of four Mexican leather chairs and a small round leather-topped table. After

several shopping trips to Guadalajara, I decided that the furniture we could afford was of poor quality and shockingly expensive.

I am sometimes slow to catch on, but my wife would mutter as she served the evening meal, "It would be nice if I had some room to put down the dishes," and things like that. I agreed to make a table next, and she, knowing my limited ability, kept it simple by suggesting a Parsons design.

Pine is the usual wood in this area, but I finally found a hardwood called ollamel and started to design the table. As the wood was not kiln-dried and seemed a little green, I decided not to build the legs or sides of solid 4x4s and chose instead to use four 1x4s for the

legs, with the edges cut at 45° and glued up with a spline. At the corners I had six pieces of wood with their ends cut on a 45° angle, all meeting at once. The corner joints were glue-blocked and screwed, and I crossed my fingers. As Tage Frid has so often said, "Wood is going to move." But so far the joints have held up well; only one has opened about ⅓₂ in., which I can doctor up. For the top I set smoked glass into a rabbet.

As the table progressed, I kept asking my wife to give me some idea for the chairs. Finally we sat down with *Fine Woodworking's Biennial Design Book* (The Taunton Press, 1977). My wife picked the Michael Rosen chair on page 27. I made six of them without his consent, consoling myself that perhaps he would not mind, imitation being the sincerest form of flattery.

The table and chairs are great and the swivel back on the chairs was a stroke of genius on Rosen's part. Now we have a couch, two living-room chairs, a china cabinet and a dressing table in the planning stages. This should keep me out of the cantina for a while. I think I have created a monster in that table saw. □

Table and chairs, made with the homemade table saw.

Q & A

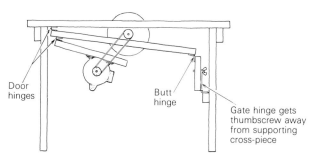

Door
hinges

Butt
hinge

Gate hinge gets
thumbscrew away
from supporting
cross-piece

A reader writes . . .

. . . William Taylor's wooden table saw (above) reminded me of one I built 26 years ago out of scrap ¾-in. plywood and 2x4s. It hadn't the refinements of mortising and routing heads; I needed to do some carpentry, not cabinetmaking.

But as it had to handle full sheets of plywood and other bulky lumber, and moreover, as I had not thought of tilting the tabletop to adjust blade height, I mounted my ball-bearing mandrel (also from Sears) on the top of a hunk of 1x6 and my washing-machine motor on the underside. The motor mount was hinged on the side farthest from the mandrel, so that the weight of the motor tightened the V-belt. This assembly was hinged to the underside of the table, or the frame, I forget which; a smaller scrap of lumber, hinged to the other end of the 1x6 and slotted to accommodate a thumbscrew, completed the height-adjustment mechanism. My fence was a well-seasoned 2x2, spaced from the blade by laborious measurement and C-clamped to the table. The saw paid its way through bookcases, window frames and countless other projects for several years until I felt flush enough to replace it with a radial-arm. And for my purposes, it turned out to be the better tool!—*Louis B. Hall, Anaheim, Calif.*

This wooden, 10-in. table-saw has a robust sliding table with fixed crosscut fence. It can crosscut wide panels as accurately as cast-iron machines costing ten times as much.

A Wooden Tablesaw
An attractive, shopmade alternative to cast iron

by Galen Winchip

Early in my woodworking career, I remember arranging to use a friend's big radial-arm saw to make critical crosscuts on wide panels for cabinets I was building. We spent hours fussing with the saw's adjustments, only to have it cut each panel frustratingly out of square. I longed for a sliding crosscut table—standard equipment on the heavy, industrial tablesaws that were way beyond my price range.

I had looked at the sliding tables then appearing as options on medium-duty saws, but they seemed flimsy and certain to sag when crosscutting heavy boards. Worst of all, these

devices were fitted with as many adjustment knobs, screws and levers as a radial-arm saw has, making them far from the set-it-and-forget-it crosscut machine I wanted.

I decided that the only way I'd own a sliding table was if I designed and built one myself out of wood. I had already constructed a half-dozen wooden woodworking machines, including panel saws, jointers (see pages 30 through 36) and lathes. I've found them to be well up to the rigors of daily use and, like a vintage wooden hand plane, they have the friendly feel that's absent from their cast-iron counterparts.

From *Fine Woodworking* magazine (July 1983) 41:28-33

Photos: Pete Krumhardt

The saw's sliding table mechanism is self-centering and self-adjusting, and it won't bind or loosen as the wooden rail swells and shrinks. The guide rail and rip fence are laminated from thinner stock for stability.

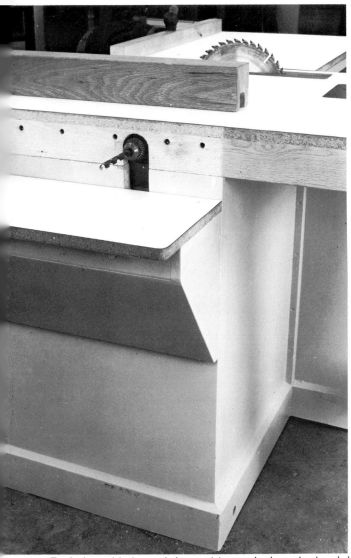

For horizontal boring and slot-mortising, a chuck can be threaded onto the saw's extended arbor. The auxiliary table can be set in two positions: flush with the main table, or 5 in. below it.

I built two tablesaws with complicated tilting-arbor mechanisms, but because I wanted my third saw, described in this article, to be easier to build, I opted for a fixed arbor. I didn't include an adjustable miter gauge either, relying instead on jigs fastened to the sliding table. Most of the adjustments on this machine are achieved by planing or jointing a small amount of wood from a critical surface, or by inserting paper shims. Because I didn't have mortising machinery at the time, I extended the saw's arbor and added a table for horizontal boring and mortising. Of course, you can modify the design to suit your own needs. After I'd built my saw, alternatives and modifications kept coming to mind, and because I've included these changes in the drawings, the photos and drawings don't correspond exactly. If you do modify, keep in mind some basic wooden-machine-building principles, which I've outlined below.

Wood vs. cast-iron—If you set out to build a wooden chair, you wouldn't look to one made of plastic as your structural model, so it follows that cast-iron woodworking machine mechanisms shouldn't serve as models for wooden ones. Cast-iron is an unyielding, predictable material which can be machined into parts that will maintain close tolerances. Wood expands and contracts with the seasons, so you must design mechanisms that won't swell and seize up in summer, then shrink out of precision in winter.

The rail I devised for my sliding table is an example of one such mechanism. As the photo above shows, it's an angled-section member which supports guides shaped so that the table's weight keeps them accurately centered, regardless of dimensional changes caused by moisture or wear. There's no play in this mechanism, but the compromise is friction. The table doesn't move as freely as do commercial models that roll on steel bearings.

For a given cross-section, cast iron is about ten times as rigid as wood, thus wooden members must have larger cross-sections for equivalent stiffness. Obviously, cast iron is harder and denser too, so it can bear concentrated loads that would crush wood. The best way to achieve rigidity in wooden machines while avoiding crushing is to distribute loads widely. In a cast-iron saw, the arbor bearings might be mounted 2 in. or 3 in. apart, but in my wooden saw, they are about 19 in. apart. Spreading out these mounting points also masks minor construction inaccuracies and distortions caused by uneven movement of wooden components.

My favorite wood for machines is well-seasoned, straight-grained hard maple, though I've had good luck with cherry, beech and oak. Whichever wood you pick, it's a good idea to let it live in the shop for a few months so it can reach equilibrium moisture content before you work it. I always cull out the highly figured pieces because they are more likely to twist, bow or cup. You can further counterbalance some of the wood's inherent instability by laminating several thin pieces into one larger one, as I did for the saw's sliding-table guide rail and rip fence.

For sheet stock, I prefer particleboard with a density of at least 45 lb./cu. ft. It's cheap and strong, and can be finished nicely with paint or covered with plastic laminate. Fiber-

Fig. 1: Wooden tablesaw construction

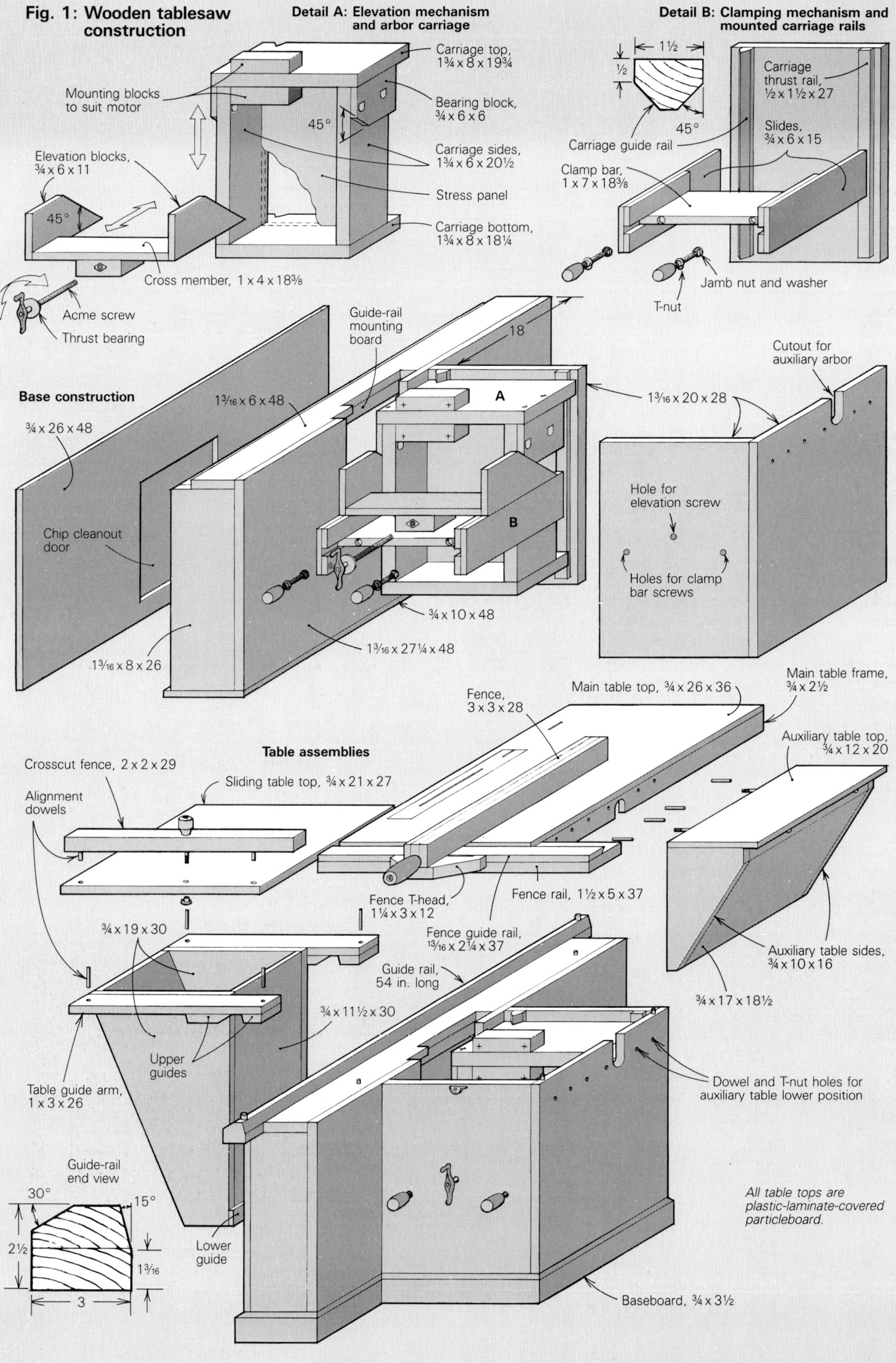
Detail A: Elevation mechanism and arbor carriage
Carriage top, 1¾ x 8 x 19¾
Mounting blocks to suit motor
Bearing block, ¾ x 6 x 6
45°
Carriage sides, 1¾ x 6 x 20½
Elevation blocks, ¾ x 6 x 11
45°
Stress panel
Carriage bottom, 1¾ x 8 x 18¼
Cross member, 1 x 4 x 18⅜
Acme screw
Thrust bearing
Detail B: Clamping mechanism and mounted carriage rails
1½
½
45°
Carriage guide rail
Carriage thrust rail, ½ x 1½ x 27
Slides, ¾ x 6 x 15
Clamp bar, 1 x 7 x 18⅜
Jamb nut and washer
T-nut
Base construction
Guide-rail mounting board
18
¾ x 26 x 48
1 3/16 x 6 x 48
A
B
1 3/16 x 20 x 28
Cutout for auxiliary arbor
Chip cleanout door
Hole for elevation screw
Holes for clamp bar screws
¾ x 10 x 48
1 3/16 x 27¼ x 48
1 3/16 x 8 x 26
Table assemblies
Fence, 3 x 3 x 28
Main table top, ¾ x 26 x 36
Main table frame, ¾ x 2½
Auxiliary table top, ¾ x 12 x 20
Crosscut fence, 2 x 2 x 29
Sliding table top, ¾ x 21 x 27
Alignment dowels
Fence T-head, 1¼ x 3 x 12
Fence rail, 1½ x 5 x 37
Fence guide rail, 13/16 x 2¼ x 37
¾ x 19 x 30
Guide rail, 54 in. long
Auxiliary table sides, ¾ x 10 x 16
¾ x 17 x 18½
¾ x 11½ x 30
Upper guides
Table guide arm, 1 x 3 x 26
Dowel and T-nut holes for auxiliary table lower position
Guide-rail end view
30°
15°
2½
1 3/16
3
Lower guide
All table tops are plastic-laminate-covered particleboard.
Baseboard, ¾ x 3½

boards such as MD44 could also be used. Particleboard has one quality that cast iron can't match: it muffles the piercing, high-frequency whines that are rough on the ears. I don't recommend the lower-density particleboards sold for a song as shelving at the local discount lumberyard, because their larger particles are bound together with less adhesive, making them weaker and more difficult to join reliably.

Building the saw—As figure 1 shows, the saw consists of a particleboard cabinet that houses the motor, arbor and arbor-raising mechanism. A second particleboard cabinet—built in the form of a box-beam for strength and rigidity—supports the sliding table. The two are screwed and glued together to form a T-shaped pedestal that enhances the saw's stability by spreading its 400 lb. over a wider area than a cast-iron saw would occupy. I built my cabinets out of 1 3/16-in. and 3/4-in. particleboard joined with glue and screws. Where possible, I reinforced the corner joints with glue blocks. If you want a lighter, more portable saw, build the cabinets out of plywood. Five-eighths to 3/4-in. plywood should be rigid enough.

The blade is lowered and raised by the arbor carriage (figure 2), a box-like frame made of 1 3/4-in. thick hard maple glued and doweled together. Both the motor and the arbor bearings are bolted to the carriage, whose vertical travel is guided by two rails—one V-shaped guide rail and one flat thrust rail—screwed to the back of the saw cabinet. It's raised by two wedge-shaped elevation blocks that bear against similarly shaped blocks glued to the sides of the carriage. To operate the elevation mechanism, I chose a 5/8-in. Acme-thread veneer-press screw. I discarded the swivel end and bought a flange-mounted ball thrust bearing at the hardware store. A small shoulder made by filing down the diameter of the veneer screw transfers the thrust to the screw's threaded collar, which is mounted on the raising mechanism.

I mounted the vertical carriage guide-rails first, then built the carriage frame, installing a 3/4-in. plywood stress panel inside it to keep it square. I lapped the V-rail into the guide by moving the carriage back and forth over a sheet of sandpaper taped to the rail, a method that also works for the sliding-table guides, as shown in the photo on page 17. Thickness the flat carriage rail so that the edges of the top and bottom members of the carriage are about parallel to the back of the saw cabinet. If the carriage rocks on the guides, plane a bit of wood off the flat rail to correct the problem.

I originally designed the arbor carriage to include the clamp bar shown in the drawings but not in the saw photographed for this article. The bar will lock the carriage firmly in place, but I never installed it. The machine works fine for sawing and drilling, but the carriage assembly vibrates when slot-mortising. The clamp would probably cure this. One other variation between the drawings and photos: I've drawn the V-shaped carriage rail on the sliding-table side of the saw rather than the other way around, as shown in the photos. Due to the motor location, the carriage's center of gravity is on the sliding-table side, and positioning the rails this way should give the carriage better balance and smoother action.

The arbor spins in two 1-in. ID, self-aligning, cast-iron pillow blocks bolted to the top of the arbor carriage, as shown in the photo at right. I turned my arbor shaft according to

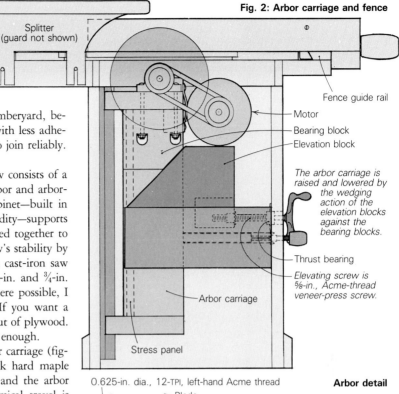

Fig. 2: Arbor carriage and fence

Splitter (guard not shown)

Fence guide rail

Motor

Bearing block

Elevation block

The arbor carriage is raised and lowered by the wedging action of the elevation blocks against the bearing blocks.

Thrust bearing

Elevating screw is 5/8-in., Acme-thread veneer-press screw.

Arbor carriage

Stress panel

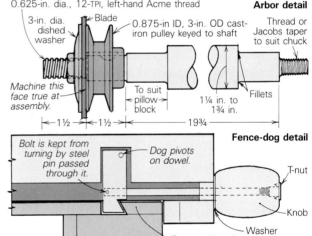

Arbor detail

0.625-in. dia., 12-TPI, left-hand Acme thread

3-in. dia. dished washer

Blade

0.875-in ID, 3-in. OD cast-iron pulley keyed to shaft

Thread or Jacobs taper to suit chuck

Machine this face true at assembly.

To suit pillow block

Fillets

1 1/4 in. to 1 3/4 in.

1 1/2 · 1 1/2 · 19 3/4

Fence-dog detail

Bolt is kept from turning by steel pin passed through it.

Dog pivots on dowel.

T-nut

Knob

Washer

Fence guide rail

A V-shaped guide rail and a flat thrust rail steady vertical travel of the arbor carriage. For better balance, the V- and thrust rails should be reversed, as in figure 1.

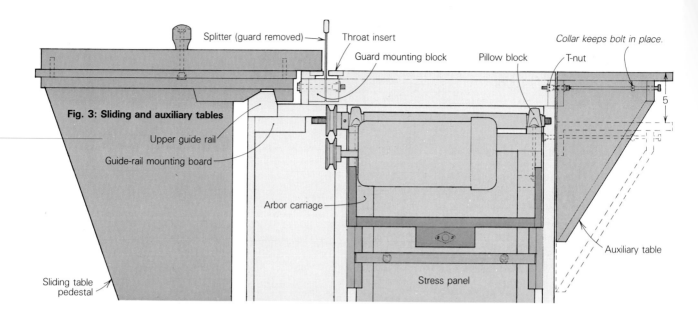

Splitter (guard removed) — Throat insert

Guard mounting block   Pillow block   T-nut   *Collar keeps bolt in place.*

Fig. 3: Sliding and auxiliary tables

Upper guide rail

Guide-rail mounting board

Arbor carriage

Auxiliary table

Sliding table pedestal

Stress panel

the detail in figure 2. Machine the arbor out of stress-proof steel rather than mild steel. To keep stress risers from developing at the inside corners where the shaft diameter is turned down, have the machinist leave small fillets at these points. The auxiliary end of my arbor is machined to take a screw-on chuck, but if you do much slot-mortising, I suggest that you install a collet instead.

Once the arbor shaft has been machined so that the bearings and pulley are a light press fit, these parts can be installed, and the face of the pulley remachined to serve as the blade flange. The pulley must be either cast iron or solid machined steel, not stamped steel or die-cast white metal.

When it's time to calibrate the saw, you can shift the pillow blocks in their slotted holes to align the blade parallel to the sliding table's travel. Insert sheet-metal shims under one of the pillow blocks to square the blade to the table surface.

The motor is bolted to two blocks glued and doweled to the arbor carriage. I used a 1½-HP, fully-enclosed, fan-cooled motor. Since my saw is connected to a large dust-collection system, there's plenty of air swirling around to cool the motor. If dust collection isn't used, cut some cooling slots in the side of the saw cabinet.

The sliding table—The most critical assembly is the sliding table and its guide rails. The table consists of a triangular particleboard pedestal to which the two guide arms are attached. As the photo on p. 13 shows, the sliding table simply hangs on the upper guide rail, and it can be lifted off when it's not needed. The upper rail should be laminated, sawn to the cross-sectional shape shown in figure 1, and jointed true. The upper-rail mounting board, a 1½-in. thick maple plank glued beneath the top of the sliding-table cabinet, should also be machined true so that it won't bow the rail when it's attached. I glued the upper rail to the saw with a "paper joint" like that used in bowlturning, so it can be removed for remachining or for replacement. It's also bolted, since that was the most convenient way to clamp the glueline.

The sliding table's upper guides are glued and doweled to the arms, and positioned so that the guides rest on the inclined surfaces of the rail, leaving a small clearance gap between the underside of the arm and the top surface of the rail, as shown in the drawing above. This space is important—it

ensures that the guides will ride on the angled surfaces of the rail and it allows for wear. To make two identical arms and guides, I fabricated them as one assembly 6 in. wide, then ripped them in half to make two pieces 3 in. wide.

With the arms glued and screwed to the sliding-table pedestal, the assembly can be hung on the machine. The table's lower guide rides against the saw's baseboard (thrust rail), a member whose thickness must be adjusted so that the top of the sliding table will remain in the same plane as the main table throughout its travel. True up the table travel by trial and error, planing a taper on the baseboard if necessary. Lap the table guides to the rail, one at a time, using the sandpaper method described earlier and pictured on the facing page. Fit properly, the guides will push sawdust in front of them rather than packing it up into clods that will hinder smooth travel of the table.

Final assembly—The saw's main table is made of ¾-in. particleboard screwed to a frame that sits atop the saw cabinet, aligned by dowels and held fast by two draw latches. With the latches popped open, the saw table can be lifted off and the arbor carriage removed for maintenance and cleaning, an operation that requires no tools. To keep the sliding and main tables in vertical alignment, I equalized the effects of seasonal movement by orienting the annual rings in the guide rail horizontally and those in the main table frame vertically.

The auxiliary table, attached to the saw with dowels and bolts threaded into T-nuts (figure 3), has only two positions: flush with the main table (where it supports extra-long or wide stock), and 5 in. below the main table (for drilling or mortising). To create a smooth, durable surface, I covered all three tables with white plastic laminate. Make sure that the tables are in proper alignment before you cover them.

I strongly recommend that this and any tablesaw be equipped with a blade guard, a splitter or riving knife, and anti-kickback pawls. My guard assembly is from an old Rockwell Unisaw. It's bolted to a block glued to the inside of the main table frame. To adjust the knife in line with the blade, I inserted thin metal shims between the guard and the mounting block.

I prefer a fence whose length ends just before the splitter. This type of fence is less likely to cause a kickback, because

G. Winchip

With sandpaper taped to the guide rail, the table guides can be lapped to a perfect fit.

once the wood has been pushed past the blade's cutting edge, it won't bind against the back of the blade. For stability and ease of fabrication, I made the fence out of three pieces of oak laminated to the 3-in. finished thickness. The fence is glued and doweled to a T-head, and it's locked in place with the wooden dog mechanism shown in the detail in figure 2. I relieved the T-head so that it bears against the fence guide rail on just two points. By planing a small amount of material from one of these contact points, I can make coarse adjustments in the fence so that it's parallel to the blade. Finer adjustments can be made by planing a slight taper on the fence guide rail.

The crosscut fence is fastened to the sliding table by dowels and a bolt threaded into a T-nut. Make some test cuts with the fence clamped in place, and once you've got a perfect 90° cut, drill for the dowels and bolt the fence down. Adjust it later by planing a taper on its front side.

With the saw built and calibrated, you can paint the particleboard with an oil-based primer, followed by a coat or two of enamel paint. I finished the solid wood parts with Watco oil and then paste-waxed the sliding parts.

Aside from the lower cost (about $300 for this saw in 1983), I've found that the greatest advantage to building my own machines has been scaling their features to meet my needs. On this saw, for example, the tables could be made larger, or the crosscut capacity made greater, by lengthening the guide rails and supporting pedestal. My machine accommodates a 10-in. blade, but the design could be modified to accept a 12-in. blade and perhaps a 3-HP motor.

The machine described here has been in use at the time of this writing for 2½ years at the Iowa State University woodworking shop, a high-abuse place if there ever was one. So far, it has required only routine cleaning and lubrication, plus an occasional tightening of the arbor mounting bolts. In our shop we have two other saws, a 10-in. Rockwell Unisaw and a 14-in., 5-HP Oliver. Often these two machines sit idle while students wait in line to use the wooden saw. They say its smoothness of operation, its adaptability to jig-work and its amiable disposition make it a more pleasant tool to use. □

Galen Winchip teaches woodworking and computer-aided manufacturing at Iowa State University at Ames.

Testing the wooden saw

When I flew out to Iowa this spring to try Winchip's wooden tablesaw, I had in mind comparing it to the sliding-table-equipped Rockwell Unisaw I've owned for three years. Having heard student raves about the wooden saw, I wasn't surprised to find it nicer on a couple of counts.

I did some ripping first, immediately discovering that the fence on Winchip's saw works better than the Unisaw's does. It's easier to position and clamp without the opposite end hopping out of alignment, as a lot of factory metal fences always seem to do, even on relatively expensive saws.

Apart from their size and construction material, I discovered the major difference between these two saws when I tried some crosscuts. With a couple of 8-ft. long, 15-in. wide panels on the sliding table, it took some muscle to make the cut—about the same effort you'd exert opening a heavy door. By contrast, the Unisaw table will slide one-handed. Although it's stiffer, the wooden table has no play and seemed more predictable than its steel counterpart, passing over the guide rail with an even swish instead of the clatter of steel on steel. A half-dozen crosscuts I checked were about 0.003 in. out of square across a 15-in. wide board. That's okay by my standards; slicing it finer calls for hunting down the renegade mils with a hand plane, a task that I suspect is no less frustrating than tickling the many adjusters on a steel table. I think Winchip is right about the guides' self-adjusting aspect, so the wooden saw should need less attention than a steel one.

The arbor carriage works as effortlessly as any I've used. Not having it tilt is a shortcoming I can live with, if only because it costs a thousand bucks less. The guard on this saw is a gem. It pivots handily out of the way for fence-setting, and it can be removed and, most importantly, reinstalled in seconds. I didn't much like the horizontal boring/mortising feature, though. For boring, 4500 RPM is too fast, and without a fence to guide it, impaling a chunk of wood on the bit is scary. Adding the clamp bar and a larger auxiliary table to accommodate fences and clamp jigs would help, especially for slot-mortising. I'd make two other changes: the sliding-table guide rail needs to be 2 in. longer, so that a full 24-in. wide panel can be crosscut, and a 3-HP motor would provide the extra power the saw needs to rip thick stock quickly, something it can't do with the smaller motor. —*Paul Bertorelli*

Winchip crosscuts two 15-in. wide panels on his wooden tablesaw.

P. Krumhardt

Making and Modifying Machines **17**

Shop-Built Panel Saw
Cutting plywood sheets down to size

by William F. Nelson

The counterbalanced saw carriage rides on steel-tube guide bars. U-bolts sheathed with short lengths of steel tubing act as bearings.

To support my woodworking hobby I practice architecture. Last year when we decided to move our offices, I offered to build the cabinets, and my partners accepted the proposal without hesitation. After drawing the cabinets and working up the bill of materials, which called for 75 sheets of plywood, I suddenly realized that my small shop had neither the space nor the equipment to handle that volume of material. Despite awful visions of wrestling dozens of cumbersome pieces of plywood around the shop and over the table saw, I was committed to the project and had to proceed.

A couple of weeks before, I had been in a woodworking-equipment store in Houston. One of the things that had caught my attention was a panel saw, the kind with a vertical frame for holding large panels and with a circular saw mounted in a sliding carriage. I certainly couldn't afford to spend the $850 the thing cost then, so I decided to make one.

I began by making a freehand sketch of the frame and the saw carriage, and was able to solve most of the construction problems on paper. The basic triangulated framework was fabricated from ordinary thin-walled electrical conduit and Unistrut steel channels, which I bought from an industrial supply store. Unistrut channels are commonly used to build warehouse shelving units and pipe racks. Because I have an acetylene welding rig, I decided to braze the metal parts of the frame together (figure 1a), but you could make it just as strong by using an assembly of wood top and bottom rails drilled to receive the vertical tubing members, fastening them together with sheet-metal screws through the back side of the wood into the tubing (figure 2). The framework must be rigid; it shouldn't rack or twist.

When the metalworking was done, I added the horizontal wooden strips and the wooden stock-support shelf at the bottom. I fastened the wood to the metal tubing with countersunk sheet-metal screws, which meant drilling pilot holes through one wall of the tubing. Be sure that the support shelf is perfectly straight and square to the frame. The saw carriage must clear the shelf and the blade must travel through it to complete the cut; the measurements given in the drawing accommodate 4x8 panels. For metric size plywood (about 5 ft. square), make the frame 1 ft. taller.

The part of the design that gave me trouble was the sliding saw carriage and guide bars. It was easy enough to make and attach the tubular guide bars to the frame, but providing for sliding bearings between the carriage and the bars was another matter. Finally I decided to use U-bolts on the carriage sides and to reduce friction and binding against the guide bars by making roller bearings from short lengths of stainless-steel tubing, whose inside diameter was the right size to fit over the U-bolts (detail A).

The guide bars are attached to the center tubular uprights at the top by means of right-angle flanges, threaded rod and nuts, as shown in detail B. The flanges can be either brazed or bolted to the uprights. Nuts on the threaded rod allow the guide bars to be adjusted so that the saw carriage will travel at a precise 90° to the base on which the workpiece rests, with no play between carriage and guide bars. At the bottom of the frame, the guide bars are fastened with a threaded rod to a ⅛-in. steel plate which is attached to the Unistrut bottom rail.

The saw carriage itself was the only part that I couldn't make in my shop. Because the design required channel-shaped flanges at each side to accommodate the U-bolts, I had to have it bent (brake-formed) in a sheet-metal shop. Two pulleys at the top of the uprights (one of them is fastened to an arm that is welded to the frame) and a counterweight complete the saw-carriage assembly. Without the counterweight, the saw is difficult to manage and will not stay at the top of the frame while you position the stock. To determine the exact weight to counterbalance the saw, I experimented with a plastic gallon jug filled with water.

My inexpensive 7¼-in. circular saw bolts to the carriage through the saw's base and is reinforced by a hose clamp and 18-ga. steel strap around the motor housing. I use a carbide-tipped blade because the glues in plywood and particleboard quickly dull standard blades. I installed a toggle switch at the top of the frame so I can pull the saw into the cut with the tubular crossmember on the carriage rather than by grasping the trigger switch in the plastic handle. I connected the saw to my dust collection system by setting a 3-in.-to-4-in. step-up PVC drain coupling astride the sawblade housing; a flexible hose fits snugly into the 4-in. part of the coupling (see photo above).

The saw is easy to use, and will produce accurate finish cuts the full width of a 4x8 plywood panel. It has been a real time-saver, too. Without rushing I was able to cut seven sheets of plywood into 62 finished pieces in 90 min. My cabinetmaking project took only 10 weeks, working evenings and weekends. During that time I also built myself a desk and credenza. I have since found the panel saw useful in ways I hadn't anticipated. Because it cuts at a perfect 90°, it's just the right tool for crosscutting long boards. With casters, the saw can be moved around the shop and then stored where it's least in the way. □

William F. Nelson lives in Beaumont, Texas. Photo and drawings by the author.

From *Fine Woodworking* magazine (March 1982) 33:90-91

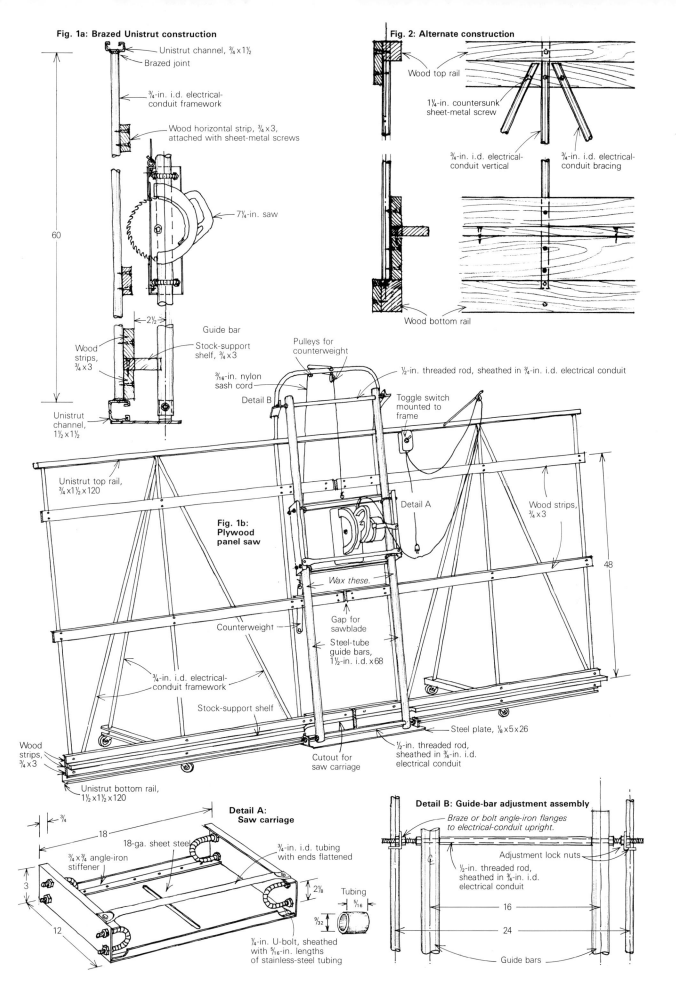

Fig. 1a: Brazed Unistrut construction

Unistrut channel, ¾ × 1½

Brazed joint

¾-in. i.d. electrical-conduit framework

Wood horizontal strip, ¾ × 3, attached with sheet-metal screws

7¼-in. saw

60

2½

Guide bar

Stock-support shelf, ¾ × 3

Wood strips, ¾ × 3

Unistrut channel, 1½ × 1½

Fig. 2: Alternate construction

Wood top rail

1¼-in. countersunk sheet-metal screw

¾-in. i.d. electrical-conduit vertical

¾-in. i.d. electrical-conduit bracing

Wood bottom rail

Pulleys for counterweight

³⁄₁₆-in. nylon sash cord

Detail B

½-in. threaded rod, sheathed in ¾-in. i.d. electrical conduit

Toggle switch mounted to frame

Detail A

Wood strips, ¾ × 3

Unistrut top rail, ¾ × 1½ × 120

Fig. 1b: Plywood panel saw

48

Wax these.

Gap for sawblade

Counterweight

Steel-tube guide bars, 1½-in. i.d. × 68

¾-in. i.d. electrical-conduit framework

Stock-support shelf

Wood strips, ¾ × 3

Unistrut bottom rail, 1½ × 1½ × 120

Cutout for saw carriage

Steel plate, ⅛ × 5 × 26

½-in. threaded rod, sheathed in ¾-in. i.d. electrical conduit

Detail A: Saw carriage

¾

18

18-ga. sheet steel

¾ × ¾ angle-iron stiffener

¾-in. i.d. tubing with ends flattened

3

2⅛

12

Tubing

⁵⁄₁₆

⁹⁄₃₂

¼-in. U-bolt, sheathed with ⁵⁄₁₆-in. lengths of stainless-steel tubing

Detail B: Guide-bar adjustment assembly

Braze or bolt angle-iron flanges to electrical-conduit upright.

Adjustment lock nuts

½-in. threaded rod, sheathed in ¾-in. i.d. electrical conduit

16

24

Guide bars

Making a Panel Saw

Sears saw serves as the basic machine

by Larry Kellam

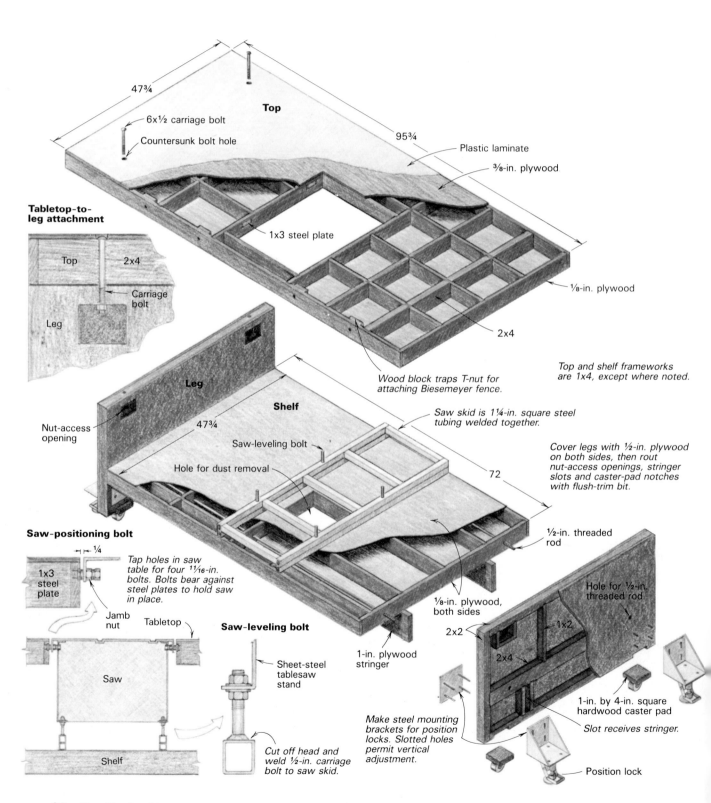

Top

47¾

6x½ carriage bolt

Countersunk bolt hole

95¾

Plastic laminate

⅜-in. plywood

1x3 steel plate

⅛-in. plywood

2x4

Tabletop-to-leg attachment

Top

2x4

Carriage bolt

Leg

Wood block traps T-nut for attaching Biesemeyer fence.

Top and shelf frameworks are 1x4, except where noted.

Leg

Shelf

Nut-access opening

47¾

Saw-leveling bolt

Hole for dust removal

Saw skid is 1¼-in. square steel tubing welded together.

72

Cover legs with ½-in. plywood on both sides, then rout nut-access openings, stringer slots and caster-pad notches with flush-trim bit.

½-in. threaded rod

Hole for ½-in. threaded rod

Saw-positioning bolt

¼

1x3 steel plate

Tap holes in saw table for four 1¹⁄₁₆-in. bolts. Bolts bear against steel plates to hold saw in place.

Jamb nut

Tabletop

Saw-leveling bolt

⅛-in. plywood, both sides

2x2

1x2

2x4

Saw

Sheet-steel tablesaw stand

1-in. plywood stringer

1-in. by 4-in. square hardwood caster pad

Slot receives stringer.

Shelf

Cut off head and weld ½-in. carriage bolt to saw skid.

Make steel mounting brackets for position locks. Slotted holes permit vertical adjustment.

Position lock

From *Fine Woodworking* magazine (March 1985) 51:68-70

In the ten years I've been building furniture, kitchen cabinets and store fixtures, my two biggest problems have always been lack of space and the absence of an additional pair of hands. To deal with the space problem, I've mounted each of my major power tools on casters so I can roll the machine I need to the center of the shop and go right to work.

Finding an extra pair of hands hasn't been as easy. I've always worked alone, which is fine until it comes to tossing around heavy 4x8 sheets of particleboard. You wouldn't believe the pain I used to put up with just to cut that stuff on my little 27-in. by 40-in. tablesaw. I tried some alternative solutions: roughing sheets with a circular saw and straightedge; ripping them on my radial-arm saw with cobbled-up extension tables. Then I got the idea of housing my tablesaw in a big, roll-around worktable. As the photo shows, my saw table is little more than a Sears 12-in. tablesaw, a Biesemeyer T-Square saw fence and a large table. Should the need arise, the saw can be completely dismantled.

While the Sears saw is by no means industrial-quality, I've never had any problems with it, so I couldn't see spending a small fortune on a better one. For about $60, I had the surface of the cast table ground to take out a nasty $\frac{1}{16}$-in. warp. The Biesemeyer T-square saw fence is the backbone of my design. The joy of being able to set a fence up to 48 in. from the blade in about two seconds borders on the euphoric. I'm consistently getting truly straight and square carcases, and the reason for this is that I'm getting truly straight and square cuts. Thank you, Mr. Biesemeyer.

Basic construction—The table consists of four large panels: the top, the shelf that supports the saw, and the two legs. Each of the panels is a torsion box—a light wooden gridwork core that is skinned over with plywood. I positioned the saw to the right of center because, unlike most people, I rip with the fence on the left side of the blade. But you can suit yourself. Right or left,

what's important is that there's enough room to set the fence 48 in. away from the blade. This allows you to cut to the center of a 4-ft. by 8-ft. sheet. I use this saw only for cutting panels and ripping, so I didn't extend the miter-gauge grooves into the table. If you want to extend the grooves, use thicker plywood for the top.

I made the torsion-box frames from clear fir. If I were to do it again, I'd probably use $3\frac{1}{2}$-in. wide pieces of $\frac{3}{4}$-in. ply, simply because it's straighter. So the grid parts would stay put during glue-up, I assembled them with $\frac{1}{8}$-in. deep dadoes.

Before gluing on the plywood skin, I positioned the Biesemeyer fence's angle-iron mount on the front edge of the top. I drilled holes for the mounting bolts and inserted a T-nut on the inside of each hole. I glued a small block of wood over each T-nut to make sure the nut could never come off. Once the plywood is glued down, the T-nuts are inaccessible.

I glued plywood across the entire top and bottom of each grid, and cut the openings later with a router fitted with a flush-trim bit. The top is $\frac{1}{4}$ in. smaller than a plywood sheet, so I could neatly trim the edges with the router. Contact cement works fine for gluing the $\frac{1}{8}$-in. plywood to the grid, and the plastic laminate to the top. You can fasten the thicker plywood with white or yellow glue and screws.

Assembly—The legs are held together by two 76-in. long, $\frac{1}{2}$-in. dia. threaded rods that pass through the shelf. I had these made at a machine shop for about $30, but you could also couple shorter lengths of threaded rod. The two plywood stringers slip into their mortises (don't glue them) and the shelf simply rests on the stringers. The saw goes in place on the shelf, and rests on a frame made from $1\frac{1}{4}$-in. square steel tube, which a blacksmith made for $100. Oak or maple would also do, and cost less. Four carriage bolts welded to the frame are used to level the saw.

To position the top, I used the bolt holes through the top panel

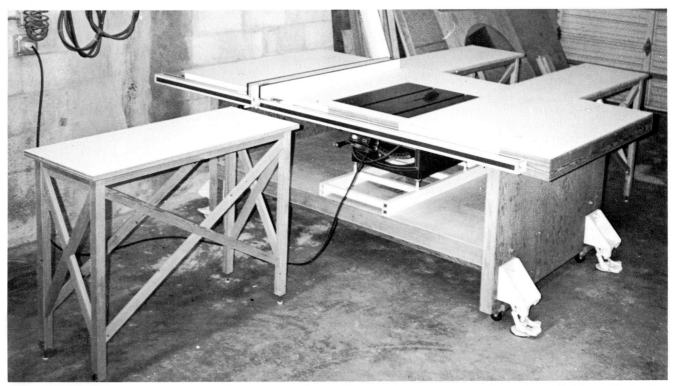

Four torsion-box panels and a Biesemeyer fence convert a Sears tablesaw to an accurate, versatile panel saw. Outrigger-like position locks extend to hold the rolling table in place. Auxiliary infeed and outfeed tables can be positioned for more panel support.

Shopbuilt sliding table

by Rick Williams

I made a sliding table for my Sears saw from scrap plywood, and produced the ugliest saw in the world. It rolls on six ball-bearing nylon roller-skate wheels—four ride on top of the track, the other two on the vertical plywood track support. I made the track from a steel clothesline pole, but any sturdy, straight pole about 7 ft. long would do.

Everyone who sees my sliding table pushes down on the outside corner of the table, and when it moves up and down they ask, "Doesn't this cause any problems?" No. Since the workpiece itself must be on both the saw table and the sliding table at the same time, the workpiece actually holds the table in place.

I've made several other modifications to the 10-in. saw, such as replacing the metal legs with a plywood box. The box has a large drawer that wheels in from the end to catch the dust that used to fall on the floor and then rolls out for emptying. I've also made a safety guard that suspends from the ceiling. It combines an anti-kickback device and a dust-collection system.

I replaced the 1-HP motor with a 1.5-HP, 220-volt motor on a 24-volt relay. I've hooked up a three-way switch setup with one switch at the front of the sliding table so I don't have to climb under a 4x8 panel to turn on the saw, and one switch on the front of the saw for when I'm working on smaller pieces.

I'd estimate the total cost of the project (including saw, new motor, and sliding table) at $500. Every time I lay a piece of ¾-in. ply on the thing and slide it through a cut, I'm amazed that anything that looks so strange could cut so well. ☐

Rick Williams is a cabinetmaker in Stanley, Kans. Photos by the author.

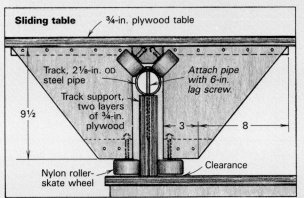

Sliding table — ¾-in. plywood table

Track, 2⅛-in. OD steel pipe

Attach pipe with 6-in. lag screw.

Track support, two layers of ¾-in. plywood

9½

3   8

Nylon roller-skate wheel

Clearance

This homely setup is a Sears tablesaw outfitted with a sliding table cobbled from scrap plywood, a metal clothesline pole and six nylon roller-skate wheels. The plywood saw stand contains a wheeled drawer that slides in to collect sawdust and rolls out for emptying. The plywood and acrylic blade guard (below) is connected to a dust-collection vacuum system. The guard swings up and away when not needed.

as a guide and drilled through the top 2x2s in the legs. Then I secured the top to the legs with four ½-in. dia. carriage bolts. Lastly, I fastened the Biesemeyer fence to the top.

The height of the saw is adjusted with the leveling bolts. When the saw is flush with the top, tighten the bolts in the table casting against the steel plates mortised into the saw opening.

To keep the table from rolling around in use, I attached four position locks (made by Bassick Div., Stewart-Warner Corp., 960 Atlantic St., Bridgeport, Conn. 06602) to the legs with steel brackets. The bolt holes in these brackets are slotted, so it's easy to level the table on an irregular floor.

Frankly, I'm a little embarrassed about the amount of money I've channeled into this project. All told, I've invested about $1,000. That includes the $300 I paid 10 years ago for my saw—today (1985) the same saw costs more than $600. Was it worth it? Yes. Every nickel. Besides, anything I build for the shop, I build to last a lifetime. I look upon my shop as a reflection of me and my work—a showroom, so to speak—and therefore I feel that everything that goes into it should be efficient, neat and well thought out. It's good for business. ☐

Larry Kellam is a professional cabinetmaker in Miami, Fla.

Steeling away
Starting from scratch

by John Gallup

Lately I've been dissatisfied with the quality of the steel in tools I get at the local True Value, so I decided to make my own. The process is quite simple, and with practice anyone can get good results. To get started, you'll need 20 or 30 tons of high-grade iron ore, 15 tons of low-sulfur coal, oxygen, and a dab of molybdenum.

The iron ore I use comes from the Mesabi range in northern Minnesota. Taconite, a low-grade pellet with less iron content, will work, but you'll need more of it. A coalyard should be able to fix you up with the coal, but if you prefer to use charcoal, refer to Eric Sloane's *A Reverence for Wood* for instructions on how to make it. The oxygen is essential to the Bessemer process, which results in a better steel, and you can order as many tanks as you need from a welding supply house. You'll need the molybdenum only if you're going to make sawblades and the like; I get mine from the big Climax, Colo., facility.

Okay, now we're ready. Load a few tons of coal into a coke oven battery and heat it for about three weeks. The natural-gas tap to your house may not be big enough, but you can dig it up out to the street and run a larger pipe in from there. Check with the local utility company about getting a larger meter, and watch out for sparks. When the coal is cooked, it's called "coke," and makes the hot fire you'll need in the blast furnace. Using tongs and heavy potholders, transfer it there, and hurry so it doesn't cool off. Specially designed railroad cars are quicker.

Load the furnace with ore and start heating. When it's molten, the various impurities will cook off or be left as slag. Experiment will teach you just how much oxygen to inject and when. Pour the white-hot steel into molds for five-ton pigs, and hustle them over to your rolling mill. I built mine out of scrap, but be sure to use good-quality metal—the rollers are under quite a bit of stress when they squeeze that squarish 2000° pig out into the bar stock you'll need to make plane irons and chisels. If the steel cools off before you've finished working it, drop the pig into a firebrick-lined pit and cook it some more. You can't be too careful here. When those five-ton

pigs are shooting back and forth between the rollers they sometimes get loose, and there go your insurance rates, right through the roof.

Now you've got about five tons of bar stock. Give it a few days to cool (if you do this in the winter it will really help the heating bill). A trip hammer is handy for cutting it to length. Don't forget to allow for tangs on your chisels. Take a piece over to the Rockwell hardness tester and check it. If it's below C60-64, you didn't add enough carbon back when the steel was molten. But

don't worry. You can always melt it down and start again.

Once you get the fundamentals down, all kinds of possibilities open up. A few years' apprenticeship with a tool-and-die maker in a foundry will teach you all you need to know to cast your own plane bodies and saw tables. A drop forge is handy for making flat pieces, and will save you a lot of tedious anvil work. Once you start making your own steel, you will never again be frustrated with nicked chisels and broken router bits. □

From *Fine Woodworking* magazine (May 1980) 22:32-33

Making and Modifying Machines **23**

Building a Walking-Beam Saw

Poor man's band saw has almost unlimited capacity

by Mark White

A walking-beam saw uses two parallel arms or beams, and a thin sawblade tensioned between them. The arms can be made of either wood or metal, and they pivot on pins or bearings. A twisted piece of line or a turnbuckle is used to tension the blade, which moves up and down, powered by either a treadle or a motor via a flywheel and crank.

The saw works like a band saw with two notable exceptions. First, since the cutting action is reciprocal, it is neither as smooth nor as continuous as that of a band saw. Second, since the walking-beam saw has only a single section of blade to worry about, it can be used to crosscut stock of almost infinite length. A band saw's width of cut is limited by the diameter of its wheels, but its length of cut is virtually unlimited. The length of cut a walking-beam saw can make is limited primarily by the length of its arms and by the configuration of its supporting members. While a circular saw is generally better for ripping long boards, the walking-beam saw can be used for ripping long stock by mounting the blade at a 90° angle to the arms and adopting a fairly short stroke.

The major advantage of the walking-beam saw is the fact that it can be easily and inexpensively constructed by the average home craftsman. However, it will do some things that the band saw cannot. It can cut an inside hole in a large piece of material, such as through mortises in the legs of a heavy trestle table. It can cut substances such as meat, bone, asbestos board, and metal—things that usually require extensive cleanup or which gum up the works or strip teeth from a band saw. Blades for the walking-beam saw are cheap and easily replaced with little or no adjustment necessary for different widths. The saw can be constructed in various sizes. While a band saw with wheels much bigger than 14 in. is usually quite expensive, a walking-beam saw with 8-ft. or 10-ft. arms will cost only slightly more than one with 3-ft. arms.

The prospective use of the saw will dictate its relative size and the rigidity of its frame. The saw (figures 1 and 2) was designed for trim work and for the precision cutting of boat frames and small parts. It has arms that measure about 3 ft. from the central pivot bearing to the sawblade bearing. When the width of the supporting frame is taken into account, useful throat depth is about 33 in.—enough for most

Fig. 1: Using his walking-beam saw, White cuts through an 8-in. hardwood block. The saw is well suited for contour cutting, crosscutting and ripping both thick and thin stock, but long rippings require special attachments for the arms. Drive mechanism with ⅙-HP motor produces 144 cutting strokes per minute.

Bill of materials (all dimensions in inches)

Arms—2 pcs., 2x4x54
Upright supports—2 pcs., 2x8x38
Block between uprights—2x8x6
Table supports—2 pcs., 2x6x48
Legs—4 pcs., 2x3x40
Side rails—2 pcs., 2x3x56
Cross rails—2 pcs., 2x3x32
Main bearing support (near crank)—1 pc., 3x4x41
Table—1 pc. of plywood, approx. 1¼ thick by 23 sq.
Main drive pulley—2 pcs., ½x24x24 ACX or CDX plywood; 1 pc., ⅜x24x24 ACX or CDX plywood
Pivot pins—2 pcs. 1-in. rod, approx. 7½ long, cold-rolled steel
Crank—1 pc., 1-in. cold-rolled steel rod from 18 to 20 in. long
Counterbalance—1 pc., ¼x2x6 steel flatbar
Blades—any dimension and style desired, suggest pruning-saw blades, 20 in. between pins to start
Turnbuckle—⅜ in., min. opening 6 in., max. opening 10 in.
Blade brackets and tensioner supports—approx. 50 in. of ¼ or ⅛x1 steel
1—⅜-in. steel clevis or shackle
Bracket and tensioner bearings—approx. 10 in. of ⅛ or ¼ brass pipe
Leg bolts—16 ea. ⁵⁄₁₆x3½ carriage bolts with washers and nuts
Crank and drive bearings—3 or 4 1-in. pillow-block bearings with zinc fittings
Drive motor—⅓ to 2-HP motor with 2-in. or 3-in. pulley
Misc. nuts, bolts, washers, screws and nails to hold motor, brackets and pieces in place—best determined at construction, rather than from a prescribed list.

Photos: Mark White; Illustrations: Ric Lopez

work. As a general rule, the arms should be about 6 in. longer than the anticipated maximum length of cut.

The arms—Once the arm length has been determined, lay out and construct a set of arms. Straight-grained ash, cherry, and basswood are good choices; they're tough, hard, stable and fairly light for their strength. The top arm is essentially an idler, which tensions and aligns the top of the blade. The bottom, driving arm has a heavier forward section to take the strain of the up-and-down motion imparted by the eccentric drive. A hole, bored a few inches back from the blade, receives the bearing for the drive crank (figure 3).

As with most reciprocating saws, the part of the stroke that does the most work is that part that draws the workpiece toward the table as it cuts. But there is a considerable difference between a cheap saw with a blade that moves merely up and down, and one on which the blade moves into the cut and backs off on the return stroke. The difference can amount to as much as a threefold increase in cutting efficiency and tooth life. One of the features that gives the walking-beam saw its efficiency is the fact that this automatic blade advancement can be easily built into the machine during construction simply by making the forward part of the top arm a little longer than the bottom arm. The parallel arms will then move the blade away from the cut on the up stroke and into the cut on the down stroke (figure 4).

On a saw with a blade length of 20 in., I would make the top arm about ¾ in. longer than the bottom arm. Thus, the distance between the arm pivot and blade bearing hole is 34 in. on the bottom arm and 34¾ in. on the top arm. A small saw with a 6-in. blade should probably have the top arm a scant ³⁄₁₆ in. to ¼ in. longer than the bottom arm. As a result of the relatively short stroke of the blade and the elasticity of the parts, the actual forward/backward motion of the blade is probably less than half of the difference built into the arms. Nevertheless, this difference will add considerably to the saw's cutting efficiency.

Wood/metal bearings—While all of the bearings in the walking-beam saw could have been commercial roller bearings, I went with wood/metal on seven out of ten of them to save time and money. The main pivot bearings for the arms were fashioned from pieces of 1-in. steel rod about 7½ in. long. I bored test holes in a scrap of koa, the wood I used for the arms, with a number of different bits to make sure the hole would be snug. The blade bearing, tensioner bearings and one arm-drive bearing were fashioned from 2-in. lengths of ⅛-in. brass pipe. The blade holders and tensioner brackets I made from ¼-in. by 1-in. mild steel flatbar, as shown in figure 5 on the next page.

Assembly of the arms and frames—The metal bearings that were to run in wood were cleaned up with a file and polished with fine sandpaper. The tensioner supports and blade holders were assembled permanently on the arms. A bit of grease in each hole ensured initial lubrication. Oil holes (¼ in.) drilled before assembly make lubrication easy.

I fitted the arms with a blade and set them in a trial position on a piece of 2x8 stock in order to get an idea of placement for the pivot pins. I tried to get the arms parallel to each

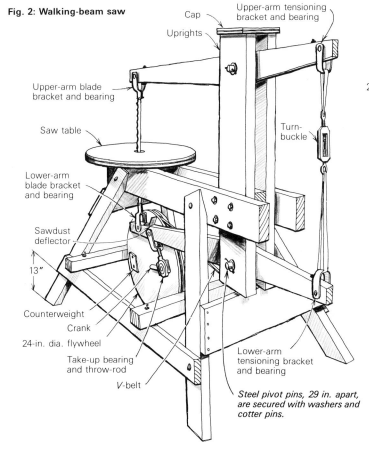

Fig. 2: Walking-beam saw

Cap
Upright
Upper-arm tensioning bracket and bearing
Upper-arm blade bracket and bearing
Saw table
Turn-buckle
Lower-arm blade bracket and bearing
Sawdust deflector
13"
Counterweight
Crank
24-in. dia. flywheel
Take-up bearing and throw-rod
V-belt
Lower-arm tensioning bracket and bearing

Steel pivot pins, 29 in. apart, are secured with washers and cotter pins.

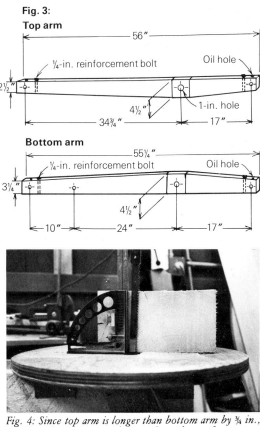

Fig. 3:
Top arm
56"
¼-in. reinforcement bolt
Oil hole
2½"
34¾"
4½"
1-in. hole
17"

Bottom arm
55¼"
¼-in. reinforcement bolt
Oil hole
3¼"
4½"
10"
24"
17"

Fig. 4: Since top arm is longer than bottom arm by ¾ in., blade angles into cut on downstroke and away from cut on upstroke, increasing cutting efficiency and blade life.

Fig. 5:
Top blade bracket

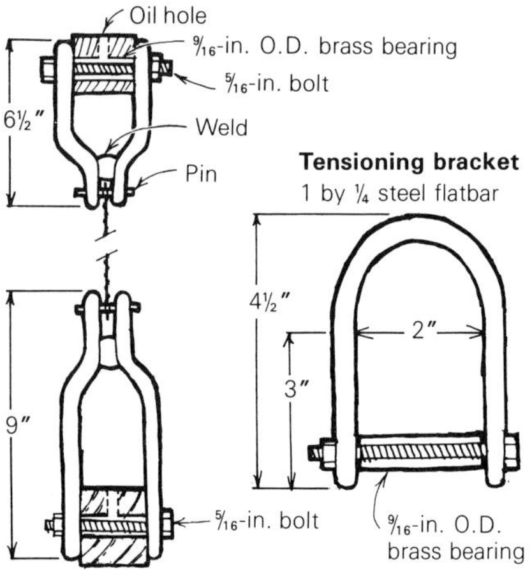
Oil hole
$\frac{9}{16}$-in. O.D. brass bearing
$\frac{5}{16}$-in. bolt
6½"
Weld
Pin
Tensioning bracket
1 by ¼ steel flatbar
4½"
2"
3"
9"
$\frac{5}{16}$-in. bolt
$\frac{9}{16}$-in. O.D. brass bearing

Bottom blade bracket

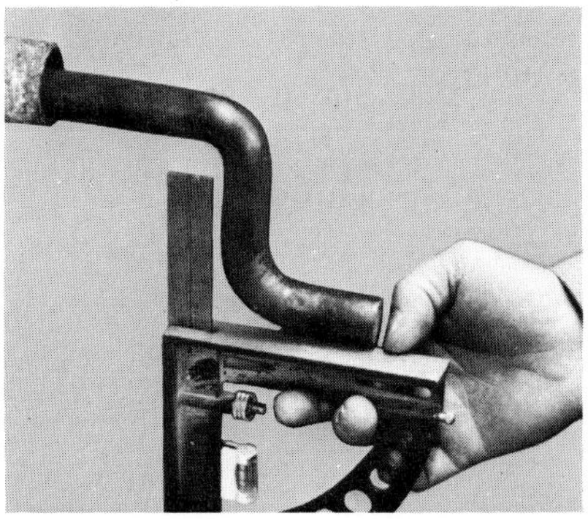

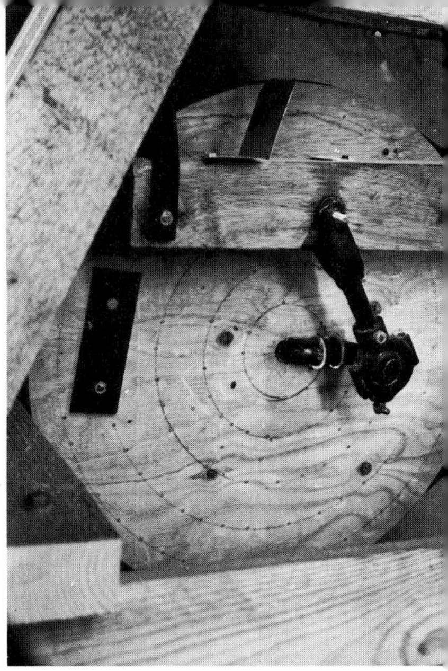

Fig. 6 (above): Crank rod is checked for squareness after being heated cherry red and bent into shape. Fig. 7 (right): Crank, takeup bearing, throw-rod and U*-shaped coupling connect flywheel to lower arm of saw. Metal plate bolted to flywheel opposite crank acts as counterbalance.*

other—and then spread the turnbuckle ends an extra ½ in. to allow for bearing wear and blade stretch. I noted the vertical distance between pivot pins and cut two pieces of 2x8 plank to serve as upright supports for the arms. These I cut about 12 in. longer than the pin-to-pin distance. They were clamped together and bored for the pivot pins on a drill press to ensure proper alignment. I cut a small block ⅛ in. thicker than the arm, and glued and nailed it in place between the uprights where they would be bolted to the two table-support members, which I cut from 2x6 stock. They were glued and lightly nailed in place on the upright. Then the whole assembly was bolted together with four ⅜-in. threaded rods. The pivot pins were lightly greased and inserted into the assembly, securing the arms (rocking beams) in position.

The assembly was held upright while four 2-in. by 3-in. legs were attached to the table support members. The joining cheeks of the legs were beveled at 15°, splayed to the front and rear and attached with nails, bolts and glue. After leveling the unit, I attached braces and stretchers to stabilize the legs and to support the motor and drive system.

The drive crank—I took my 20-in. piece of 1-in. steel rod over to the local auto shop to use their cutting torch. The section of rod was heated cherry red about 7 in. from one end and inserted into two sections of pipe to bend it to a perfect 90° angle. A friend applied more heat as the metal was being stretched to prevent cracking. After cooling, a section about 4 in. past the first bend was heated cherry red and bent away from the first to complete the crank (figure 6).

The wooden flywheel—The next task was to make a belt-driven flywheel to turn the crank. My power source was an ancient electric washing-machine motor of ⅙ HP. I assumed that it turned at a standard 1,725 RPM. As large a flywheel as practical would give the poor little drive motor a hefty mechanical advantage. I formed the wheel from three plywood discs, the two outer ones of ½-in. plywood scribed to a 24-in. circle and the inner one of ⅜-in. plywood scribed to a 23⅝-in. circle. Then I bored a 1-in. hole in the center of each disc, spread glue over the mating surfaces of the discs and used the 1-in shaft to align them while I nailed them together, evenly spacing the nails on concentric lines for balance.

The crank was fastened to the completed flywheel with two *U*-bolts fashioned from ¼-in. threaded rod. It took about 40 minutes of wedging, bolt tightening and loosening, and fiddling to get the wheel to run true. Once it did, I smeared a lot of epoxy into the cracks and crevices. This seemed to help hold it in alignment, as it continues to run true.

The two pillow-block bearings were installed on the shaft, and support members were added to carry the shaft and motor. The flywheel was mounted so that the throw from the crank was properly aligned beneath the lower arm. I fastened a 1-in. takeup bearing to a short section of ½-in. steel pipe and pinned it in place with a small $\frac{5}{16}$-in. bolt (figure 7).

Adjusting the stroke—With the blade tightened and the arms braced at the upper limit of their stroke, I raised the crank to its upper limit also. On the lower arm I temporarily bolted into place a *U*-shaped piece of ¼-in. by 1-in. flatbar and set the takeup bearing (crank bearing) and pipe throw-rod in place. The pipe was then cut to a length that bridged the gap between the bearing and the *U*-shaped bracket. Then I welded the throw-rod into position at both ends.

Installing the motor—The completed throw-rod was mounted on the crank and bolted into the lower arm. I turned the flywheel by hand and moved the arms up and down to continue the motion. I bolted a piece of ¼-in. by 2-in. steel flatbar about 4 in. long to the wheel to counterbalance the rotating weight of the crank. A 2-in. pulley was mounted on the motor, which was bolted to a ¾-in. plywood base. Part of the bracket and the crank-rod bearing had to be dismantled to install the *V*-belt. This done, the motor was drawn tight against the belt, and I temporarily nailed the base down. With the motor running and the large pulley spinning, I used a small turning gouge to put a mild bevel on the insides of the flywheel pulley groove. Then I repositioned the motor in order to draw the belt up tight.

I let the saw run for a couple of hours while the pieces wore together. A periodic shot of heavy gear oil on the rubbing surfaces and in the oil holes helped considerably. I tacked small flaps of leather over the holes to keep out dirt and grit.

The table—I made the table from a piece of 1¼-in. plywood flooring, screwing it in place on the frame, square with the sides of the blade. I fastened two butt hinges to one side of the frame and to the table. If I need to cut stock at an angle, I remove the mounting screws and pivot the table until the desired angle is achieved. Wedges and a small turnbuckle can be used to hold the table in place. A larger table can be fastened to the existing table for cutting large stock.

Tuning—I had to make sure that the blade ran true on its up-and-down course (viewed from the front). Turning the flywheel slowly by hand revealed that the blade had some side-to-side movement which was caused, I found, by the upper blade bracket being a little crooked. I cured the problem by turning the bracket around and moving the blade over a bit on reassembly.

With a 2-in. drive pulley on the motor and a 24-in. flywheel, the saw produces 144 strokes per minute. While this is a little slow for efficiency's sake, that's about all the little ⅙-HP motor can handle without tripping its breaker. A ½-HP motor with a 3-in. or 4-in. pulley (or a smaller flywheel) would give a better turn of speed. But I have no trouble zipping through a heavy chunk of 8-in. by 12-in. timber. A piece of wood 8 in. thick is about the upper limit simply because the 11-in. stroke on a 20-in. blade leaves only about 8 in. for the wood being cut on the table. A longer blade or a shorter stroke would provide for a greater depth of cut.

Blades—When I designed this particular saw, I decided to use a standard 20-in. pruning-saw blade, available at almost any hardware store. The one difficulty with pruning-saw blades is that they are fairly wide and are designed to cut in both directions. This is fine for cutting firewood, but not very good for precision cutting where greater control is needed. Short sections of a band-saw blade would cut more precise-

ly. Woodcraft (41 Atlantic Ave., Box 4000, Woburn, Mass. 01888) supplies blades of any length. I would choose a blade from ½ in. to ¾ in. wide with three or four teeth per inch.

Because band-saw blades are thinner and cut in only one direction they don't catch and hold on the upstroke. Those needing very narrow blades should think about shaving the arms down a bit near the ends and using lightweight blade brackets and a lightweight tensioner. This will reduce the oscillating mass and thus reduce the strain on thinner blades.

Ripping and resawing—A walking-beam saw designed for ripping usually has a moderate throat, and the blade is set at 90° to the arms. The arms must be club-shaped at the ends with a radius sawn around those ends so that the blade stays vertical and in the same plane as it moves up and down. Pins driven into the ends of arms hold the blade 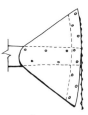 instead of blade brackets and the blade flexes around the ends of the arms, just as it would on the wheels of a band saw.

The walking-beam saw is cheap to make and operate, very quiet to run, and fairly efficient. As with any cutting tool, safety precautions are advised. The greatest danger seems to lie in having the workpiece wrested from your grasp and then attempting to grab it back instead of turning the machine off. Practice, a moderate speed, a sharp, thin blade and some common sense will go a long way toward making your experience with this saw a pleasant and rewarding one. □

Mark White teaches arctic house construction and boatbuilding at Kodiak (Alaska) Community College.

Treadle Band Saw

With a kit and plans for a 12-in. band saw supplied by Gilliom Mfg. (1700 Scherer Pkwy., St. Charles, Mo. 63303) and a number of scavenged parts, Andrew Maier of East Orange, N.J., built a treadle-powered band saw for use in a high-school shop. Intrigued by Richard Starr's foot-powered lathe (see pages 99 to 100), which uses a five-speed gear cluster to achieve different operating speeds, Maier decided that the same drive mechanism could be adapted for use with a band saw. Friends discouraged the idea, saying that he'd never be able to develop and sustain enough muscle power to cut stock of usable dimensions. But Maier carried through his scheme, getting parts for the drive system from a used bicycle shop and an auto junkyard, where he bought a Volkswagen flywheel and front-wheel bearings for the drive shaft. The finished machine, he says, will cut rapidly and smoothly through stock 2 in. thick and smaller, but it's slow going through pieces 4 in. thick or more. Maier was very pleased with the machine's performance. (For other readers' experiences in building band saws and other machines from Gilliom kits, see the letters on pages 92 and 93.) □

Maier's band saw, right, has frame, housing, column and table made entirely of wood. So this saw can be foot driven, a threaded-rod drive shaft fits into tapered roller bearings (above), which are mortised into cross members in frame. Drive pulley, flywheel and five-speed sprocket cluster were all purchased as used parts. It can, of course, be equipped with an electric motor.

Photos: Gina Scalzulli

Radial Saw Meets Computer

A cross-cutting robot for the small shop

by Lewis Buchner

About seven years ago, as my woodworking business went through the transition from a one-man shop in a garage to a six-person operation with more machinery and space, I was asked to manufacture cabinets for a computerized medical instrument. The job promised to be a bread-and-butter item that could augment my custom cabinet and furniture business, so I decided to take a crack at it.

It proved to be quite a challenge. Because each cabinet had to be accurate within 0.015 in. to accommodate the instrument's panels, we had to cut the parts precisely. We made jigs that slid down a fence past a tilted radial-arm saw; we tried fancy ball-bearing attachments for the shaper table and a host of hold-down, slide-along, slip-back, bevel-cut gadgets. Warped or cupped boards and material that varied in thickness (as much as 0.025 in. in a single plywood sheet) gave us the biggest problems.

After much hair-tearing and a failed search for machinery remotely within our budget, we concluded that we should

Photos by the author

To position the wood for sawing, Buchner built this Plexiglas sliding table, which glides on linear-motion bearings riding on steel rods. The wood is clamped to the table via vacuum pressure, and the computer positions the stock by moving the table through a rack-and-pinion gear connected to a stepping motor.

An accurate cut is vital to Buchner's folded-box technique. The V-grooves are made in one pass, cutting through all but half the $\frac{1}{28}$-in. thick face veneer on the outside face of the plywood. Tape reinforces the joint, acting as a hinge when the cabinet is folded and glued up.

either bail out of the box business or create our own robot to do the job for us. I called a brainstorming meeting at the shop one night with our foreman and a couple of friends, one an electronics engineer and computer nut, the other a machinist and inventor. The challenge of building such a smart machine was appealing, and we agreed that each person would develop an aspect of it that was within his area of expertise.

We decided we would make our boxes by cutting five accurately spaced V-shaped grooves in a plywood panel as wide as the cabinet's depth. The grooves would be cut through the plywood core and about halfway through the face veneer on the opposite side of the panel. Once cut, the plywood could be folded on the grooves, transforming them into miters and creating an instant box.

If our machine was to work, we had to accurately control two things: the depth of cut and, to compensate for variation in the plywood thickness so that the case's inside dimensions would be consistent, the distance between grooves. We started with an old 16-in. DeWalt radial-arm saw, refurbished by the local DeWalt service center so that it would cut more accurately. We had the blade custom-made—a 10-in. diameter, 2-in. thick steel disc with eight large triangular carbide teeth. Because of the mass of the cutter and the healthy size of the cut, it would be impossible to operate the saw by hand, so we built a hydraulic-pneumatic system to move the saw.

To get the critical accuracy between V-grooves, we needed to position the stock in front of the blade precisely, time after time. Stop blocks set on the saw fence would have been too slow and inaccurate, since each box had to be cut slightly differently. So we built an 8-ft. bed that slides back and forth in front of the saw. This bed, which rides on linear-motion bearings and steel rods, is motivated by a rack-and-pinion gear attached to a computer-controlled stepping motor. The stepping motor has 200 poles and rotates its shaft one pole for every pulse that it receives from the control circuitry.

We made the bed itself of 1-in. thick Plexiglas with a 1-in. square grid routed into it. At the leading edge of the bed, we drilled a small hole where vacuum pressure from a pump enters the grid. Once the plywood blank is positioned on the grid and the vacuum is actuated, several hundred pounds of force eliminates any warp or cup and allows the cutter to operate unhindered by clamps.

With the saw calibrated and working, it's amazing how quickly the boxes can be made. First, the operator measures the thickness of the plywood at each of the five points where a groove is to be cut. Using a chart we made up, he sets thumbwheels on the saw's control panel that tell the computer the distance between the V-grooves.

Next, he applies tape to the back side of the panel to support the thin veneer left after the cut is made. He places the panel on the saw table, turns on the vacuum and pushes the start button. The computerized control circuit is pro-

From *Fine Woodworking* magazine (May 1983) 40:98-99

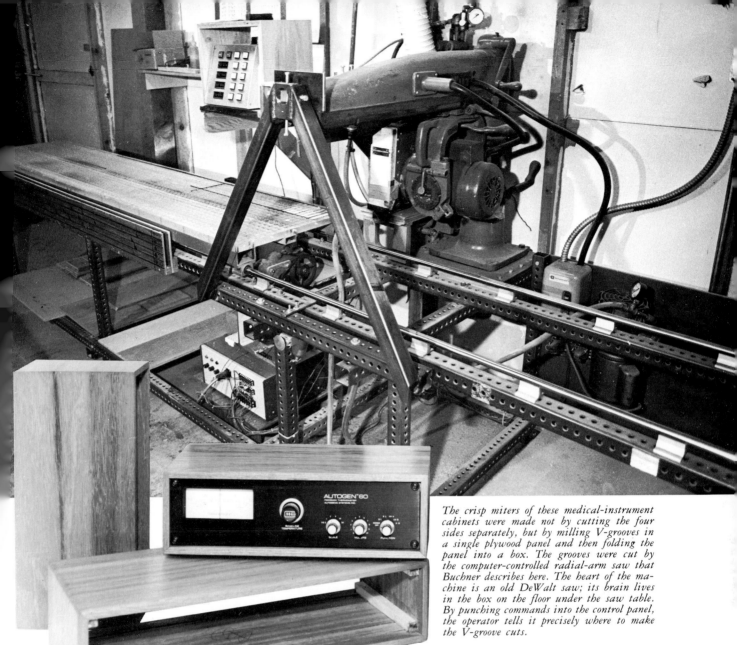

The crisp miters of these medical-instrument cabinets were made not by cutting the four sides separately, but by milling V-grooves in a single plywood panel and then folding the panel into a box. The grooves were cut by the computer-controlled radial-arm saw that Buchner describes here. The heart of the machine is an old DeWalt saw; its brain lives in the box on the floor under the saw table. By punching commands into the control panel, the operator tells it precisely where to make the V-groove cuts.

grammed to make an initial groove about an inch in from the end of the blank. This groove is the zero point, from which all the other distances are measured. The computer sends out pulses to the stepping motor, telling it where to position the sliding bed. When the bed comes to rest, a solenoid activates the cylinder that drives the cutting head. When one cut has been completed, the stepping motor moves the bed the appropriate distance to the next cut. We found that bed movement is accurate to within 0.005 in.

It takes about 30 seconds to mike the blank and enter the numbers on the control panel, and about a minute for the machine to do its work. During this time, the operator can mike and tape the next blank. Once a blank is positioned on the table, the machine does everything automatically, except turning the vacuum on and off, which is done by hand. The V-grooved panels are taken to another room where they are glued up, sanded and finished.

One of the remarkable things about our V-groove saw is how well it has held up. By now, it has cut more than 5,000 boxes, running for a few days each week. Last year, when I returned to one-of-a-kind furniture work, I sold the saw to a woodworker friend, who tells me that it's still running strong. During the time I owned the saw, I experienced no major breakdowns, and did little more than replace hydraulic seals, sharpen the blade and blow the dust off it. We spent $7,500 to build the machine in 1977, including buying and programming our own electronic chips to run the thing. You could probably do it much more cheaply now. Anyone with basic computer knowledge could program an Apple or other personal computer to direct a machine—the hardest part would be connecting the computer to the various switches, solenoids and motors that actually run the machine. Except for the stepping motor, we bought most of the hardware for our saw from electronic and industrial supply houses.   □

Lewis Buchner makes furniture in San Francisco.

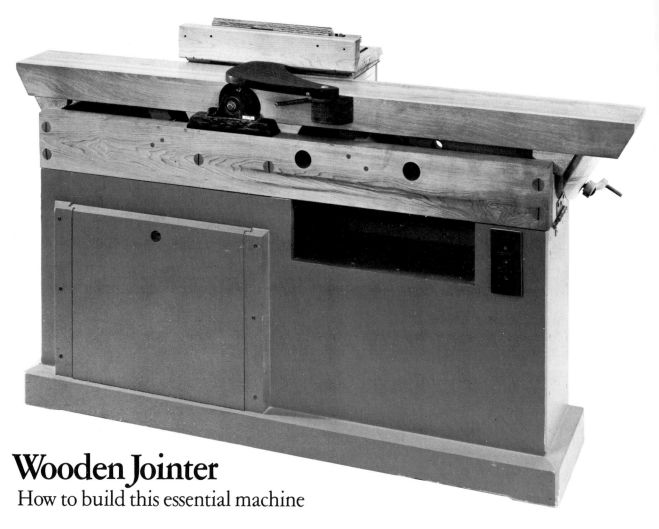

Wooden Jointer
How to build this essential machine

by Galen Winchip

Seven years ago I walked into a local hardware store to buy an odd assortment of stuff. "What are you going to make?" asked the quizzical gentleman waiting on me. "A wooden jointer," I replied, trying to sound confident. He was both astonished and skeptical, and did his best to persuade me to buy the jointer on display in the store. Despite his warning that a jointer is a precision tool and not the kind of thing you just throw together in your shop, I bought the items on my list and thus embarked on my first tool-building venture.

That first jointer worked, but it left several things to be desired. So I determined to make a jointer that would perform as well as a commercial model. I subsequently tested five designs, each one simpler, more reliable and more precise than the one before. Finally, I

arrived at the design for the jointer shown here. It requires no exotic, hard-to-find hardware or materials, and it doesn't call for any tricky methods of construction. Its performance rivals that of an industrially produced machine, though its price (about $350 in 1981) is considerably less, and its feel and appearance are friendlier. After using this jointer for about 18 months, taking it from one job site to another, I'm very happy with its design and with the results it produces.

Like certain of its industrial-duty,

cast-iron counterparts, my wooden jointer incorporates four sets of inclined ways or wedge-shaped bearing blocks. As shown below, these provide the means for raising and lowering the tables. The wedges on the bottom of each table (elevation blocks) ride up and down on the stationary ways (bearing blocks) attached to the frame assembly. This system is especially suitable for a wooden jointer because it supports each bed at four points, two at each end, eliminating the possibility of drooping tables and providing very

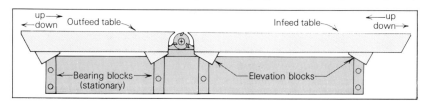

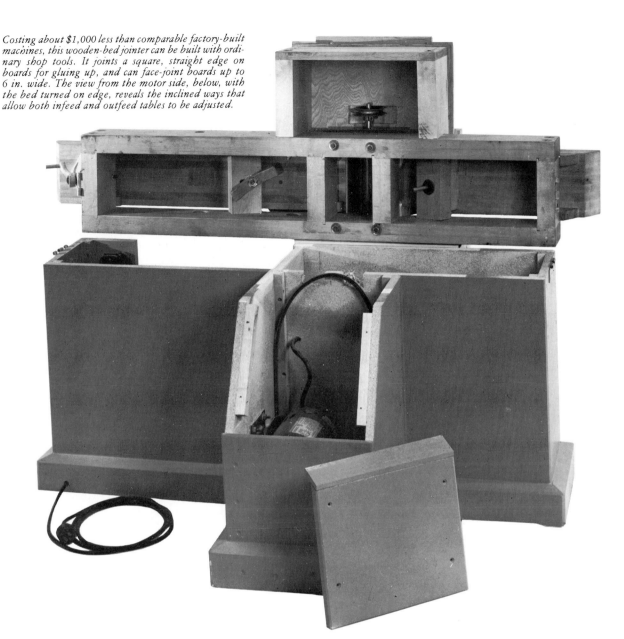

Costing about $1,000 less than comparable factory-built machines, this wooden-bed jointer can be built with ordinary shop tools. It joints a square, straight edge on boards for gluing up, and can face-joint boards up to 6 in. wide. The view from the motor side, below, with the bed turned on edge, reveals the inclined ways that allow both infeed and outfeed tables to be adjusted.

stable working surfaces. I've jointed a lot of long, heavy stock with this machine, and found it can easily cut a true edge on an 8/4 board, 8 ft. long and 10 in. wide.

The cutterhead is the heart of the machine, so you should get one that is well-balanced and perfectly round (square cutterheads are dangerous) and that has been turned and milled from a single piece of bar stock. It should have a cutting arc of about 3 in. and a hefty shaft, ¾ in. in diameter. Mine was turned and milled by a machinist friend, who got the shaft too small for my liking. I'll soon make a new one with a ¾-in. shaft, which will minimize vibration and increase durability. You can have a machinist do this work for you as I did, or you can buy a cutterhead as a replacement part from a woodworking-

machinery distributor. The cutterhead shaft runs in two self-aligning, ball-bearing pillow blocks, which you can get at any well-stocked industrial-supply or farm-supply store.

For driving the cutterhead, use a 1-HP or 1½-HP, 3,600-RPM motor. Select a pair of pulleys that will turn the cutterhead about 5,000 RPM (about 4,000 surface feet per minute).

The infeed and outfeed tables are laminated from quartersawn, face-glued boards. I used ¾-in. beech, but maple or another hard, heavy wood would do. Since the finished tables are 3 in. thick, you should rip the laminae to a rough width of around 3¼ in. to allow for a preliminary and a final surfacing of both sides. Use yellow (aliphatic resin) glue, and allow the tables to sit for several weeks before initial sur-

facing. The gluelines need time to cure thoroughly, and the laminated slabs need time to stabilize.

The tables shown here are proportioned to my own preferences: the infeed table is 10 in. longer than the outfeed because I find this easier for jointing long, heavy stock. But you can make them of equal length, as is common practice, or you can experiment to learn what suits you best. The same holds true for the dimensions of the fence. You can make one fence for the kind of work you do most, or you can make several of different sizes for different jobs. Since you're making your own, you aren't limited by what some manufacturer decides is the average size.

The jointer frame consists of two sides and three sets of blocks—two pairs of bearing blocks and a pair of clamping

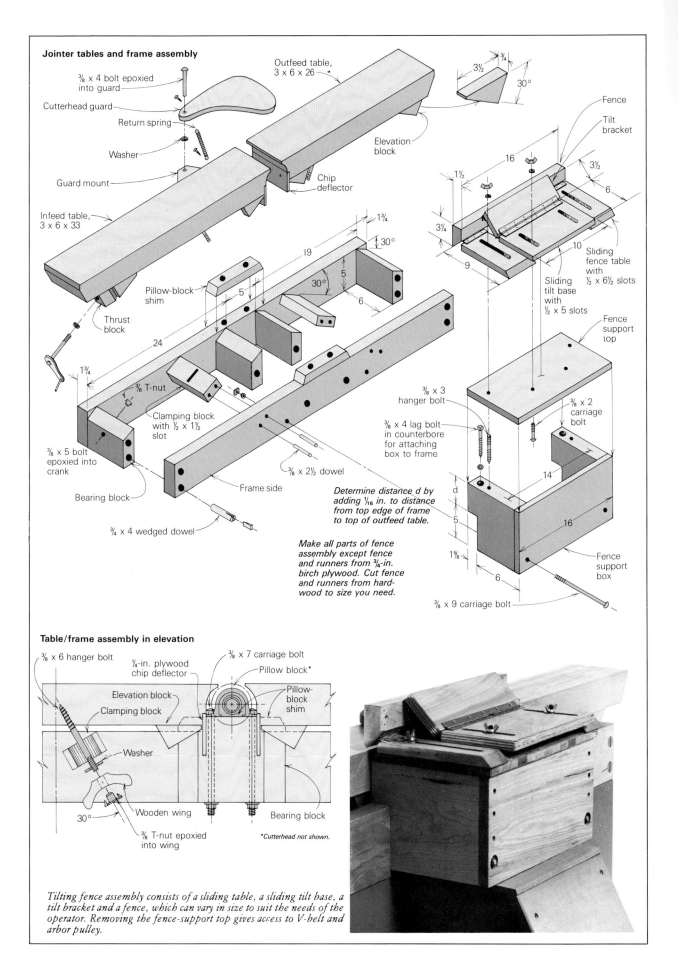

Jointer tables and frame assembly

⅜ x 4 bolt epoxied into guard

Cutterhead guard

Return spring

Washer

Guard mount

Infeed table, 3 x 6 x 33

Thrust block

Outfeed table, 3 x 6 x 26

Elevation block

Chip deflector

30°

3½

¾

Fence

Tilt bracket

16

1½

3¾

9

3½

6

10

Sliding fence table with ½ x 6½ slots

Sliding tilt base with ½ x 5 slots

Fence support top

Pillow-block shim

30°

30°

5

5

6

19

1¾

24

1¾

⅜ T-nut

Clamping block with ½ x 1½ slot

⅜ x 5 bolt epoxied into crank

Bearing block

¾ x 4 wedged dowel

Frame side

⅜ x 2½ dowel

⅜ x 3 hanger bolt

⅜ x 4 lag bolt in counterbore for attaching box to frame

⅜ x 2 carriage bolt

14

16

d

5

1⅝

6

Fence support box

⅜ x 9 carriage bolt

Determine distance d by adding ¹⁄₁₆ in. to distance from top edge of frame to top of outfeed table.

Make all parts of fence assembly except fence and runners from ¾-in. birch plywood. Cut fence and runners from hardwood to size you need.

Table/frame assembly in elevation

⅜ x 6 hanger bolt

¼-in. plywood chip deflector

⅜ x 7 carriage bolt

Pillow block*

Elevation block

Clamping block

Pillow-block shim

Washer

30°

Wooden wing

⅜ T-nut epoxied into wing

Bearing block

Cutterhead not shown.

Tilting fence assembly consists of a sliding table, a sliding tilt base, a tilt bracket and a fence, which can vary in size to suit the needs of the operator. Removing the fence-support top gives access to V-belt and arbor pulley.

blocks. The top edges of the bearing blocks are beveled at 30°, and the clamping blocks are slotted for clamping bolts. The clamping blocks, though not beveled, are set at a 30° angle to the top of the frame. The drawing (facing page) dimensions and locates these parts. Make sure when cutting duplicate parts that their dimensions and angles are precisely the same. This can be done by ripping and beveling a single board and then crosscutting identical parts to finished length. All the blocks must be oriented at a true 90° to the frame sides, and the clamping blocks ought to be positioned as close as possible to the center bearing blocks. The outer bearing blocks should be flush with the ends of the frame sides.

To add strength and to help position the parts during clamping, I cut narrow tenons on the bearing blocks and dadoes in the frame sides to house them. But you need not go to this trouble to get similar results—just clamp the frame sides together with the bearing and clamping blocks between, and then tap them into their exact positions with a mallet. This done, tighten the clamps, and bore for dowels through the frame sides into the blocks as shown in the drawing (¾-in. dia. holes for the bearing blocks, ⅜-in. dia. holes for the clamping blocks). The dowels will let you place the parts accurately when gluing up and will reinforce the frame assembly. The ¾-in. dowels are slotted and wedged. Since you're gluing end grain to long grain, epoxy is best; size the end grain before gluing and clamping. When the glue has set, sand the dowels flush with the frame sides.

The base, which you'll probably want to make while your table laminations are aging, is of ¾-in. high-density particleboard. Plywood will suffice, but it's more expensive and not as rigid or heavy. With a plan view that resembles a T, the stand is constructed using corner cleats, screws and yellow glue. This type of base has several advantages. One is that the motor is enclosed in a separate compartment, protected from dust and shavings. Another is that the shavings, being contained in a single bin, are easily removed. A third advantage of the T configuration is that the weight of the machine and the base rests on the three extreme points, and thus leveling is never required.

Surfacing the tables is easy if you have access to a thickness planer and a

Particleboard base contains separate compartments for the motor and for chips and shavings. Door to shavings bin slides up and down in rabbeted cleats. Opening in side under the infeed table gives quick access to the wing nut that must be loosened for making changes in depth of cut. The T configuration of the base concentrates the machine's weight on three points, eliminating the need to level it to the floor.

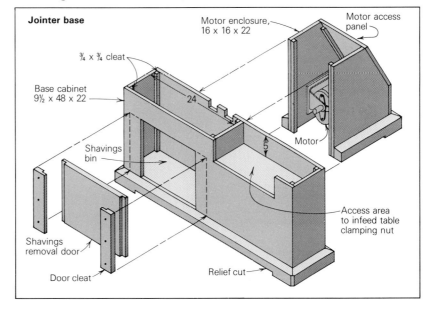

Jointer base

Motor enclosure, 16 x 16 x 22
Motor access panel
¾ x ¾ cleat
Base cabinet 9½ x 48 x 22
24
Shavings bin
5
Motor
Access area to infeed table clamping nut
Shavings removal door
Door cleat
Relief cut

jointer wider than the one you're making. If you can't find a friend who'll let you use his, or a school shop where you can do this work, you'll probably have to pay to have it done at a local millwork or cabinet shop. You could even do it with hand planes, winding sticks and a straightedge, but you must be very patient to get the results required.

Begin by jointing one face of each table, being careful to take light cuts and to avoid sniping the ends. Then run

both tables through the thickness planer for several light passes to bring them within ⅛ in. of their finished thickness. Again, be careful to set the planer's bedrolls properly to prevent snipe on the final pass.

Now place both tables upside down on a perfectly flat surface, butt them end to end, and separate them about 2 in. Get two small boards, each about 9 in. long, 2 in. wide and exactly ¾ in. thick, and put one across the outer edge of each table. Place the frame assembly upside down on the two boards, which will hold the frame ¾ in. above the bottoms of the tables. Position the frame and tables relative to one another, and check the spacing between the two tables to make sure there's room for the rotating cutterhead. Apply some yellow glue (or epoxy) to the top edges of the elevation blocks, and slide them into place between the inclined surfaces of the bearing blocks. Since the angles are complementary, the fit should be perfect. When installing the elevation blocks, don't wedge them too tightly under the bearing blocks; just bring the mating surfaces into light, uniform contact. If all eight elevation blocks are not exerting equal pressure against the bearing blocks, the tables will rock.

Securing the tables to the frame is accomplished by two ⅜-in. by 6-in. hanger bolts. The wood-thread ends are screwed at a 60° angle into the table bottoms. The machine-thread ends pass through the slots in the clamping blocks and are retained by homemade wing nuts (optional on the outfeed table). These have wood bodies with T-nuts epoxied into their centers. After the glue holding the elevation blocks in place has thoroughly dried, remove the frame assembly and bore angled pilot holes in the tables for the hanger bolts and screw them into place. Long hanger bolts are used in stairway handrailing; if you can't find any, buy a couple of long lag bolts, cut their heads off and die-cut National Coarse machine threads onto their unthreaded shoulders.

Now you can put the tables onto the wedged ways and clamp them in place with the wing nuts. Loosen each nut slightly and check to see that each table rides freely up and down the inclines and that there is no rock or play anywhere. If you detect any rocking, carefully remove a small amount of wood from the bearing surface of the opposite elevation block and check again.

When the tables fit and slide correctly, return the whole assembly (frame and tables) to your flat reference surface. With both tables resting flat on this surface, tighten the clamping nuts. Now take the whole thing back to wherever you did your initial jointing and surfacing, place your jointer upside down on the borrowed jointer and surface both tables in a single pass. Take a very light cut (1⁄32 in. or less) and check down the length of both tables at once

with an accurate straightedge. If they are truly straight and in the same plane, you can take your jointer back to your shop and continue construction. If not, find the source of the error (it could be in the iron machine), eliminate it and take another light cut the full length of both beds. Remove as little stock as possible, since you may want to surface the tables again in the future, should they warp out of true or their surfaces get badly gouged and pitted.

Surfacing complete, trim the tables to final width and cope an appropriately curved area where each table will extend over the cutterhead. The bandsaw is best for this. Don't cut the arcs so the blade exits on the top surface of the table, but rather so it exits on the end, about 3⁄16 in. below the top. This will produce a little land that makes the ends of the tables stronger, and leaves the straight lines across the tables intact. Keep the throat opening narrow.

The elevating mechanism for the infeed table consists of a ⅜-in. by 5-in. bolt epoxied into a wooden crank, a thrust block glued to the bottom of the infeed table and a T-nut countersunk into the end bearing block. The ⅜-in. National Coarse bolt has 16 threads per inch. Because the bolt moves the table up and down a 30° incline, and the sine of 30° equals 0.5, one revolution of the crank will move the table 1⁄32 in. vertically, a handy reference. You could mount a depth-of-cut indicator on one of the bearing blocks.

To change depth of cut, back off the clamping nut just enough to free the table, turn the crank to raise or lower it and retighten the nut. Excessive torque isn't necessary to hold the tables securely on their ways. For making the fine adjustments on the outfeed table, I keep the nut snug and smartly strike the end of the table with a wooden mallet to raise it slightly, or strike the end of the frame to lower it—similar to the way you tune a wooden handplane. Since the nut stays tight, you seldom need access to it. Mine doesn't even have wooden wings attached; I use a wrench when it needs adjusting.

To install the cutterhead, first dimension a pair of pillow-block support shims, which will hold the cutterhead at the proper height. Fiddle with the thickness of each shim to level the cutterhead with the tables. Screw the shims into place, replace the cutterhead and pillow blocks and mark the centers for

four holes to be drilled through the shims and frame sides. The diameter of the holes should be slightly larger than the ⅜-in. carriage bolts that will hold the pillow blocks in place. These bolts may have to be retightened from time to time, because seasonal shrinkage might loosen them. For safety, use self-locking nuts.

The fence assembly is mounted on a three-sided hardwood box. Its sides are notched to fit over the edge of the frame side, and it is held in place by two carriage bolts and two lag bolts. The plywood top of the fence-support box should sit about 1⁄16 in. higher than the level of the outfeed table. This clearance allows the fence table to slide freely across the jointer beds.

The fence itself can be made to any reasonable size, though its dimensions need not change those of the sliding fence table or the hinged tilting bracket and base. To make the table and tilting brackets, get some good ¾-in. birch plywood, and cut the three pieces to the sizes shown in the drawing on page 32. Then cut two slots in the sliding table and two in the tilting bracket base. For hinging the parts together, you can cut a continuous hinge into three lengths or use three pairs of butt hinges. You may want to attach hardwood sled-type runners to the sides of the sliding table, as I have done. These will wear longer than plywood and will look better. Depending on the diameter of your arbor sheave, you might have to cove out an area on the underside of the fence support top to keep the belt from rubbing the wood. The fence table is locked in place by two wing nuts screwed onto ⅜-in. hanger bolts that extend through the table slots. The tilting bracket base is secured also by wing nuts screwed onto carriage bolts that extend through the fence table.

The cutterhead guard must be made of a sturdy hardwood (I used padauk). You may alter its standard shape as you please, so long as it moves easily away from the fence when stock is pushed against it and so long as it covers the unused portion of the rotating knives. The guard has a ⅜-in. bolt epoxied to it, and this bolt pivots in a hole in a mounting block that is screwed to the sides of the infeed table. A washer on the bolt between the mounting block and the bottom of the guard will ensure that the guard swings just clear of the jointer beds. A small tensioning spring holds

A look underneath the infeed table shows the positions of elevation blocks, clamping stud (hanger bolt) and thrust block, which contains elevation screw and crank. In the jointer frame underneath, you can see the inclined bearing blocks (ways), the slotted clamping block and the large
wooden wing nut. The unfilled holes in the side of the frame remain from author's earlier experiment with a different means of securing the table
to its ways. They have nothing to do with the existing arrangement.

Staff

Staff

Left, Winchip strikes end of jointer frame with a mallet to lower the outfeed
table, as in tuning a wooden handplane. Index and middle fingers on left
hand detect the slight movement of elevation block as it travels minutely
down the ways. Above, he joints the edge of an 8-ft., 5/4 red oak board.

Making and Modifying Machines   **35**

the guard against the fence and against the stock being jointed.

I finished the machine with Watco oil and waxed the tops of the tables and the sliding surfaces on the wedged ways. The base I painted grey. No finish, however, makes wood completely impervious to moisture—I had to make slight adjustments in the outfeed table as its thickness changed minutely with the seasons. To correct any rocking or droop that might develop, insert paper shims between the bearing and elevation blocks. To spring-joint boards for gluing up panels, you could shim up the two inner elevation blocks on the outfeed table so that it slopes down from the cutterhead. A couple of pieces of notebook paper would be about right. Remember that the orientation of the outfeed table (both its angle and its

height) determines whether the jointed edge will be slightly concave or slightly convex. If the table is high in relation to the knives, the jointed surface will be convex; if low, it will be concave. Also, it's a good idea to check the tables occasionally for proper alignment. Crank the infeed table up to the exact height of the outfeed table and then lay your straightedge across both beds. If there's any deviation from a true plane, remedy the error with paper shims between the bearing and elevation blocks.

Having spent quite a few years working in university wood shops, I'll be first to admit that industrial-duty machine tools offer greater built-in precision than shop-made machines. But the differences are small, and the advantages of being able to build your own machines are great. My first woodworking

machines were home-workshop quality and were far inferior in terms of precision and stability to the shop-built ones I now use. Experience taught me that good work depends as much on the skill and sensitivity of the craftsman as on the built-in precision of the machinery. I have often observed students getting less than satisfactory results using good tools simply because they believe that machines should do accurate work in spite of the operator. The truth is, of course, that the operational skills and intuitive understanding of the craftsman are necessary to the precision cabinetmaking demands. ☐

Galen Winchip is a professional woodworker and industrial-education instructor in Ames, Iowa. For more on wooden jointers, see page 79.

Jointer safety

Some of the nastiest woodworking accidents result from careless or improper use of the jointer. A cutterhead rotating at 5,000 RPM looks seductively harmless; with its knives blurred into invisibility, all you see is a shimmering steel cylinder. Yet jointers regularly gobble up fingers, thumbs and sometimes hands. Surgical restoration is almost impossible—repairing tissue lost to a jointer is like trying to remake an original board from a pile of shavings. Such a nightmare can be avoided by being careful every time you use the jointer.

Before switching the machine on, make certain that the knives are firmly tightened in place. A loose knife can grab the work or come flying out of the cutterhead at high speed. Never use a jointer unless the cutterhead guard is in place. Even with the guard in place, large chips can be hurled from the machine with enough force to injure eyes. So always wear your safety goggles when jointing stock. Some jointers are equipped with a rabbeting table, and you must remove the guard to use this feature. But a jointer is not the best machine for rabbeting. It's better to use your table saw or spindle shaper or router. They do this job more safely and more efficiently. Though most jointers will cut as deeply as ¼ in. or more, you shouldn't take a cut any deeper than ⅛ in. in a single pass. You risk injury from kickback when taking too deep a cut, and you put unnecessary strain on the motor.

When jointing the edge of a board, keep your fingers well away from the table surface. When face-jointing stock, even

thick stock, always use a push-block. Stock shorter than 12 in. should not be machine-jointed, so if your finished pieces will be less than a foot long, joint the longer board before you cut it up. For jointing stock thinner than ½ in., you should make a massive push-block, like the one shown below made by John Alcock-White for jointing one face of the ⅜-in. stock he laminates for bandsaw boxes. The block should be as wide and as long as the stock being jointed, and 4 in. to 6 in. thick.

Used over a long time for repetitive operations, the jointer's incessant drone can lull the operator into inattention. In such a semiconscious state, an accident is liable to happen. So be especially vigilant when your work is boring and your attitude perfunctory.

Posture and stance are also important. Learn to feed stock across the tables without overreaching and losing your balance. Adopt a posture that will allow you to exert consistent downward and horizontal pressure on the stock. This not only contributes to safety, but also affects the results of your work. When feeding, allow the machine to cut at its own pace. Don't force work into the cutterhead, or try to hurry the board across the tables. A slow to moderate feed rate is best, though pausing or creeping along during a cut can score the surface of the wood and overheat the knives.

The knives should be kept sharp, and should all be maintained at the exact height. You can touch up the edges periodically with the judicious use of a slipstone, but when knives are knicked or dulled beyond reason, you should have them reground. Instruct the person doing this to remove the same amount of steel from each knife. Improperly ground knives will put the cutterhead out of balance, which causes vibration and can lead to an accident, and will definitely bring about premature bearing failure. When sharpening, maintain the original bevel angle. If you try to hone or grind a secondary bevel on the edges, the result will be increased noise and vibration, and decreased cutting efficiency.

Constant alertness, common sense and a knowledge of cutterhead dynamics are the best safeguards against accidental injury. Used properly, a machine jointer makes a woodworker's task immeasurably lighter and introduces a high degree of precision into the work.   *—John Lively*

A Sanding-Disc Jointer
Tapered disc on tilted arbor allows fine adjustment

by H.B. Montgomery

There are various methods for obtaining perfect edges on workpieces from thin veneers to ¾-in. thick hardwoods. With a simple guide jig and a tapered sanding disc mounted on a tilting-arbor table saw, I am getting perfect edges, ready for gluing in a matter of minutes.

A tapered sanding disc can be machined from a piece of ⅜-in. thick aluminum. I prefer a 10-in. disc with 2° to 3° of taper. Use a heavy backing plate while cutting the taper, or the edge will curve away under the pressure of the cutting tool and the surface will not be true. Three degrees is the maximum taper you can expect the sandpaper disc to adhere to. I use Sears pressure-sensitive sanding-disc cement and cut a 3-in. hole in the center of the sandpaper. Use paper-backed sanding discs; cloth or fiber-backed discs will not stay on.

The advantage of a tapered disc is that when mounted on the saw arbor and tilted to compensate for the taper, only a small portion of the disc is at 90° to the saw table, and that portion is moving practically parallel to the grain of the work being fed past. Also, because the arbor is tilted, the crank that raises and lowers the arbor can be used for fine adjustment of the lateral depth of cut of the disc.

The guide jig, which runs between the rip fence and the sanding disc, consists of a top and bottom plate (¾-in. hardwood plywood), a hardwood clamping reinforcement strip, two carriage bolts with wing nuts and two registration dowels. The jig should be slightly longer and wider than the stock you will be jointing. Crown the reinforcing strip about 1/16 in. to even out clamping pressure, and fasten it to the top plate from the bottom, about 1 in. back from the edge, with two countersunk wood screws located about 3 in. on either side of the center. Placing the screws farther apart might bend the

plywood to the slight arc of the reinforcing strip. Now clamp the two plates together and drill through at the ends of the reinforcing strip for the two carriage bolts. Countersink the bolts and tighten the wing nuts. Drill a hole in each side of the far edge of the jig to receive ½-in. by 1¼-in. registration dowels, as shown. Loosen the wing nuts, install the dowels and retighten the jig.

With the sanding disc on the saw, raise the arbor to its full height and, checking with a try square, tilt the arbor until the disc face is exactly 90° to the table, measured directly over the arbor. This is the only critical adjustment for the jointing operation. Lower the disc to 1¾ in. above the table and set the rip fence so the jig just fits between the two. Turn on the power and run the jig through several times on each edge, raising the arbor slightly between passes, until its edges are true and parallel.

To use the jig for jointing two veneers, lay the pieces side by side as they will be joined, face up, and fold them together with the good faces inside. Clamp this "book" in the jig with only 1/16 in. or so protruding, set the rip fence for the lightest cut and pass the work-loaded jig past the rotating disc. Raise the arbor between passes for a deeper cut until the veneers are flush with the jig edge; depending on the grit size on the disc, from .005 in. to .025 in. can be removed with one pass. I recommend 120 grit for finished edges.

The horizontal locating dowels work best for thin stock. The jig can handle up to ¾-in. thick stock (1½ in. thick total) with a 10-in. disc, but with thick stock vertical registers should be used. □

H.B. Montgomery, a retired mechanic, lives in Seminole, Fla.

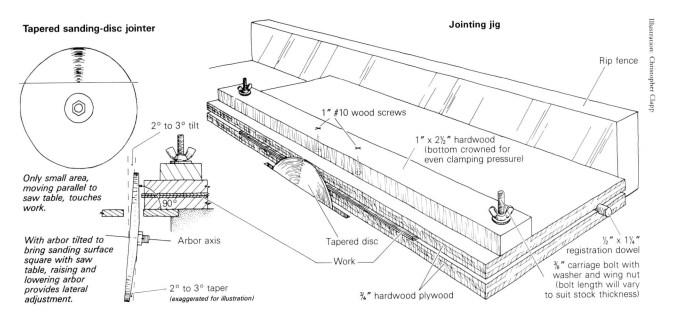

Tapered sanding-disc jointer

Only small area, moving parallel to saw table, touches work.

With arbor tilted to bring sanding surface square with saw table, raising and lowering arbor provides lateral adjustment.

2° to 3° tilt

90°

Arbor axis

2° to 3° taper
(exaggerated for illustration)

Jointing jig

Rip fence

1" #10 wood screws

1" x 2½" hardwood
(bottom crowned for even clamping pressure)

Tapered disc

Work

¾" hardwood plywood

½" x 1¼" registration dowel

⅜" carriage bolt with washer and wing nut
(bolt length will vary to suit stock thickness)

Illustration: Christopher Clapp

A Low-Tech Thickness Sander
Homebuilt machine is accurate and cheap

by T.R. Warbey

I make dulcimers, so I need thin pieces of wood sanded to fine tolerances after resawing. Last summer I made an abrasive thicknesser that handles stock down to 0.040 in. The machine cost me less than $20 (1980).

My thicknesser uses a drum made of plywood discs glued together and mounted on a steel shaft. The two end discs have ¼-in. grooves routed in them, and the steel shaft is drilled through with two ¼-in. holes to coincide with these grooves. Insert 3-in. lengths of steel rod into the holes when all the discs but the end ones are glued and in position on the shaft. Apply glue to the end discs and position them over the two rods.

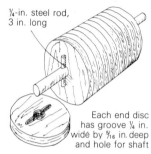

¼-in. steel rod, 3 in. long

Each end disc has groove ¼ in. wide by 5/16 in. deep and hole for shaft

Clamping the assembly locks the drum onto the shaft. When it's dry, I take it to the local machinist to be turned true.

Next mount the drum/shaft in pillow blocks on wooden spacers on a heavy plywood base. On my machine, the base is the top of a stand to support the machine and to house the motor. For the work-support table under the drum I used 1-in. maple only about 15 in. long, to minimize flexing. The table is hinged at one end (a full-length piano hinge is best) and sits on a wedge at the other.

I glue sanding-belt material to the drum using contact cement, but I use white glue for the joint at the belt ends. Dip the ends in boiling water to remove the abrasive, and dry prior to gluing. Lap the ends at an angle to the axis, a standard belt-gluing procedure.

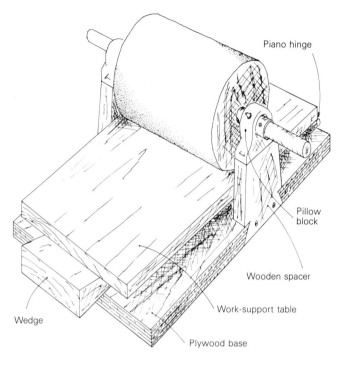

Piano hinge

Pillow block

Wooden spacer

Work-support table

Wedge

Plywood base

I sand both softwoods and hardwoods using 50-grit closed-coat aluminum-oxide belting. My machine is driven by a ¾-HP motor; the 6-in. diameter drum turns bottom toward me at 1600 RPM. I stand at the wedged end, place the work on the table and gently push it in under the drum, which sands and thicknesses at the same time. When one side is done, turn the work over, shift the wedge in a little and sand the other side until your stock is the desired thickness.

The machine is light enough to carry outside; this way I don't have a dust problem. Even so, I wear a mask. My next problem is how to change grits and keep it simple. □

EDITOR'S NOTE: We've come across a number of machines similar to Warbey's thickness sander. One made by Bob Meadow (a lutemaker and resident woodworker at Peters Valley Craftsmen, Layton, N.J.) is shown at right. It has a screw adjustment instead of a wedge to raise and lower the table. Two threaded rods are pinned to two timing pulleys and synchronized by a toothed rubber (timing) belt, which ensures even support. To true his drum, Meadow slid coarse sandpaper under the rotating, roughcut drum. (It is even possible to turn round an octagonal blank, already in the pillow blocks, from a tool rest mounted on the frame.) This both trues the drum and corrects any slight misalignment to the table. (For another version, see p. 79.)

According to R.E. Brune, of Evanston, Ill., another maker, the drum-type thickness sander has been around for several centuries as a luthier's *filertier*. Other variations can be found in the data sheets compiled by the Guild of American Luthiers (8222 S. Park Ave., Tacoma, Wash. 98408). Among the refinements is an answer to Warbey's problem of changing grits simply. *GAL Quarterly* editor Tim Olsen recommends using a steel drum (see data sheet 48). Not only is this more stable than a wooden one, but the sanding strip can be applied with a light, spray-on rubber cement (Olsen uses Weldwood Spray 'n' Glue), which bonds weakly with the steel and is easily removed. Wrapping the strip helically and securing the ends with masking tape provide an adequate hold.

Thickness sander by Bob Meadow uses a pair of synchronized machine screws to raise and lower the table. The machine is powered by a 1½-HP motor that turns the cylinder 1150 RPM.

From *Fine Woodworking* magazine (March 1980) 21:50

An Abrasive Planer
Automatic feed and rigid bed offer exceptional accuracy

by Michael Horwitz and Michael Rancourt

Stringed-instrument makers, marquetarians and boxmakers all deal with thin stock that must be thicknessed accurately. Luthiers in particular need to thickness tops, backs and sides often as thin as 0.080 in., and to make bindings and rosette components that commonly measure 0.010 in. or less. Knived planers can rarely handle stock less than ⅛ in. thick, and they produce a scalloped surface. An abrasive planer increases the possibilities for both production and design in thin stock. Simple drum-type sanders that are hand-fed (as on page 38) give modest results and do provide an alternative to tedious hand-planing or to purchasing thicknessed wood. However, to the woodworker involved in light production and/or requiring great accuracy, an automatic-feed, continuous-belt abrasive planer can prove valuable. In the seven machines we have built, a rigid bed provides advantages over the conveyer bed of other abrasive planers currently available. The machine detailed here can handle with greater accuracy the most delicate pieces of wood, and its cost and size make it feasible for the small shop. With the construction drawings on the next page, some mechanical know-how and basic machining, a superior abrasive planer can be home-built.

Construction — We make our planers, a 12-in. and an 18-in. size, on a movable base. It consists of eight pieces of angle iron and a half-lapped 2x6 maple frame. The angle iron forms a table whose legs are bolted to the frame, which rides on casters. The top surface of the angle-iron table is 31½ in. high; from it hang the motors (the machine has two motors) and on it is mounted the machine's superstructure. This consists of another 2x6 maple frame into which we mortise 2x4 uprights, attached from beneath with lag bolts. Two cross braces keep the uprights parallel, and two diagonal braces hold them perpendicular to the base.

The machine has two belt rolls: a lower sanding roll, which drives the belt, and an upper belt-tensioning idler. These we make of hardwood plywood discs, stacked and glued together on cold-rolled steel shafts, then turned and sanded with 50 grit. Leaving the bottom roll rough gives necessary belt grab. To prevent warping, the rolls are sealed with sanding sealer and polyurethane. The upper roll is then covered with ³⁄₁₆-in. cork (applied with contact cement) to help belt tracking. A locking pin system keeps each roll from turning on its shaft.

The bearings for the belt rolls are sealed roller-type with double-width races, and must be press-fit onto their respective shafts. The sanding-roll bearings are pressed into housings held in place with setscrews in two steel mounts. The mounts are 1-in. thick

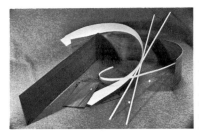

Left, stock thicknessed on abrasive planer, the thinnest pieces to 0.005 in. Below, Michael Horwitz at the 12-in. model.

milled forks, welded to ½-in. steel plates bolted to the machine base. The idler is supported by two belt-tensioning arms that pivot from the uprights on ¾-in. steel rod pinned to the arms. Cutouts drilled with a circle cutter on the insides of the arms receive the bearings for the idler. A snug fit here ensures consistent belt tracking. Slots in the ends of the swing arms receive threaded rods. These pivot from steel angle brackets bolted to the top of the uprights. Each of the two adjustment handles, which control both belt tension and tracking, is a homemade rod-coupler pressed and pinned into a piece of maple shaped like a giant wing nut.

The bed is a piece of ⅝-in. hot-rolled steel covered with Formica. Attached to the underside of the bed by five machine screws is a ¾-in. cold-rolled steel rod, which serves as a pivot mounted in Oilite bearings at either end. One end of the pivot is in a fixed maple block; the other adjusts to true the bed parallel to the sanding roll. A piece of threaded rod with a handwheel attached raises and lowers the bed to adjust depth of cut. The rod passes at a 6° angle through a tapped block, welded to a steel cross member. The end of the threaded rod is turned to a soft point to achieve a smaller and more positive contact. A dead stop (two jam nuts on the threaded rod) keeps the bed from contacting the sanding roll.

The accuracy of this machine is achieved in good part by driving the stock past the sanding surface at a steady rate. The three rubber drive rolls are chain driven by a ¼-HP, 18-RPM gear motor. It produces a feed rate of 9 SFM. We made the drive rolls by cutting to length 2-in. medium-hard rubber cylinders and slipping them onto the cold-rolled shafts. We then ribbed the rubber on the table saw and fixed it to the shaft with ¼-in. roll pins. The feed-roll shafts rotate in oilite bearings pressed into collars welded on the end of steel swing arms that pivot on the frame. Tension springs attached between the

arms and the frame provide downward pressure on the stock. Adjustable arm length compensates for chain slackening.

The abrasive belt for the 18-in. machine is driven by a 3-HP, 1725-RPM, totally enclosed, fan-cooled motor, the 12-in. machine by a 2-HP motor. The motor's speed is reduced slightly by a 3½-in. pulley on the motor and a 4¾-in. pulley on the roll. These produce a belt speed of 1,700 SFM. The motor is equipped with an overload button, and all electrical components are matched according to motor amperage.

A vacuum hood mounted directly over the space between the sanding roll and the front drive roll collects dust immediately as it leaves the board. The entire evacuation unit, including the ¼-in. Plexiglas guard, is hinged so it can be swung away during belt changes. For safety, Plexiglas also encloses the drive system and the idler.

For passing many boards through the machine in succession, we designed a stacking attachment to receive stock at the outfeed end. It is a collapsible birch-plywood shelf,

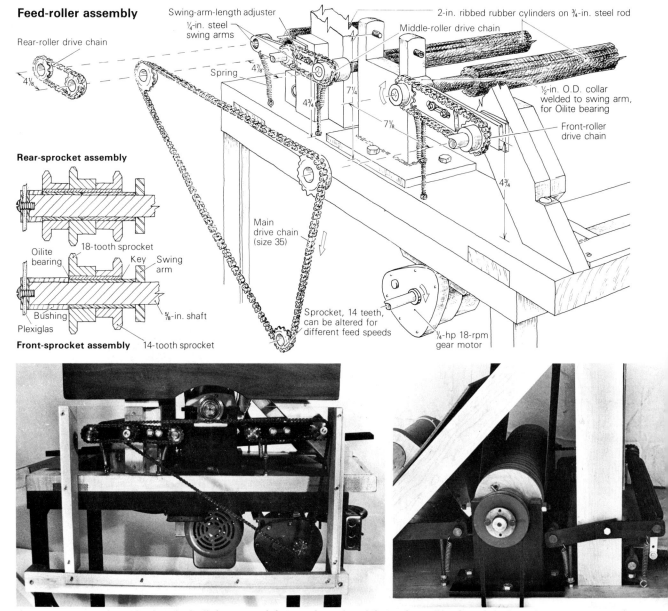

Feed-roller assembly

Rear-roller drive chain

4⅛

Swing-arm-length adjuster

¼-in. steel swing arms

Spring

4⅞

4¾

7¼

7⅛

2-in. ribbed rubber cylinders on ¾-in. steel rod

Middle-roller drive chain

½-in. O.D. collar welded to swing arm, for Oilite bearing

Front-roller drive chain

4¾

Rear-sprocket assembly

18-tooth sprocket

Oilite bearing

Key

Swing arm

Bushing

⅝-in. shaft

Plexiglas

Front-sprocket assembly   14-tooth sprocket

Main drive chain (size 35)

Sprocket, 14 teeth, can be altered for different feed speeds

¼-hp 18-rpm gear motor

A ¼-HP gear motor drives the three feed rolls by means of chains and sprockets, left. Sanding roll, right, is belt-driven by 3-HP motor at right-hand side of machine. Bed-truing adjuster can be seen attached to back of 2x4 upright.

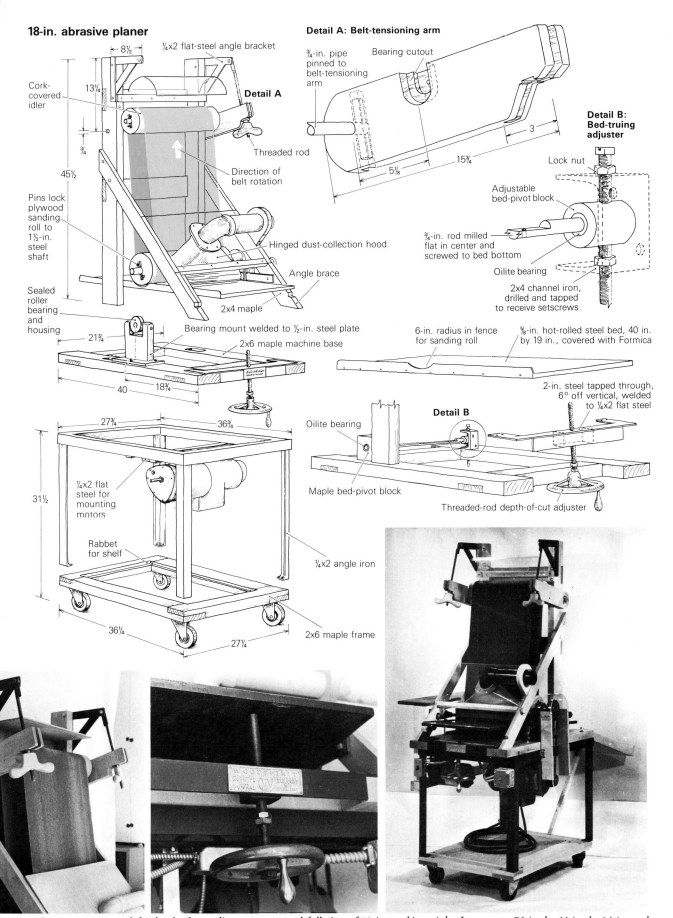

18-in. abrasive planer

8½

¼x2 flat-steel angle bracket

13¼

Detail A

Cork-covered idler

¾

45½

Threaded rod

Direction of belt rotation

Pins lock plywood sanding roll to 1½-in. steel shaft

Hinged dust-collection hood

Angle brace

2x4 maple

Sealed roller bearing and housing

Bearing mount welded to ½-in. steel plate

21¾

2x6 maple machine base

40   18¾

Detail A: Belt-tensioning arm

¾-in. pipe pinned to belt-tensioning arm

Bearing cutout

3

15¾

5⅛

Detail B: Bed-truing adjuster

Lock nut

Adjustable bed-pivot block

¾-in. rod milled flat in center and screwed to bed bottom

Oilite bearing

2x4 channel iron, drilled and tapped to receive setscrews

6-in. radius in fence for sanding roll

⅝-in. hot-rolled steel bed, 40 in. by 19 in., covered with Formica

2-in. steel tapped through, 6° off vertical, welded to ¼x2 flat steel

27¾   36¾

¼x2 flat steel for mounting motors

31½

Rabbet for shelf

36¼

27¼

¼x2 angle iron

2x6 maple frame

Oilite bearing

Detail B

Maple bed-pivot block

Threaded-rod depth-of-cut adjuster

Belt-tensioning arms, left, depth-of-cut adjuster, center, and full view of 18-in machine, right. It measures 76 in. by 44 in. by 34 in. and weighs 800 lb.

Photos: Raymond P. Bub; Illustrations: Christopher Clapp

hinged from the rear of the base. The rear feed roll eases each piece down onto the stacking shelf.

Operation — To install the belt, loosen the setscrews that retain the sanding roll. Tilt the roller assembly, remove the drive belt and then the roll itself. At the tensioning arms the idler can be removed, passed through the abrasive belt and replaced. Then pass the lower roll through the belt and replace it in the steel mounts. To tension and track the belt, tighten the two wooden wing nuts so that each side is firm but not forcibly stretched. For an initial tracking check, bump the motor on and off. Final tracking is achieved with the motor running. Keep a close eye on the belt for a while, as even a 5° turn of the wing nuts takes minutes to show up as belt movement. Don't get the belt too tight. Tracking can be achieved by loosening as well as tightening the wing nuts.

To get accurate results, the bed must be absolutely parallel to the sanding roll. After turning on the two motors and the vacuum, run narrow test boards through the machine at the sides of the roll, compare their thickness and true the bed using the bed adjuster at the right-hand side of the machine (detail B in the drawing). To begin sanding, lower the bed, using the handwheel at the front, beyond the thickness of the board and pass the board under the feed roll. As the board goes under the sanding roll, raise the bed slowly until light contact is made. Now that the bed is adjusted to the board's thickness, the depth of cut depends on grit, wood density and width of the board. For example, 0.050 in. can be removed from a 10-in. Sitka spruce board with 36 grit, 0.025 in. with 60 grit. In wood as dense as Brazilian rosewood, the maximum cut might be 0.015 in. with 60 grit on an 8-in. board.

Saddle jig with two cam clamps.

Special jigs can hold even the shortest pieces of wood, which to guitar builders can mean the accurate thickness-ing of nuts, saddles and bridge blanks. By taping strips of stock to support boards, one can make custom bindings and rosette components. In the repair of a rare Torres guitar, we matched the original binding with maple purfling strips measuring 0.005 in., a size thinner than those available commercially.

You might consider several options to improve the machine. They include a variable-speed feed motor to accelerate taking light cuts, and a more powerful sanding motor to make heavier cuts. Another possibility is a thickness-calibration system using two dial indicators that would eliminate manual measuring of stock thickness.

The only maintenance necessary on this machine is an occasional oiling of the drive chain, and keeping the machine clean. The vacuum system, which is hooked up to a shop vac, picks up 99% of the dust produced; to achieve accuracy of ± 0.003 in. across the whole width of the planing surface, a relatively dust-free situation is necessary. □

At the time of this writing (1980), Michael Horwitz and Michael Rancourt ran Woodspirit in Pownal, Vt. They have since moved on to other enterprises.

And a Disc Sander

by Donald C. Bjorkman

As the price of tools becomes astronomical, I rely more and more on equipment I build in my own shop. Having been given a ¾-HP, 1750-RPM motor retired from pumping well water, I felt I was on my way to the sander of my dreams. As with many such projects, procuring parts was most demanding. The materials list at right tells where I got my supplies and what I paid for them in 1979.

As I planned to have my sander last me a long time, and because it would cost about one-eighth as much as a comparable commercial machine, I felt I should go first-class on components. I also wanted a sander that would satisfy as many sanding needs as possible. With this in mind I designed a dual 16-in. variable-speed sander with two adjustable tables. As I use both sides of the discs, I have four disc surfaces, each with a different sanding grit: two outboard with tilting tables and two inboard with a stationary table.

Besides the motor, the basic components include ball-bearing, self-aligning pillow blocks to guide the ¾-in. shaft, a hardwood frame joined with mortise and tenon and ⅜-in. Finnish birch plywood for the cabinet stress panels and the sander table. The 30-in. by 44-in. table consists of three layers of plywood laminated together (using slightly curved clamping members and quick-set clamps) to give a strong 21-ply top, 1⅛ in. thick.

Putting the motor down low in the cabinet keeps it out of the dust, allows access to both sides of the discs and makes for a more stable machine. The shaft is fitted with step pulleys. This is helpful when going from rough sanding to medium and then to fine. With 16-in. discs I have found that speeds over 2000 RPM burn the wood and that speeds less than 1000 RPM are too slow for good cutting, so I use a 3/3½/4-in. step pulley on the motor and a 4/4½/5-in. step pulley on the shaft. For smaller discs, faster speed could be used.

My only complaint with the machine was the lack of a dust-collection system, which I have recently remedied. As shown in the drawing, the discs run in slots that prevent dust from entering the cabinet. I cut two half-circles of tempered hardboard and glued plywood spacers around the edges. I sanded flat the mouths of two Sears corner nozzles and epoxied them over openings in the hardboard. The covers are attached with wing bolts and T-nuts, and the nozzles connected to a vacuum, which removes most of the dust. □

Don Bjorkman is a professor of fine woodworking and furniture design, industrial design and interior design.

Bjorkman's 16-in. disc sander incorporates tilting tables and uses all four surfaces of the discs. Pulley guard removed for photo.

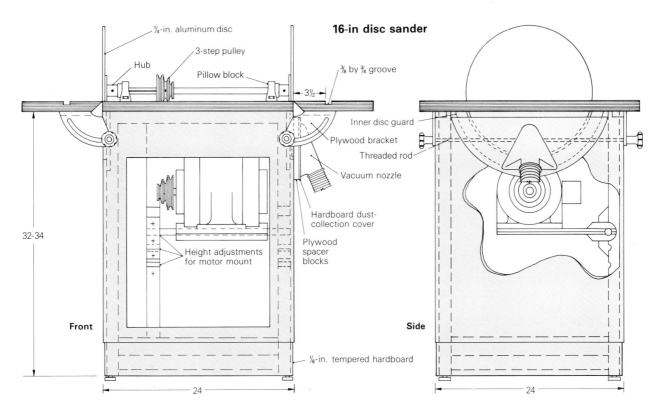

16-in disc sander

¼-in. aluminum disc

3-step pulley

Hub

Pillow block

⅜ by ¾ groove

3½

Inner disc guard

Plywood bracket

Threaded rod

Vacuum nozzle

Hardboard dust-collection cover

Plywood spacer blocks

Height adjustments for motor mount

32-34

Front

⅛-in. tempered hardboard

24

Side

24

Materials list		
Quantity	Purchased parts	Approx. cost (Spring, 1979)
	Local lumberyard	
2	⅜x60x60 birch ply	$33.00
5	2x2x34 maple	10.00
8	1½x1½x24 maple	
4	⅛x4x24 hardboard	
2	⅛x8x18 hardboard	1.00
	Machinery supplier	
1	Manual switch	9.00
24 in.	¾-in. shaft w/keyway	20.00
2	¾-in. ball-bearing pillow block	26.00
2	¾-in. bore step pulley	15.00
4	Adjustable glides	4.00
1	V-belt	3.00
	Metals company	
1	¼x16x32 aluminum plate	21.00
	Hardware store	
6 ft.	Electrical cord	2.50
1	Electrical plug	1.50
2	Cord connectors	.50
1	Tension spring	2.00
24 in.	1¹/₁₆-in. continous hinge	3.00
24 in.	2-in. continuous hinge	3.00
4	½x20 T-nuts	1.00
4	½x20x1½ wing bolts	1.00
	Bolts, washers, screws	4.00
	Gilliom Mfg., 1700 Scherer Pkwy., St. Charles, Mo. 63303	
4	Lock knobs	5.00
2	3 flange hubs	6.00
	Brookstone Co., Vose Farm Rd., Peterborough, N.H. 03458	
4	Thread inserts ⅜-16	1.50
	Sears	
2	Corner nozzles (#14277)	3.00
		$176.00

Layout for parts from two sheets of Finnish plywood

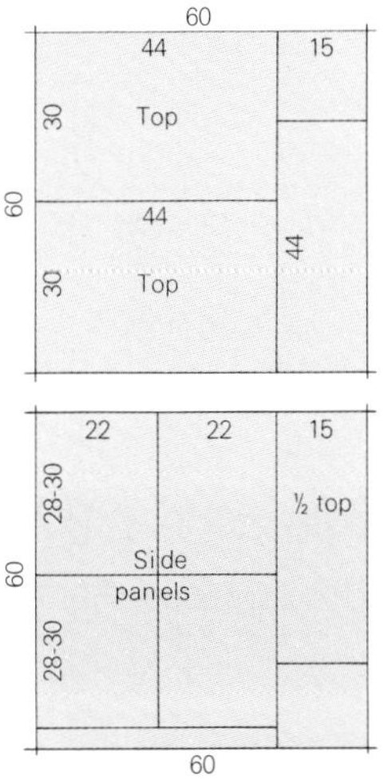

60

44 | 15
30 | Top
60
44 | 44
30 | Top

22 | 22 | 15
28-30 | ½ top
60 | Side panels
28-30

60

The motor is counterbalanced on its pivot with a spring.

Upper corner bracing is set into groove in frame.

An Inflatable Drum Sander

Rubber sleeve conforms to work

by Robert L. Pavey

*Walnut bird,
11 in. high by 8 in. wide,
sanded on homebuilt
pneumatic drum sander.*

An inflatable sanding drum is an invaluable tool for shaping and smoothing wood and other materials—both convex and all but the tightest concave surfaces can be executed with style. The sanding surface conforms to irregularly shaped work and, unlike a hard-backed sanding drum, does not leave deep sanding marks. You can inflate it hard for fast cutting, then release some pressure to make it soft for smooth finishing. It is also easy to change sanding sleeves: Simply release the air pressure, slip off one sleeve, slip on another, reinflate and on with your work. Whether you have compressed air in your shop or a bicycle pump, it takes only seconds.

Making a pneumatic sanding drum is easy. It can be run on a lathe or be driven as mine is by a ⅝-in. shaft supported by pillow-block bearings and powered by a 1725 RPM, ⅓-HP motor. I get variable speeds from half to twice that RPM with a double-flange, spring-loaded pulley system that effectively changes the diameter of the drive pulley by levering the pulleys away from or toward one another. The materials for the drum itself should be available locally:

—1 12-in. length of ½-in. water pipe

—1 tire valve stem

—1 tube silicone rubber sealant

—1 shaft adapter to fit your drive

—1 rubber stopper, ½ in. dia.

—1 10-in. length of 3-in. diameter rubber tubing (Goodyear Spiroflex 2001 water discharge hose works well)

—4 ¾-in. shaft bushings

—2 ¼-in. to ⅜-in. thick by 3½-in. dia. discs: wood, polyethylene, nylon or other material

—wire or strong, thin cord

—1 piece of canvas 12 in. by 12 in.

—2 pieces of ⅛-in. cord, 12 in. long

—Sandpaper and glue to make the sanding sleeves

EDITOR'S NOTE: For those who do not want to make their own, pneumatic sanding drums, their separate parts (with or without drive) and various-sized sanding sleeves are available from Sand-Rite Mfg. Co., 1611 N. Sheffield Ave., Chicago, Ill. 60614.

First cut the ½-in. pipe to length using a pipe cutter. The burr this leaves serves as a flange inside the pipe that will prevent the tire stem from slipping out. The other end of the pipe should be reamed to remove the burr. The tire stem must be turned down to fit snugly into the pipe. Chuck the cap end in a drill or lathe and file while it turns. Then slip the stem through the pipe and before pulling it tight against the flange, place some silicone rubber sealant under the flange to form a seal. Pull tight and let dry.

The next step is to mount the shaft adapter to the opposite end of the pipe. First drill and tap a set-key hole in the pipe approximately ¼ in. from the end to keep the pipe from slipping on the shaft adapter. It's a good idea to use a threaded shaft adapter and to tap a thread in the pipe to fit it.

Before attaching the adapter, insert in the pipe a tight-fitting rubber stopper liberally coated with silicone rubber sealant to form an airtight seal ahead of the shaft adapter. A ⅛-in. hole drilled through the pipe between the stopper and the valve end permits air to enter the drum chamber.

Next construct the ends of the drum. First ream the four ¾-in. bushings to fit over the pipe, which will be approximately ²⁷/₃₂ in. Also drill and ream the center holes of the discs. Place the bushings and the discs on the pipe as shown in the drawing. Before tightening be sure to apply liberal amounts of silicone rubber sealant on each side of the discs next to the bushings; position and tighten the bushings to hold the discs in place 9 in. apart outside to outside.

After the silicone rubber sealant is dry, place the assembly on your drive and turn down the two discs to a 3³/₁₆-in. diameter. This corrects for any wobble in your shaft or off-centering of the hole drilled in the discs. Next turn a groove in the center of each disc for gluing the diaphragm. This groove should be deep enough to permit the wire or cord windings to be pulled below the surface of the completed drum. This will

Sheets of cloth-backed sandpaper with a strip of sand removed and glued over on the back form sleeves for the sander.

The drum, showing tire valve stem (sealed with silicone), wire wrap, canvas sleeve with drawstring, and pillow blocks bearing the belted shaft.

From *Fine Woodworking* magazine (March 1980) 21:48-49

Inflatable sanding drum

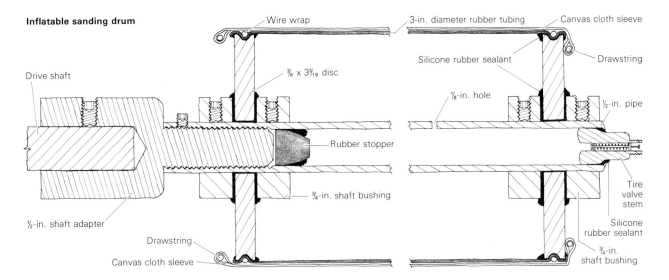

Drive shaft

Wire wrap

3-in. diameter rubber tubing

Canvas cloth sleeve

3/8 x 3³/₁₆ disc

Silicone rubber sealant

Drawstring

1/8-in. hole

1/2-in. pipe

Rubber stopper

3/4-in. shaft bushing

Tire valve stem

1/2-in. shaft adapter

Drawstring

Canvas cloth sleeve

Silicone rubber sealant

3/4-in. shaft bushing

protect the windings and the protective cover from damage.

Now comes perhaps the most difficult step, that of attaching the diaphragm and obtaining an air-tight seal. The 3-in. diameter rubber tubing should be longer than the drum in order to be able to hold it in place while wrapping and gluing the binding wire or cord. Silicone rubber sealant applied liberally on the inside of each disc will aid in forming an airtight seal. Pull the wire or cord tight so that it bites into the rubber, pressing it tight against the discs. Let the sealant dry thoroughly before testing. If you detect minor air leaks, these may be sealed using bicycle-tire sealing materials. The diaphragm is then covered with a canvas cloth stitched and tied with a drawstring down over the ends.

The last step is to prepare the sanding sleeves to be placed over the drum. First wrap the 9-in. by 11-in. sheet around the drum and mark the sheet at the point of overlap. Scrape a strip of abrasive off one end of the paper, apply glue and then clamp until set. Once the glue is dry, place the sleeve over the deflated drum, inflate and use. For dust collection, I have mounted a 3-in. by 6-in. vacuum nozzle (not shown in the photos) behind the drum. A Sears Shop-vac takes care of most of the dust. My drum rotates counter-clockwise, and I hold work sometimes above, sometimes below it. Try using different pressures and see how it affects your work; you will be amazed at the fine, smooth finish you can achieve on ir-

regularly shaped pieces of wood without leaving flat spots, ridges and sanding marks.

Hand-held adaptations — I am sure that by extending the length of the water pipe to accommodate two handles slipped over the ends, with bearings between the inside diameter of the handles and the outside diameter of the pipe, you would have the beginnings of a rolling-pin sander. The handles could be turned-and-bored wood or plastic or metal pipe. The tire-valve stem would remain protruding from one end of the spindle pipe. To power the unit, a shaft adapter or a plug fixed to the other end of the pipe could be turned to fit a flexible-drive-shaft or portable-drill chuck.

The hand-held adaptations I have actually made are single-handle designs made from nylon bar stock. Efficient use of standard 9x11 sheet sandpaper determined the various drum sizes, all smaller than the original design and ideal for sanding holes and tight curves. To use a 5½-in. by 9-in. half-sheet, the drum must measure 9 in. by 1⁵/₁₆ in. in diameter. Taking into consideration ¹/₁₆ in. for the inflatable sleeve and ¹/₁₆ in. for the canvas covering, the disc has to be turned to 1³/₁₆ in. To use a 5½-in. by 4½-in. quarter-sheet, the drum measures 5½ in. by 1³/₁₆ in. in diameter and the discs must be turned to 1¹/₁₆ in. And to use a 4½-in. by 2¾ in. eighth-sheet, the drum measures 4½ in. by ¾ in. in diameter and the discs must be turned to ⅝ in. These drums were constructed similarly to the large one, however the spindle and discs are one unit turned from 2-in., 1½-in. and 1-in. nylon bar stock, respectively. For a drive shaft I drilled and tapped a hole in the end of the bar stock and screwed in a ⅜-in. bolt, then cut the head off. This shaft can be mounted on any ⅜-in. chuck drive (flex-shaft or portable drill). To attach the tire-valve stem to the opposite end of the shaft, first remove the rubber from the metal portion of the valve stem. Then drill a hole in the end of the spindle, into which the valve stem can be driven for a tight fit. This hole should be deep enough to go past the disc portion of the spindle in order that the ⅛-in. hole that permits air to flow into the chamber can be drilled across the spindle to meet it. The diaphragms for these smaller drums were made from thin-wall latex rubber tubing, attached, sealed and covered as on the larger drum. □

Drum sander smooths irregular contours of a bandsawn bird.

Bob Pavey, a research scientist, lives in Western Springs, Ill.

Photos: Milton Fanta; Illustration: Christopher Clapp

Some Abrasive Facts

by Lyle Laske

Abrasives fall into two categories: natural mineral and synthetic mineral. Natural minerals include flint, garnet and emery. Since 1900 the synthetic minerals aluminum oxide and silicon carbide have become more and more popular, both in industry and in the home shop. Because of the superior qualities of synthetics and also as a result of the development of power tools, sanding has become a shaping method as well as a finishing method.

Abrasive hardness is routinely measured on two scales. The Mohs scale runs from 1 (talc) to 10 (diamond). Ratings are determined by abrading a soft mineral with a harder one; they do not indicate equal or proportional differences. The Knoop scale, which goes from 1 to 8500, determines hardness with a pressure indenter, and more accurately measures the proportional hardness of minerals. Toughness, which differs from hardness, is determined by a ball-mill test: rotating a given grit in a steel drum with steel balls for a standard period of time and noting how much of the grit survives at the original size.

Each abrasive has advantages and disadvantages, and comparing them will help you choose the right one for the job at hand.

Flint is used in an inexpensive sandpaper. Because its sharp edges break down quickly, it is not used in production work, but is good for sanding resinous and waxy surfaces and for removing paint and sealers, which clog sandpaper quickly.

Flint *(quartz)*
Color: *buff*
Mohs: *6.8 to 7.0*
Knoop: *820*
Toughness: *20%*

Garnet *(almandite)*
Color: *reddish-brown*
Mohs: *7.5 to 8.5*
Knoop: *1360*
Toughness: *60%*

Emery *(corundum and magnetite)*
Color: *grey to black*
Mohs: *8.5 to 9.0*
Knoop: *1750*
Toughness: *80%*

Aluminum oxide
Color: *tan or white*
Mohs: *9.4*
Knoop: *2050*
Toughness: *75%*

Silicon carbide
Color: *greenish-black*
Mohs: *9.6*
Knoop: *2480*
Toughness: *55%*

Garnet abrasive is obtained by crushing semiprecious garnet jewel stock and heat-treating it to increase its natural hardness and toughness. It is used for production woodwork and sanding between coats of paint and sealers. In use, garnet fractures, and thus will generate new cutting edges. The furniture industry prefers garnet because it is less expensive than aluminum oxide and because garnet's cutting edges scrape rather than scratch the wood. This promotes finish consistency and resistance to burning on most end-grain sanding operations. Garnet is manufactured in grits from 12 to 320. It is not recommended for metal.

Emery, the second hardest natural mineral after diamond, is the toughest abrasive listed here. However, because it has round, blocky, heat-generating cutting edges, it is usually used with lubricants to polish metal. The dull fracture and lack of chip clearance make it unsuitable for woodworking.

Aluminum oxide is made of heat-treated bauxite and lesser amounts of titania. There are only four minerals harder (three synthetic and diamond). Its heavy, wedge-shaped cutting edge is the reason for its toughness. Aluminum oxide is well suited to high-speed sanding machines working hardwoods and hard metals; its higher cost is offset by its durability. However, when sanding resinous softwoods which clog the cutting edges, thus shortening the work life, and where burning is a problem, garnet is a more economical abrasive.

Silicon carbide is made from heat-treated silica sand and petroleum coke. Only boron carbide and diamond are harder. Of all abrasives, silicon carbide has the longest cutting edges and the best concave sides for chip clearance. Unfortunately it breaks down rapidly on hard metals and reacts chemically with ferrous metals. Because of this it is commonly marketed in finer grits—from 180 to 600, although grits as coarse as 24 are useful on particle board and plywood. The best uses for silicon carbide are in sanding soft materials, hardwoods and low tensile-strength materials such as stone, plastic and glass. Silicon carbide abrasive is also used for sanding hard lacquers, varnish and baked-enamel finishes.

Abrasives are sold by grit size, a measure of how coarse or fine they are. Three grading systems are commonly used. The *grit symbol*, the oldest, is an arbitrary system. Number 4½ is the coarsest and 10/0 is the finest. The grit symbol is being de-emphasized by manufacturers. The *mesh number* or *grit number* indicates the approximate number of apertures per running inch in the vibrating silk or wire screen that sorts that grade of stock. Thus 120 grit means there are 14,400 (120 × 120) openings per square inch; discounting the size of the silk thread, each opening (and each grit that falls through it) is about 0.0052 in. across. *Simplified labels* used on flint sheet and emery cloth—Extra Fine, Fine, Medium, Coarse, and Extra Coarse—are of little use to the serious finisher since their meanings are variable.

Abrasives are applied to their backing either by gravity or electrostatically. First the backing is given a *make coat* of glue (either hide or resin, the latter being stronger). In the electrostatic process, the glued backing is conveyed in a strip above a belt conveying the sorted grit through a high-voltage field. This causes the grit to lift off the conveyor and adhere, with maximum evenness and with their sharp points (least mass) outward, to the glued backing. After the make coat has dried, a second, thinner *size coat* (again of either hide or resin glue) is applied over the abrasive surface. Resin-over-resin bonds are used for heavy-duty grinding and in waterproof papers for rubbing out finishes.

The grit can be applied to cover the complete surface *(closed coat)*, or to cover 50% to 70% of the surface *(open coat)*. The spaces in the open coat promote self-cleaning when sanding gummy or resinous materials, and extreme flexibility when bonded to cloth. For fast cutting, use light pressure to avoid heating. A closed coat has more abrading points per square inch, will last longer and produce a smoother surface. It is best for hardwoods and other hard materials that will not clog; it can be put to the work with heavy, constant pressure.

There are four types of abrasive backing: paper, cloth, fiber and combination. Paper backing is manufactured in four weights. A-weight paper, or finishing paper, is used mainly for light hand and vibration sanding. Its flexibility allows the operator to feel defects, and it conforms to small contours and narrow openings without breaking. C-weight and D-weight (cabinet) paper backings are heavier, stronger and less flexible than finishing paper. They are used for hand or vibration sanding with coarse grits and greater pressure. These papers are strong enough not to buckle, yet flexible enough to conform to irregular contours. E-weight paper (roll stock cylinder paper) is strong and durable. It is used on belt, disc and drum sanders. This paper withstands heavy pressures without becoming soft or raggy.

Cloth backings are of two types. J-weight, or "jeans," is lightweight and flexible. It is used in roll form for sanding irregular shapes, especially with pneumatic drums. X-weight, or "drills," is medium-weight, strong cloth backing. It lacks flexibility, hence it is used for mechanical sanders in high-pressure and high-tension operations.

Fiber backing—mainly for disc and drum sanding—is made from vulcanized or hardened rag-stock paper. Combination backing is sturdy and shock-resistant. Laminated paper and cloth is used for high-speed drum sanders. Laminated fiber and cloth is used for discs.

Three abrasives used in surfacing finishes should be mentioned here. Steel wool in pad or roll form is sold in grades from 0000 (very fine) to no. 3 (coarse). Pumice, made from lava, is a white powder that is combined with rubbing oil or water and rubbed with a felt pad. The common grades for woodworking are FF and FFF. Rottenstone, a brown or dark grey substance made from decayed limestone, is finer and softer than pumice and is used in the same way. □

Lyle Laske, a sculptor, of Moorhead, Minn., prepared this article with help from 3M Company and from Norton Company.

Wooden-Drum Stroke Sander
Shop-built machine saves space and money

by A.W. Marlow

Surely every woodworker, amateur as well as professional, needs a stroke sander to relieve him of the tedious, time-consuming hand-sanding of large flat surfaces. Everything about my contraption is crude and inexpensive. I built it when we were just crawling out of the Depression. Nothing was bought that could be homemade. After hand-sanding one or two tabletops, I discovered that if I wanted to eat regularly, a stroke sander was in order. So I had to match its design requirements with the money and space available.

A stroke sander is not a complicated machine. The upper part consists of an electric motor, two main drums, a tensioning/tracking idler drum and a metal framework to hold these components in the proper working relation to one another. The lower part of the machine is a table for holding the workpiece. This table is raised or lowered, depending on the thickness of the stock being sanded, and travels front to back beneath the moving sanding belt.

To operate the machine, the workpiece is laid on the table, which is elevated until the surface to be sanded is about ¼ in. below the sanding belt. With the power on, one hand moves the table in and out below the moving belt, while the other hand presses down, moving forward and back, on the smooth side of the belt with a wooden platen. The amount of pressure on the platen and its movement must be coordinated with the in-and-out movement of the table. Sanding with this machine is like trying to pat your head and rub your belly at

the same time, but once you get the hang of it, work proceeds quickly, and all that's left prior to finishing is a light and easy hand-sanding with a finer grit.

I had to have a machine that would handle stock up to 7 ft. long, but one that would occupy minimal space in my shop. So I decided to place it in a corner, where I could suspend the upper parts of the machine from the wall and support the sanding table on the top of a storage cabinet. Instead of starting with a preconceived design and buying all the hardware initially, I let the thing evolve, meeting each technical problem as it showed its ugly face and buying metal materials as I learned what was needed. The bill of materials for the ma-

A stroke sander makes short work of smoothing large, flat surfaces. Marlow built the machine below nearly 50 years ago, and used no factory-made drums or other hard-to-find materials. To make the most of shop space, he mounted the sanding table on top of a storage cabinet. End view of stroke sander, right, shows the relative positions of drive system and tensioning/tracking idler assembly. Arched block in foreground houses acme-threaded screw that raises and lowers the sanding table. Photos, except where noted: Andy Marlow.

Fig. 1: Wooden-drum stroke sander

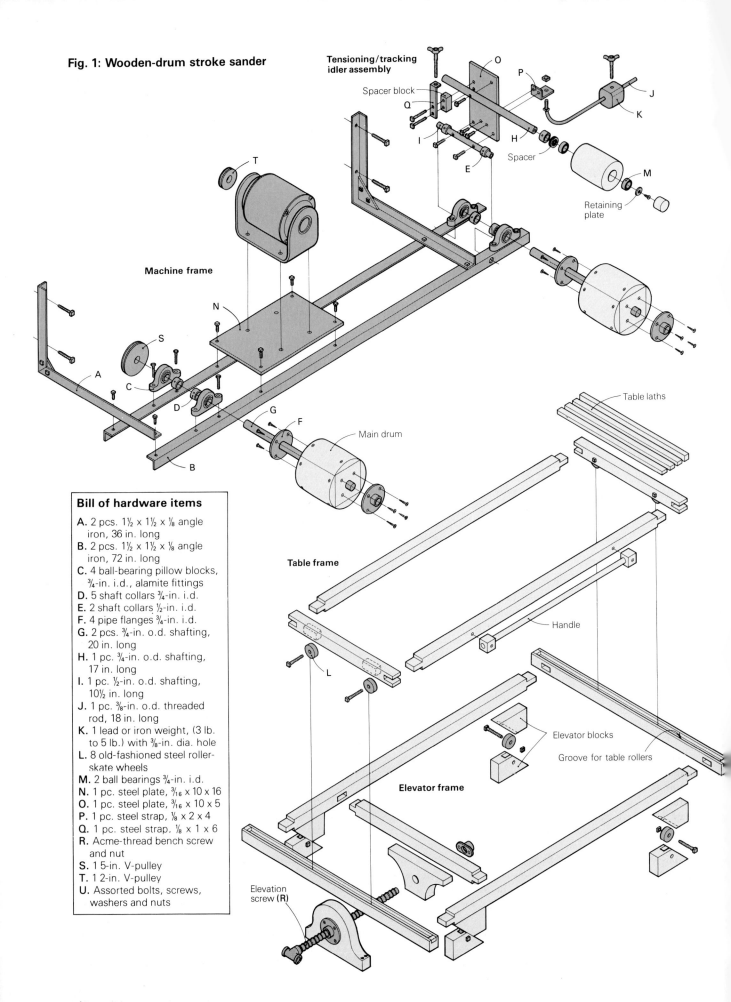

Tensioning/tracking idler assembly

Spacer block

Machine frame

Retaining plate

Spacer

Main drum

Table laths

Table frame

Handle

Elevator blocks

Groove for table rollers

Elevator frame

Elevation screw (R)

Bill of hardware items

A. 2 pcs. 1½ x 1½ x ⅛ angle iron, 36 in. long
B. 2 pcs. 1½ x 1½ x ⅛ angle iron, 72 in. long
C. 4 ball-bearing pillow blocks, ¾-in. i.d., alamite fittings
D. 5 shaft collars ¾-in. i.d.
E. 2 shaft collars ½-in. i.d.
F. 4 pipe flanges ¾-in. i.d.
G. 2 pcs. ¾-in. o.d. shafting, 20 in. long
H. 1 pc. ¾-in. o.d. shafting, 17 in. long
I. 1 pc. ½-in. o.d. shafting, 10½ in. long
J. 1 pc. ⅜-in. o.d. threaded rod, 18 in. long
K. 1 lead or iron weight, (3 lb. to 5 lb.) with ⅜-in. dia. hole
L. 8 old-fashioned steel roller-skate wheels
M. 2 ball bearings ¾-in. i.d.
N. 1 pc. steel plate, ³⁄₁₆ x 10 x 16
O. 1 pc. steel plate, ³⁄₁₆ x 10 x 5
P. 1 pc. steel strap, ⅛ x 2 x 4
Q. 1 pc. steel strap, ⅛ x 1 x 6
R. Acme-thread bench screw and nut
S. 1 5-in. V-pulley
T. 1 2-in. V-pulley
U. Assorted bolts, screws, washers and nuts

From *Fine Woodworking* magazine (July 1981) 29:47-51

chine (opposite page) includes only items that were truly needed and could be scavenged or purchased from local ironmongers and hardware dealers.

The machine frame—Begin construction by fabricating the angle-iron machine frame (figure 1) for supporting the motor and drums. Use the two 36-in. lengths of angle iron for making the wall brackets. Cut in each a 90° notch 14 in. from the end, and bend the pieces to form a right angle (with flanges to the inside, you need a right-hand bracket and left-hand bracket). Strengthen the resulting miter joint with either a weld or a strap bolted across the angle. Drill two ¼-in. holes in each vertical (14-in.) arm; then two ¼-in. holes in each horizontal arm for attaching the 6-ft. rails. These holes should be drilled on 8¾-in. centers, with the first hole ¾ in. from the end of the bracket. Now you can mount the brackets to the wall. Position them 42 in. above the floor and about 62 in. apart. This distance can be exact on a masonry wall where you must bore for expanding lead inserts, but it will vary on a framed wall where you must screw the brackets directly to the studs.

After mounting the support brackets to the wall, temporarily clamp the 6-ft. rails in place and mark them for matching bolt holes. If all is correct, the right-hand ends of these rails should overshoot the right bracket about 10 in. to make room for the tracking/tensioning assembly and the pillow blocks for the right-hand drum. Also drill four ¼-in. holes in the 10-in. by 16-in. steel plate needed for mounting the motor. This mounting plate should be attached to the rails about 20 in. from the left end, so clamp it in place here and mark for holes in the rails. Now bore two ½-in. holes in the vertical flanges of the angle iron about 7 in. from the right-hand ends. These holes will accommodate the tension/tracking-plate pivot shaft.

The only holes remaining to be drilled in the long rails are those for mounting the pillow blocks. Alignment of these is crucial for belt tracking. So rather than mark for these holes when you first clamp the rails to the brackets, it is advisable to bolt the long rails to the brackets as for permanent attachment, even though you will have to remove them later to drill the holes. Using a carpenter's framing square, scribe a centerline across both front and back rail irons about 1 in. from the right end and 11 in. from the left end. Determine the distance between the two mounting holes in each pillow block and lay out matching holes on the irons. After drilling these, bolt the frame assembly together into one unit.

The main drums—The next step is to make the main drums. Figure 2 shows the number and dimensions of the parts required for each. Buy enough No. 2 white pine to make both drums. All pieces must measure exactly 1³⁄₁₆ in. thick. First, saw the four end pieces 4¾ in. by 4¾ in. Next, mark the exact center on two of these squares. Clamp one of the marked squares on top of an unmarked one, and with a drill press, accurately bore a ¾-in. hole through both at once. Repeat this operation with the other pair. Now cut the four narrow side pieces 4¾ in. by 6 in. (precisely the same width as the squares). Then cut the wide side pieces 7⅛ in. by 6 in. long. Draw centerlines down the length of all eight pieces, and measure out 1⅝ in. on both sides of the line and about ⅝ in. in from each end. This will give two bore centers on each end of all eight pieces. Counterbore on these centers ½-in. holes

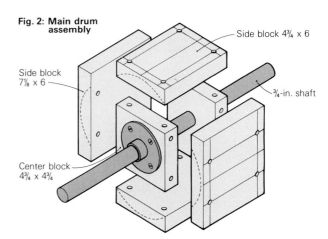

Fig. 2: Main drum assembly

Side block 4¾ × 6

Side block 7⅛ × 6

¾-in. shaft

Center block 4¾ × 4¾

Assemble the parts of the drum blank with the two end blocks held in alignment by the shaft. Remove finished blank from shaft and bandsaw it to a rough cylinder. Replace blank on shaft and mount it in machine frame, which becomes a makeshift lathe. Turn the drum true, leaving a ⅛-in. crown in the center.

to a depth of ⅝ in. Bore ¹¹⁄₆₄-in. clearance holes through the remaining wood thickness.

To keep the parts of the ends of the drum blank in alignment as you assemble them, take one of the 20-in. shafts and slide it through the holes in two of the squares. Spread the squares 6 in. apart, and be sure the grain runs from top to bottom on both blocks. Apply some yellow glue to the end grain of one of the squares, place one of the narrow side pieces flush with the end and even on both sides and screw it down tightly using 1¼-in. #8 woodscrews. Now shift the other square into proper alignment, and glue and screw it in place. If necessary, bore small pilot holes to start the screws. Turn the unit 180° and fasten the other narrow side piece. Next, attach the two wider side pieces in the same manner. You can at this point (if your bandsaw is big enough) mark out a 7-in. dia. circle on the end of each turning blank and rough-cut the circle. This will save time when turning the blanks into cylinders.

The drums are secured to the shafts with ¾-in. I.D. pipe flanges. Prepare the flanges by boring out the threads with a ¾-in. drill or by removing enough of the threads with a round file to allow the shaft to slide through. Next bore a ⁷⁄₃₂-in. hole in each hub, and thread each hole with a ¼-20 tap for receiving a setscrew. Now secure the drums, flanked by two flanges, on their shafts and slide one of the shafts into the left-hand pillow-block bearings. With the shaft collars in place, spread so they just touch the inside of the blocks, tighten all the setscrews. Bolt your motor (⅓ HP, 1,725 RPM) on its mounting plate and tighten a 2½-in. dia. V-pulley on the shaft. I recently installed another motor on my sander and its rotation is opposite from the original, so I installed the plywood outrigger shown in the photos. Slide a 4-in. V-pulley on the main shaft, position it in line with the motor pulley and tighten the setscrew. You now have a makeshift lathe for truing up the diameters of the drums.

A tool rest for turning must now be devised. The simplest is a steel bar or pipe supported at each end in some manner. Even with a good rest the RPM is so low that it would make a good turner cry, but the wood is soft and there are only two to do. Close to a 7-in. dia. is what to strive for, but more important is that there be about a ⅛-in. crown in the center. Do not allow the center to be flat or concave; that would mean

 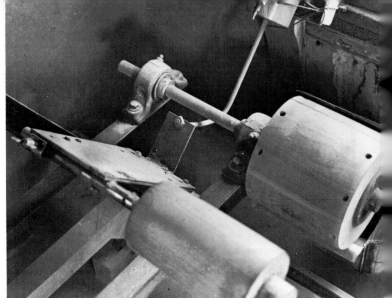

Tensioning/tracking idler assembly pivots on a ½-in. shaft in the frame to tension the belt. The idler drum rotates on a ¾-in. shaft that pivots on a bolt across the axis of the shaft. Photo: Staff.

Pivoted to its extreme left-hand position, the tension/tracking assembly can be seen in its entirety. The tensioning weight (here tied to a brick) fits onto a bent rod, which is attached to the pivoting plate by means of a flange. The thumbscrew adjustment at the top of the plate is used to control belt tracking. Photo: Staff.

trouble in tracking. Sand the turning with 60-grit paper, using calipers to be sure the ends are both the same diameter. Remove the drum and install the other to turn in like manner.

The tensioning/tracking assembly—First study the photos on this page and figure 1 (p. 48). Assuming that you've bored two ½-in. holes in the long rails to house the tensioning/tracking shaft, proceed to prepare the plate for bolting to the pivot shaft and for mounting the idler-drum shaft and tracking-adjustment screw. Drill two ¹³⁄₆₄-in. holes along the 5-in. edge of the plate as shown in figure 1. Lay this plate on top of the ½-in. shaft, which should extend equally on both sides. Mark the shaft for boring ¹¹⁄₆₄-in. holes, and drill and tap these for ³⁄₁₆-in. by ½-in. bolts. That will take care of the hinged bottom edge.

Along the top edge of the plate will be mounted the ¾-in. by 17-in. idler shaft. This shaft pivots on a ¼-in. by 1-in. hinge bolt to track the sanding belt. Bore a ⁷⁄₃₂-in. hole for the bolt 1 in. down from the top and 1 in. in from the right edge; then tap the hole for ¼-20 threads. Now bore a ¼-in. hole through the shaft 5 in. from one end.

Next prepare the ¹⁄₈-in. by 1-in. by 6-in. strap for installing on the plate. Before bending the strap, drill a ⁷⁄₃₂-in. hole ½ in. from one end, and tap this hole for insertion of the ½-in. dia. tracking-adjustment screw. At the other end, bore two ¹⁷⁄₆₄-in. holes for mounting the bracket to the plate. Now you can bend the strap 90° to produce a 1-in. flange on the threaded end. Provide a wooden spacer block (¹⁄₃₂ in. thicker than ¾ in. so the shaft can move freely) for mounting the strap. Bore this block for clearance holes and insert the bolts through the strap and the block. Then take the assembly over to the plate and position it in the upper left-hand corner, straddling the idler shaft. Pivot the idler shaft until it is precisely parallel with the top edge of the plate; then shift the strap and block up or down to equalize the space between the flange and the block. Mark and bore two ⁷⁄₃₂-in. holes and tap them for ¼-20 threads.

The photo above right shows a flanged 2-in. by 4-in. plate bolted to the bottom of the tensioning/tracking plate. This smaller plate is for mounting the tension bar and weight. The bar is best made from a ³⁄₈-in. threaded rod about 18 in. long;

it is equipped with a 3-lb. to 5-lb. weight (more if necessary), which slides up and down the rod and is fixed at the proper place with a thumbscrew. Bore one end of the plate to receive the rod, and bore two ¼-in. holes in the other end for mounting bolts. Bend the plate 90° to produce a 1½-in. flange on the end with the two holes. Then center the small plate on the tensioning/tracking plate so the mounting holes are about 1 in. above the pivot shaft. Mark and bore two ⁷⁄₃₂-in. holes for attaching the weight plate; tap them and then bolt the small plate in place.

Now slide a shaft collar onto each end of the pivot shaft, and insert the shaft in the two ½-in. holes in the long rails, taking care to center the plate between the rails and to spread the collars so they just touch the inside edges of the angle iron. Tighten the setscrews to secure the collars.

Now turn to making the idler drum. Dimension two pieces of wood 7 in. by 4½ in. by 2 in. thick. Down the center of each piece, plow a groove ¾ in. wide by ³⁄₈ in. deep. When the two halves are glued together, these channels should align to make a ¾-in. square hole through the drum blank for accommodating the shaft. Having glued up the halves and left them in the clamps overnight, cut the blank to a finished length of 6 in., making sure the ends are square. Now make a pair of tapered plugs, each ¾ in. long, ¹¹⁄₁₆ in. square at one end and ¹³⁄₁₆ in. square at the other. Seat them solidly in the ¾-in. square holes, and mark their centers for turning.

Mount the blank between centers in a lathe and turn as you did the belt drums, leaving a ¹⁄₈-in. crown in the middle. Measure accurately the O.D. of the ball-bearing race, and turn a snug-fitting recess for it ¼ in. deeper than the width of the bearing race, leaving enough wood to keep the center intact. Remove and flip the piece end for end, carefully find the centers and turn a recess in the other end. After turning, the remaining wood can be bored out on the drill press. Insert bearings, slide the pulley on the shaft and if (for any reason) it does not run true, it can be placed on the main left-hand shaft temporarily and turned true, using a flange for driving. This idler must run true to keep vibration at a minimum.

The front end of the shaft should have a tapped hole in its center for a ³⁄₁₆-in. R.H. machine screw to hold a retaining plate for the bearing. The plate can be a washer with an

Grooved track in the side member of the elevation frame accommodates skate wheels on the bottom of the traveling sanding table. Blocks glued in grooves stop the table travel. Anchor block beneath cross-member in frame holds nut for elevation screw.

O.D. larger than ¾ in. On the shaft at the rear bearing, a number of washers or a short sleeve will be needed to fill the space between bearing and collar. When a wing or thumb bolt is turned into the tapped ¼-in. hole for tracking adjustment, this unit should be operable.

The elevator frame and carriage track—To make the most efficient use of space beneath the machine, begin by constructing a storage cupboard; its top should be 29 in. high. This completed, start work on the elevator frame and carriage track (photo above). Made of softwood, the track bars are 1¾ in. square and 36 in. long. Plow grooves down their lengths, ¼ in. deep and 1/16 in. wider than the skate wheels. Stop the grooves front and rear by gluing in little blocks. The front and rear frame members, also 1¾ in. square, are 48 in. long. These are positioned 22 in. apart and tenoned into the track bars. A crossmember, to which you will later attach the elevator-screw anchor block, is tenoned into the frame members 8 in. in from the left-hand track.

The elevator frame is raised and lowered on four pairs of blocks, their mating surfaces inclined at 45°. The bottom ones (bearing blocks) are 1¾ in. thick, 2¾ in. high and 5½ in. long and are fitted with steel roller-skate wheels. The top angled corners must be mortised out sufficiently to allow the skate wheels to revolve freely when placed so the wheel's radius extends ⅜ in. above the wood. The upper blocks (elevation blocks) are grooved along their inclined surfaces 1/16 in. wider than the skate wheels and ¼ in. deep. All blocks are drilled and counterbored for attaching to frame and cabinet top with screws.

Fasten the elevation blocks to the frame, and place four shims under the frame at each corner, holding it off the cabinet top just enough to clear the bottom of the elevation blocks. Now center the frame front-to-back under the belt and position it end-to-end about 3 in. in from the extreme right of the long angle-iron rails. Apply glue to the bottoms of the bearing blocks and slide them into place under the elevation blocks. Allow the glue to set overnight; then lift off the frame and seat the necessary wood screws.

Shown in figure 1 is the elevation-screw anchor block. It's about 3 in. wide and 8 in. long and should be bored to re-

ceive the nut for the acme-thread bench screw. After the nut is installed, screw the block to the bottom of the cross-member. The position of the fixed block will depend on the length of the screw you use.

The traveling table—The sanding table consists of a carriage frame, which is fitted with skate wheels, and a slatted top for holding the workpiece. Using open mortise-and-tenon joints, make the carriage frame 22 in. wide and 48 in. long from 1¾-in. square stock. About 3 in. in from the front and rear, cut mortises for the skate wheels. Then bore the sides of the mortises for axle holes, which will allow the wheels to extend ⅜ in. below the frame. The carriage frame must travel back and forth freely in the tracks.

Now cut a bunch of laths about ⅝ in. thick, 1 in. wide and 22 in. long. The far right-hand strip should be ⅜ in. thicker than the rest, as it will act as a stop for the workpiece. Space them about ½ in. apart and fasten them to the carriage frame with glue and countersunk screws or nails.

Now fashion a handle for getting a comfortable hold on the table. I find a long, ¾-in. dowel held at each end by blocks to be good enough. All that remains is to make a platen from soft pine. It ought to be about 5 in. wide and 7 in. long and slightly beveled at the ends. Attach a handle that pleases you and when in use rub the contacting surface occasionally with a cake of beeswax.

Because this machine generates a lot of dust, I recommend that you hook it up to a dust-collection system of some kind. I have made an inexpensive dust-collection head from downspouting and scrap pieces of sheet metal, and connected the head via a flexible hose to an old blower that I scavenged from an oil burner.

Sanding belts—I use Norton Adalox 60-grit production paper, which can be purchased in 6-in. wide rolls from most industrial-supply stores and is cheaper than cloth belting. To determine the length of the belt, prop up the tracking idler and measure the distance around the pulleys and the idler with a steel tape. Add 2 in. to this and you've got the length of your belt. Now splice the ends together. Both of the ends should be cut at complementary 60° angles, using a sharp knife; these angles must be exact or the belt will not run true. Dimension two clamping blocks (2½ in. by 9 in. by ¾ in. thick) and, to pad the clamping blocks, cut 20 pieces of newspaper the same size.

With the smooth side up, bring the two ends of the belt together, and place one of the clamping blocks evenly under the joint, having first covered the block with one piece of newspaper. Using two short, thin brads, tack the belt onto the block. Then carefully butt the other end to the first and brad it in place.

Tightly woven linen makes the best splicing material. Cut two strips of the cloth 9 in. long, one 1 in. and the other 2 in. wide. Spread a thin coat of glue on the 1-in. strip and lay it evenly across the joint; coat the 2-in. strip with glue and lay it evenly over the first. Center the pad of newspaper over the splice, and clamp the second block on top. Allow to sit overnight, then remove the clamps, carefully lift the belt from the brads, and trim the excess cloth. □

The late Andy Marlow was a designer of traditional furniture and a contributing editor to Fine Woodworking *magazine.*

A Swing-Away Drill-Press Table

Versatile accessories help sand and rout

by R.J. DeCristoforo

The drill press is one of the most versatile tools in any woodworking shop, but you need special accessories to get the most from it. Many times these accessories aren't available commercially and you must make them. Here's an auxiliary swing-away table with custom-made inserts that will help you use your drill press for drum-sanding inside or outside curves, pattern-sanding and pin-routing. When the jig isn't needed, it swings out of the way, and can be used as a platform for other tools.

To construct the jig, cut two 1½-in. thick pieces of maple, birch or other hardwood, 5¼ in. wide by 19½ in. long. Clamp the pieces edge-to-edge and use a hole saw or a fly-cutter to make a hole the same size as your drill-press column. Locate the hole so that its rim is 2 in. from the end of the jig and its center is directly on the joint line.

Unclamp, and draw the outside profile on one of the pieces, as shown in figure 1. After sawing and sanding it, use it as a pattern to mark the mating piece. If you have a bandsaw, you can speed up the process by taping the pieces together and cutting both at the same time. Locate and drill the hole for the ⅜-in. carriage bolt that tightens the jig on the drill-press column.

Mark the centerline for the strap hinge on one half of the jig. Before cutting along this line, mark the location of the hinge screws, or, better yet, install the hinge and then remove it. Replace the hinge after making the cut and rounding the corner of the cut-off

Fig. 1: Swing-away drill-press table

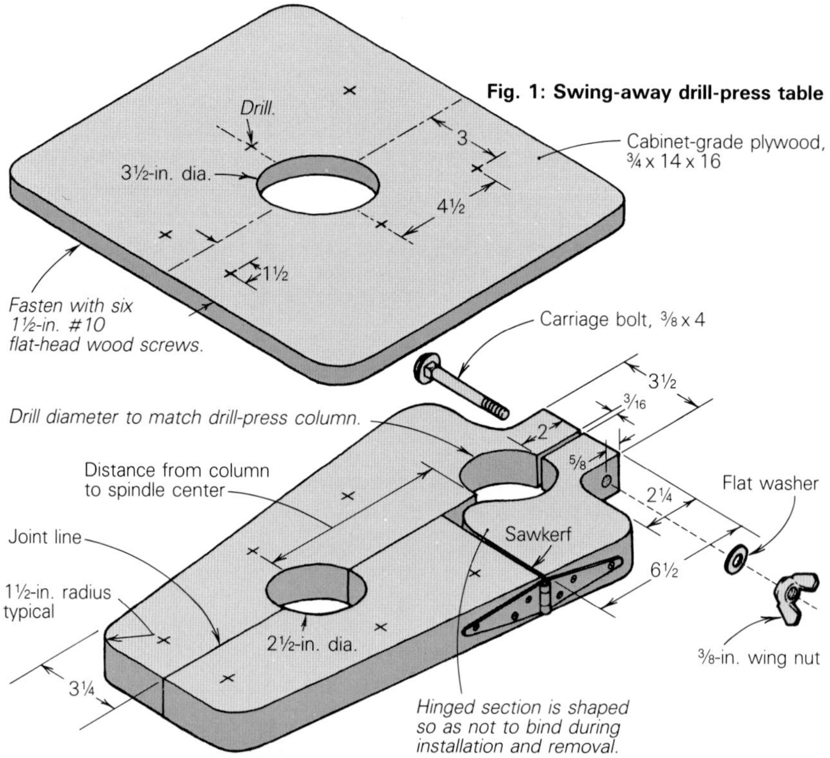

Drill.
3½-in. dia.
3
4½
1½
Cabinet-grade plywood, ¾ x 14 x 16
Fasten with six 1½-in. #10 flat-head wood screws.
Carriage bolt, ⅜ x 4
Drill diameter to match drill-press column.
3½
3/16
2
5/8
Distance from column to spindle center
2¼
Flat washer
Joint line
Sawkerf
6½
1½-in. radius typical
2½-in. dia.
⅜-in. wing nut
3¼
Hinged section is shaped so as not to bind during installation and removal.

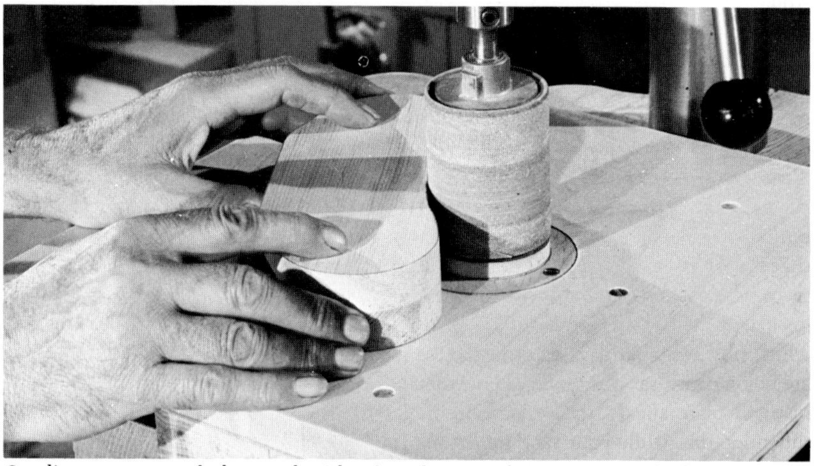

Sanding pattern tacked to underside of workpiece rides against guide disc.

Fig. 1A: Inserts

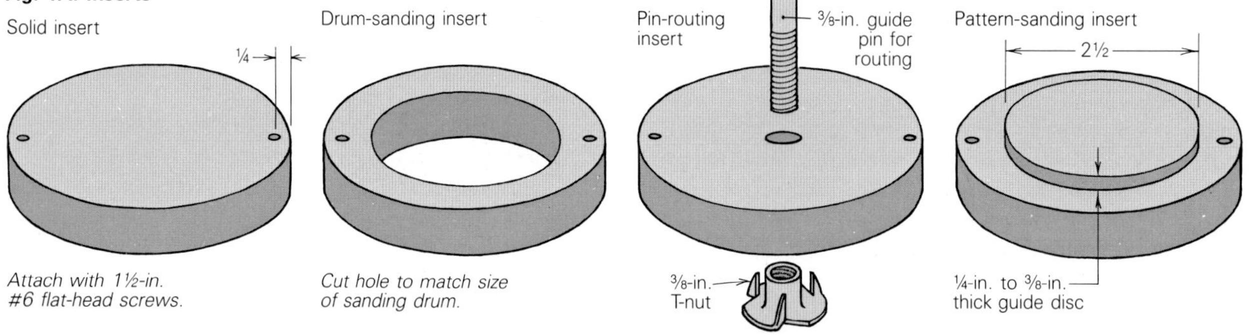

Solid insert
¼
Attach with 1½-in. #6 flat-head screws.
Drum-sanding insert
Cut hole to match size of sanding drum.
Pin-routing insert
⅜-in. guide pin for routing
⅜-in. T-nut
Pattern-sanding insert
2½
¼-in. to ⅜-in. thick guide disc

From *Fine Woodworking* magazine (May 1984) 46:58-59

piece. Remove just enough material from the corner to allow the hinged section to swing around the drill-press column. Glue the two table pieces together.

Make the top piece now, but don't cut any of the holes yet. Center the top on the base and attach it with six 1½-in. #10 flat-head wood screws. The front edge of the top should be flush with the front of the base piece. Now center the assembly on the drill-press table, secure it with the carriage bolt, and, with the drill press, drill a small pilot hole through both top and base. Take the two pieces apart, and cut the 3½-in. hole through the top and the 2½-in. hole through the base. Sand all parts carefully and then screw the top to the base. Finish with lacquer or shellac, followed by paste wax.

Now use your bandsaw, fly-cutter or hole saw to make the inserts shown in figure 1A. All the inserts are 3½ in. in diameter, to fit snugly into the jig. The solid insert provides a good surface for normal drilling and helps prevent tearout. The drum insert, designed for a 2½-in. drum, supports the workpiece so that its edges can be sanded square to surfaces. To sand inside areas, put the workpiece in place before you lower the drum.

To make the insert for pin-routing, drill the hole for the pin and T-nut while the insert is locked in the table. This ensures that the router bit and the pin, which is made from a cut-off ⅜-in. bolt, will be perfectly aligned. Alignment is crucial since a pattern, exactly the size and shape of the part you need, is tack-nailed to the bottom of a rough-cut piece. Moving the pattern along the pin enables the router bit to transfer the shape of the pattern to the rough-cut piece. Use a similar alignment procedure in making the pattern-sanding insert, which serves as a guide disc when pieces are being drum-sanded to size. Have the insert in place and mark the location of the guide disc while your sanding drum is mounted in the chuck. The sander and the guide disc must be perfectly concentric. The pattern rides the disc, so the work is sanded to match. Remember that this is a sanding operation—workpieces should be sawn as close to the line as possible. □

R.J. DeCristoforo, of Los Altos Hills, Calif., is a woodworker and author of numerous articles and books on woodworking. Photo by the author.

An Oscillating Spindle Sander
Taiwanese drill press spins and bobs

by Wesley P. Glewwe

An oscillating vertical spindle sander, whose drum moves up and down as it spins, doesn't leave the scratches that a conventional drum sander does. With a few inexpensive parts, you can turn a cheap Taiwan-made benchtop drill press into a durable, efficient oscillating sander, for a fraction of the cost of a manufactured unit, and you won't need to do any welding or machine work.

Not all Taiwanese drill presses are suitable for conversion. The one I used is about 23 in. high, weighs just under 50 lb., and cost under $100 in 1984. It is cast iron with a ½-in. chuck, a ⅓-HP single-phase motor, and stepped pulleys for variable speeds. These machines are sold under many different names (American, Duracraft, Chicago, Intergram, Sterling, Central, Guardian, etc.), but all brands are about the same. Larger, more expensive Taiwanese drill presses, about 30 in. to 38 in. tall, cost more and can't be modified because of the way the head casting is attached.

The drill-press motor will rotate the sanding drum, but you'll need to buy a reduction motor to move the spindle up and down about ¾ in. to ⅞ in. There are two types of reduction motors: one with

Photos: Blumenfeld Photography

With a few extra parts, Glewwe converted a Taiwanese drill press into this oscillating spindle sander. The sanding drum moves up and down as it rotates, eliminating scratches. The particleboard cabinet has a plastic-laminate top with different size inserts, shown hanging on the cabinet, that lift out for drum-changing.

Drawings: Karen Pease

Drill press dismantled . . .   **. . . becomes oscillating spindle sander**

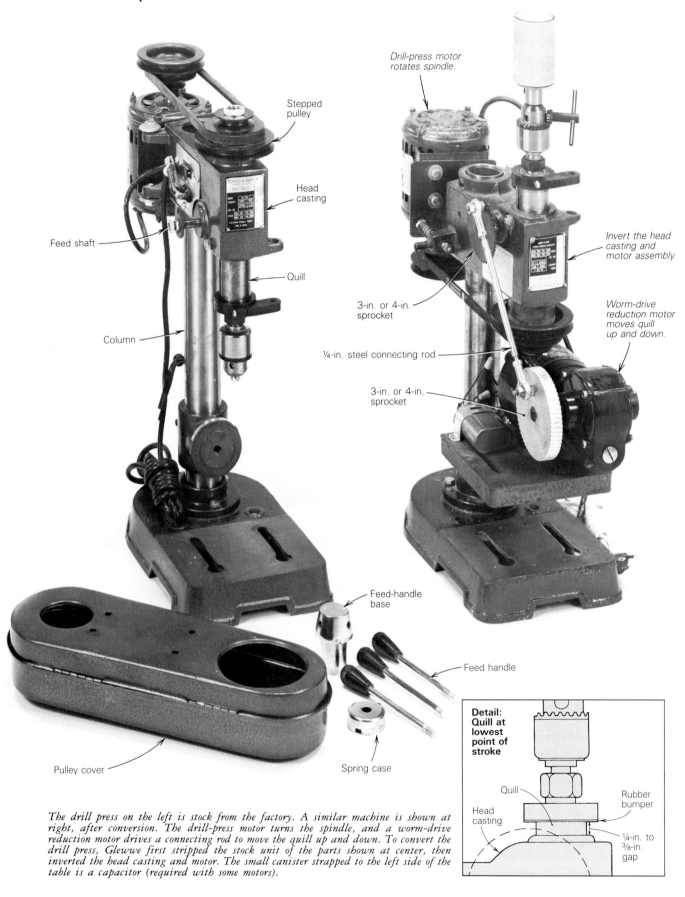

Drill-press motor rotates spindle.

Stepped pulley

Head casting

Feed shaft

Quill

Invert the head casting and motor assembly.

3-in. or 4-in. sprocket

Worm-drive reduction motor moves quill up and down.

Column

¼-in. steel connecting rod

3-in. or 4-in. sprocket

Feed-handle base

Feed handle

Pulley cover

Spring case

Detail: Quill at lowest point of stroke

Quill

Head casting

Rubber bumper

¼-in. to ³/₈-in. gap

The drill press on the left is stock from the factory. A similar machine is shown at right, after conversion. The drill-press motor turns the spindle, and a worm-drive reduction motor drives a connecting rod to move the quill up and down. To convert the drill press, Glewwe first stripped the stock unit of the parts shown at center, then inverted the head casting and motor. The small canister strapped to the left side of the table is a capacitor (required with some motors).

a sun-gear mechanism, and one with a worm-gear assembly. Either type will do, but the worm-gear motor is easier to mount because the shaft is perpendicular to the axis of the motor. Buy a motor with at least $\frac{1}{20}$ HP, rated continuous-duty with an output speed between 25 RPM and 60 RPM. My motor is a 115-volt AC, $\frac{1}{15}$-HP worm-gear type with a 60:1 ratio and an output speed of 28 RPM. It was made by Bodine Electric Co. (2500 West Bradley Pl., Chicago, Ill. 60618), but I bought it at a surplus house (Surplus Center, 1000-1015 West "O" St., PO Box 82209, Lincoln, Neb. 68501) for about $30.

Two 3-in. or 4-in. sprockets form the crankshafts that oscillate the spindle. One fits on the reduction-motor arbor, the other on the drill-press feed shaft. Each sprocket must have a setscrew or some other means of locking it on the arbor. You can substitute gears or pulleys for the sprockets, or you can make the crankshafts from flat bar stock—they don't need to be round.

The connecting rod between the sprockets is made from an 8-in. length of $\frac{1}{4}$-in. steel rod, capped by two rod ends with $\frac{1}{4}$-in. bearing inserts (available from Alinabal, Division of MPD Corp., 28 Woodmont Rd., Milford, Conn. 06460). Buy the kind with female threads where the rod attaches.

Begin the conversion of your machine by removing the stepped pulley on the quill shaft. This is a press-fit and may be tough to get off. To loosen it, give the shaft end a few sharp taps while a helper tugs on the pulley. Be careful not to break the flanges. After you get the pulley off, remove the sheet-metal pulley cover, then replace the pulley on the quill shaft. If you can't get the pulley off, just cut the cover off with a hacksaw.

Next, remove the quill-return spring, which is in a case on the left side of the head casting, and slide out the feed shaft and handle assembly. Remove the three feed handles, and with a pin punch, drive out the pin that secures the feed-handle base to its shaft. Remove the base, which is also a press-fit.

The small end of the feed shaft is slotted for the spring (which you've removed). Epoxy a metal shim in this slot to prevent the shaft from crushing when you tighten the sprocket on the shaft. Slide the feed shaft back through the head casting, and slip a few washers on the end of the shaft to take up the space originally occupied by the spring.

Now lift off the entire head assembly and invert it on the column. There are three cast-iron ribs on the inside of the head assembly. If the inverted head assembly won't slip over the column, file off the burr on the center rib.

One crankshaft sprocket goes on the feed shaft, but first drill a $\frac{1}{4}$-in. hole $1\frac{1}{8}$ in. from the center of the arbor hole for the connecting-rod end. Mount the sprocket on the shaft. Drill a $\frac{1}{4}$-in. hole through the other sprocket, 1 in. from the center of the arbor hole, and mount this sprocket on the gear-reduction motor arbor. Making sure the table isn't tilted, position the reduction motor on the worktable. Line up the upper and lower sprockets with a straightedge, and bolt down the motor.

Rotate the upper sprocket so that the rod-end hole is at four o'clock. At this position, the low point in the quill-shaft stroke, there should be a $\frac{1}{4}$-in. to $\frac{3}{8}$-in. gap between the head casting and the rubber bumper on the quill shaft. If there isn't, remove the sprocket, slide out the feed shaft, rotate it slightly, and replace it. Put a scrap piece of wood in the gap temporarily to prevent the quill from dropping while you're measuring. Now rotate the lower sprocket, by running the reduction motor, so that the rod-end hole is at six o'clock. At these positions, the quill will be at the bottom of its stroke. Now you're ready to measure for the connecting rod.

With the sprockets in the right posi-

tion, measure the distance between the rod-end threads and add $\frac{5}{8}$ in. to allow for threads. Cut the $\frac{1}{4}$-in. rod to this length and thread the ends with a die that matches the rod-end threads. Just start the rod into the rod ends—you'll need to make adjustments later. Mount the rod assembly on the sprockets with machine screws, and add lock washers and nuts, finger-tightened.

Test the action by quickly switching the reduction motor on and off. Don't plug in the drill-press motor yet. The upper sprocket should make less than half a revolution, then reverse direction. You'll probably have to adjust the length of the connecting rod to get a smooth up-and-down motion. The easiest way to make this adjustment is to turn the connecting rod farther in or out of the rod ends, but you can also raise or lower the worktable or the head casting. Don't allow the reduction motor to run continuously until you get a smooth stroke of about $\frac{3}{4}$ in. to $\frac{7}{8}$ in. with no "thumps" at the top or bottom of the quill's stroke.

You can mount the sander underneath an existing workbench in your shop, but I built a particleboard cabinet to house mine. Plastic laminate makes a good work surface for the top. The spindle protrudes through a hole in a removable insert in the worktable that lifts out when you want to change drums.

I usually plug both motors into an outlet box controlled by a single switch. Sometimes you may want only the spindle to rotate, and with this setup, all you have to do is unplug the reduction motor.

In my machine, I use 3-in. long sanding drums with $\frac{1}{2}$-in. dia. shanks (available from Singley Specialty Co., Inc., Box 5087, Greensboro, N.C. 27403). I like the kind with a clamping mechanism to hold regular sheets of abrasive paper, so I don't have to buy abrasive sleeves. These drums come in diameters from $\frac{3}{4}$ in. to 3 in. Use the larger ones for long, sweeping curves, and the smaller ones for short arcs and scrollwork.

For best results, feed the work against the rotation of the drum, and keep it moving to avoid burn marks. You also risk burns if the drum turns too fast, so adjust the rotation speed by moving the V-belt on the pulleys. □

Wesley Glewwe is a retired FBI special agent. He lives in West St. Paul, Minn., and makes wooden-gear clocks as a hobby.

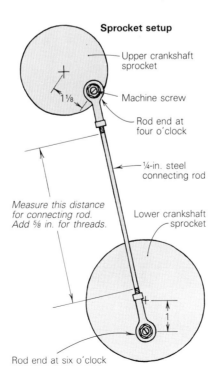

Sprocket setup

Upper crankshaft sprocket

$1\frac{1}{8}$

Machine screw

Rod end at four o'clock

$\frac{1}{4}$-in. steel connecting rod

Measure this distance for connecting rod. Add $\frac{5}{8}$ in. for threads.

Lower crankshaft sprocket

1

Rod end at six o'clock

Making Shaper Knives

by Tommy Bargeron

The shaper is one of the most useful machines to have in the serious workshop for machining edges, moldings and lippings. Only the router or a set of hand planes can even attempt to do the type of work the shaper can do, and they are no match for its speed, versatility and efficiency.

For most woodworkers and antique restorers, however, the shaper's usefulness is limited by the small selection of patterns available in the common three-wing cutters. Its range can be made infinite by using shaper collars to hold pairs of flat knives, which can easily be ground to almost any desired profile. The process is surprisingly simple and no elaborate grinding equipment is required.

Shaper collars are available in various diameters to fit most spindles. There are two basic types of collar, lock-edge and plain, and each comes with either solid or ball-bearing construction. I highly recommend the lock-edge collar because it is much safer. Knife steel for these collars is made with a serrated edge, which fits into grooves in the top of the collar and virtually eliminates the danger of throwing a knife. The lock-edge collar is approved by the federal Occupational Safety and Health Administration (OSHA). On light- to medium-duty machines, a 2-1/2-inch diameter collar is adequate. If your shaper has a variety of spindles use the

---

Tommy Bargeron is a restoration specialist with the Georgia Agrirama Development Authority in Tifton, where part of his time is spent making knives to match existing moldings.

largest. You will find an extra-long spindle helpful at times.

In a small shop where flexibility is vital, ball-bearing collars are best. They make shaping curved work safe and easy, because the stock can ride directly on the bearing. The ball-bearing collars I used cost about $100 (in 1976); plain collars were available for $60.

Knife blanks to fit the collars are made in a variety of widths and are usually sold in 24-inch bars. Shaper steel is available hardened or unhardened; I always use hardened because I do not have the knowledge and equipment for heat-treating. The depth of the cut determines bar thickness. It is advisable to make the knife at least one-third as thick as the cut is to be deep. Although this ratio can vary depending on spindle speed, wood density and so on, it is better to play it safe and not skimp. If you are trying this setup for the first time, buy several precut shaper blanks in various widths. Be sure to specify lock-edge. Later, buy a 24-inch bar of the width you use the most. Note also that it is possible to grind both ends of a blank, and also to grind several narrow profiles on one wide blank.

To add this setup to your present shaper, you must adjust its spindle speed and add a spindle lock. Lock-edge cutters are designed to run about 4,000 r.p.m., but most shapers are set at the factory for about 10,000 r.p.m. Running too fast risks thrown knives. To compute your present spindle speed, use the formula:

$$\text{spindle speed} \times \text{spindle pulley size} = \text{motor speed} \times \text{motor pulley size}$$

Plug in all the knowns, which can be obtained by measuring the diameters of the pulleys and from the motor specification plate. Then use the formula to determine the proper pulley for 4,000 r.p.m. On most machines the motor pulley is easiest to change, and you will have to buy new vee-belts of the proper length.

The compression of the spindle nut is all that holds the knives in the collar. Therefore the machine must have a positive spindle lock against which to tighten the nut. To make one, weld a short piece of 1-1/2-inch pipe to the bottom of the spindle pulley and drill a 1/2-inch hole through the pipe. A Phillips screwdriver slipped into this hole will catch on other parts of the machine and prevent the

Knives can be ground to almost any profile. Some of these knives are ground at both ends, and some carry more than one profile on an edge. Drawing shows lock-edge knives in a ball-bearing cutter.

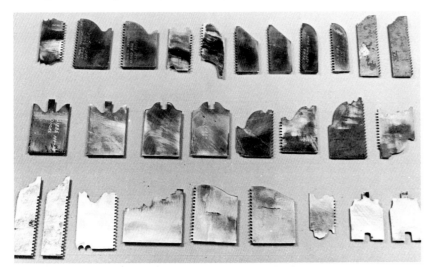
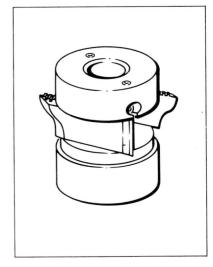

From *Fine Woodworking* magazine (Winter 1976) 5:60-62

spindle from turning while it is being tightened (see photo).

The knives are ground to shape on a conventional bench grinder with a medium or coarse grit wheel, with delicate profiles worked on an abrasive cutoff wheel. Each profile requires two matched knives. The process is straightforward and, like anything else, becomes quicker and easier with experience.

First, know exactly what profile you want to cut and make a drawing or hand shape a wooden template. Paint or spray the knife blank with the blue layout dye that machinists use. It is inexpensive, a little goes a long way, and should be available at a local machine shop or mill supply house. After the dye has dried use an awl or scriber to mark the desired pattern on the knife. The dye makes possible a very fine but highly visible line.

In designing knives, avoid long narrow sections and sharp points, which break easily. The cutting edge must have a side clearance of three to five degrees to prevent burning. And you should realize that the cut produced is not exactly the same as the pattern ground on the knife, because the knives are set on a chord, not radially, in the cutterhead. This affects the depth of the cut, not its width. Unless extreme accuracy is required this will not be significant. One way to overcome the problem when duplicating molding is to miter a piece of the original molding at the attack angle of the knife, and use this profile as a layout template.

Begin rough grinding on a conventional bench grinder. The bevel depends on the size of the shaper collar, and must be steep enough to keep the heel of the cutting edge from bumping the stock. On a 2-1/2-inch collar, I use a 45 degree angle—about five degrees greater than absolutely necessary for clearance. The width of the wheel depends on the profile being ground; they are made in widths from 1/2 to 1 inch. Remember to keep the steel cool by dipping it frequently in water. When it gets uncomfortable to hold it is too hot, and overheating can ruin the temper.

After the knife is rough ground to within 1/16 inch of the desired profile, change to a fine grit wheel and finish very carefully to the line. Sometimes it is necessary to lay out the profile again as the dye may have burned away.

Delicate profiles and moldings with sharp corners or small

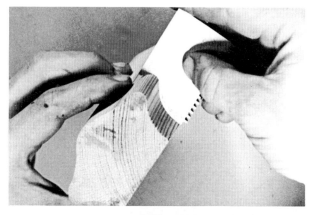

Top picture shows knife being checked for accuracy against an existing molding. At center a bead is cut using ball-bearing collars and a starting pin. At bottom a piece of pipe welded to spindle pulley provides positive lock against which to tighten spindle nut.

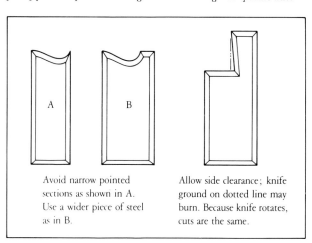

Avoid narrow pointed sections as shown in A. Use a wider piece of steel as in B.

Allow side clearance; knife ground on dotted line may burn. Because knife rotates, cuts are the same.

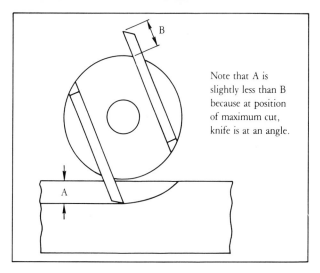

Note that A is slightly less than B because at position of maximum cut, knife is at an angle.

radii will require special grinding operations and here an abrasive cutoff wheel about 1/8 inch thick is most useful. Normally cutoff wheels are used on special industrial machinery with elaborate guards, but they do excellent work mounted on a bench grinder or on the arbor of a table saw. They cannot withstand lateral stress and you must be careful to cut directly into the wheel and avoid binding or pinching. Stay well under the maximum safe r.p.m. printed on the wheel, and guard it as much as possible, exposing only the cutting edge. On a table saw, simply raise the arbor until the wheel meets the table at the proper bevel angle, and carefully remove all sawdust to prevent a fire. I also use cutoff wheels on the table saw to cut knife blanks from 24-inch bars of shaper steel.

A jig to hold knives for grinding can be made from two pieces of scrap steel about 1/4 inch thick. Drill both pieces, tap the holes in the bottom one to accept bolts and sandwich the blank between them. A valuable aid is the diamond wheel-dressing tool. It looks like a Phillips screwdriver with diamond impregnated in the tip and can be used to shape and dress a grinding wheel to any profile.

High-speed rotary grinders, such as the Dremel, can be used with small diameter wheels to grind sharp curves. Mounted wheels for such tools can also be chucked in the drill press, with the table tilted to the correct bevel.

After the knife has been ground to the desired profile, it must be sharpened. First, remove the burrs by whetting the face of the knife on a fine stone such as hard Arkansas. Then whet the ground edge with a regular bench stone for straight or bevel cutters, and a slip stone, moon stick or Arkansas file set for curved cutters. When properly sharpened the knife should shave.

Before mounting the knives, make sure the collars are free of dirt, grease and chips. Set the bottom collar on the spindle and place the knives in its slots, allowing them to extend about the distance of the required cut. Be sure the knives are long enough to reach at least the centerline of the collar. Place the top collar over the knives, engaging the slots, and make sure the lock-edge notches fit properly. Adjust the knives to the desired cut by turning the Allen screws on the bottom collar, and hand tighten the spindle nut. Now lock the spindle and snug the nut. It is wise to place a heavy board in front of the knives when the machine is turned on, just in case.

Finally, a few cautions: Never run the spindle clockwise as this would loosen the spindle nut. Cut from the bottom whenever possible, as the knives are less exposed and there is no risk of binding. Avoid kickback by keeping the knives sharp and using hold-down fixtures. Keep the cutterhead well balanced and investigate any undue vibration. ☐

[*Author's note:* Shaper collars and knives can be obtained from the following sources: Wisconsin Knife Works, 2710 Prairie Ave., Beloit, Wisc. 53511; Forest City Tool Co., Box 788, Hickory, N.C. 28601; Charles G. G. Schmidt & Co., 301 W. Grand Ave., Montvale, N.J. 07645; Woodworkers Tool Works, 2420 E. Oakton St., Arlington Hts., Ill. 60005.]

At top, existing molding mitered to the attack angle of the knife can be used as layout template for an exact reproduction. Below, a cut-off wheel mounted on table saw arbor refines the contour that has been roughed out on a bench grinder. For safety, cut-off wheel should be used with a knife holder and guard. A diamond wheel dresser shapes grinding wheel to reverse profile of the desired cut. High-speed grinder sharpens difficult contour. At bottom Arkansas file set is used to hone knife.

Shaper Cutters and Fences

For accuracy and flexibility, make your own

by Earl J. Beck

My machine woodworking efforts started in 1934 with making a shaper from two old auto brake drums, using a plan from *Popular Science*. I have for 19 years been using variations of my own design of a single-cutter shaper collar, using mostly freehand-ground cutters, with great success, speed and safety. I got to grinding the cutters in a curious way. I was fortunate in finding a number of old cabinet planes, some of which were molding planes. I wanted to use the nice shape in one of these, but did not want to limit myself to a straight or slightly convex edge, so I ground my first cutter to match the plane iron. When I returned to the plane for the straight cuts, the grain proved difficult and the plane badly tore out the wood. As the shaper cutter didn't, I finished the job with it. I like my collection of beautiful old hand tools, but I love that shaper.

The shaper has many advantages over other tools to do the same work. Now if you enjoy pushing a carving chisel through a complex, knotty, ornery piece of wood for hours on end, fine. I like to do that myself once in a while. But more important to me is the rapid, precise contouring of wood to produce parts that fit together without a lot of hand-finishing, allowing me all the time I want for hand-detailing and removing all traces of machine work. I use a band saw, jointer and shaper, and of these only the shaper is indispensable.

Shaper and router cutters — While the shaper is my tool of choice, there are applications for the portable high-speed router for which I have been unable to adapt a shaper. So I will precede my discussion of shaper cutters with a discussion of router cutters—many of the principles are the same.

A router may be the best choice where the workpiece is large and awkward. It may also be the only machine alternative for the shaping of compound-curved stock—the contouring, for instance, of fancy chair frames that would otherwise be handcarved. To reduce handwork in making a double-wide copy of a French Provincial chair, I made a cutter for the router like the one in figure 1. I could have ground a standard cutter to shape, but I chose to braze a tungsten-carbide metal-cutting chip to a ¼-in. aircraft-quality bolt, rounding the hex head in a lathe (you could also do this by hand-grinding) and slotting it to receive the chip. The important thing with a single-edged cutter (the only type most of us want to fool with, in the absence of sophisticated precision grinders) is to have the dummy side—used only for balance—short enough that it doesn't tear up what the sharp cutter side does. So place the chip slightly off-center and sharpen the slightly longer side. Once when I did not have a large enough chip, I placed a smaller chip more than a little off-center, with no obvious disadvantage or vibration.

Being able to fashion your own cutter gives you the option of producing the same contour in different ways. A conventional ogee cutter looks like the one at *A* in figure 2. The same shape can be produced by *B*, with the advantage that the tool marks are in line with the grain and consequently easier to remove.

While there is no great point in using carbide steel rather than high-speed metal-cutting steel unless you plan to use your cutters continually on abrasive wood or you desire a permanent cutting edge, the carbide can be brazed and heated with impunity (MAPP torches are satisfactory), as overheating does not anneal them. Carbides are inherently hard and unlike tool steels do not depend on quench-hardening. Also, carbide tool bits come in shapes and sizes about right for the job, and don't require extensive sawing or grinding. If you decide to silver-solder tool steels (brazing will probably be too hot), you'll find either *T* or *M*-series high-speed steels will be harder than necessary for wood cutting. If available, the higher numbers in the *M*-series—*M15* or *M33*—will be least susceptible to annealing during silver-soldering.

If you choose carbide, you'll need a silicon-carbide grind-

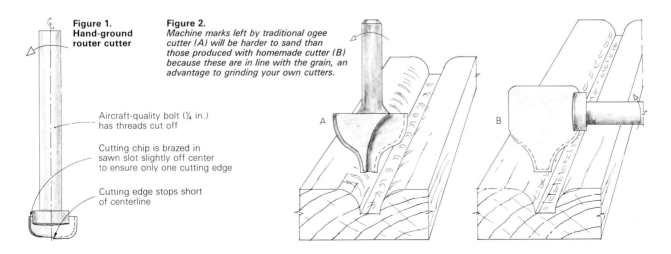

**Figure 1.
Hand-ground
router cutter**

Aircraft-quality bolt (¼ in.)
has threads cut off

Cutting chip is brazed in
sawn slot slightly off center
to ensure only one cutting edge

Cutting edge stops short
of centerline

Figure 2.
*Machine marks left by traditional ogee
cutter (A) will be harder to sand than
those produced with homemade cutter (B)
because these are in line with the grain, an
advantage to grinding your own cutters.*

A

B

ing wheel; aluminum-oxide grinding wheels are too soft. You can use the soft, green silicon-carbide recommended for this purpose, but I prefer a harder, vitrified wheel made for lapidary. The vitrified wheel is more likely to overheat and while that won't harm a brazed chip, it might melt the silver solder. It is my impression in freehand grinding, where the cutter is not rigidly held, that the vitrified wheel produces a slightly sharper edge.

Tool geometry and sharpening — I have two single-cutter shaper collar systems (figure 3)—to attempt to grind multiple cutters is impractical as it's difficult (if not impossible) to grind two or more cutters to exactly the same shape. The system *A* cutter consists of two collars separated by a post, which balances the cutter sandwiched opposite it. System *B* consists of a small cutter held in a slot in a solid-steel disc with an allen screw. For cutters up to about ⅝ in. wide at the cutting edge, system *B* is my method of choice. The small cutters are heat-treated easily with a small torch, and easily annealed for reshaping. The disc may be any useful size—for small cuts I have had success with a disc 1½ in. to 2 in. in diameter. An advantage of system *B* is that the holding disc usually doesn't interfere with the wood guide (discussed later), which may then fit closely and all but totally shield the cutter.

Through grinding cutters I attempt to achieve a wood surface that may be sanded easily, has no trace of casehardening (burnishing of the surface), and minimum or no tear-out. This combination is probably impossible, which is why production woodworking involves so much sanding. If you examine all but the finest of new furniture, you'll see that sanding frequently has been substituted for high-speed machining, giving the finished piece a buttery, rounded appearance with excessive radii on corners. Woodworkers who try to speed things up with an abrasive flap wheel know the effect.

For every wood, moisture content, machine and speed there is an optimum combination of rake (cutting) and relief

Small dovetail cutter

Small radius cutter

Allen screw

System A   System B

(clearance) angles, as shown in figure 4. The desirability of, and in production work the need for, a definite rake angle is a persuasive argument for the shaper instead of the router. The rake angles of the router cutters I have seen vary all over the place—as do their cutting capabilities. All seem to depend on the machine's high speed to compensate for a lack of attention to detail.

Over the cutting length of a shaper knife from top to bottom, the radius (r_1 and r_2 in figure 4) varies significantly, and thus so do the cutting and relief angles. On straight blades such as the ones used in jointers and planers, you can produce a smaller cutting angle by grinding a small second bevel on the face of the knives. This back-beveling gives more of a scraping than a lifting action, and it virtually eliminates tear-out. However, this tactic cannot be used for grinding shaper blades be-

Figure 4.
Cutting angle (α) is measured between the face of the blade and the radius of the cutting circle (r). As r_1 changes to r_2 along the contour of the blade, so does α change. The only way the cutting angle can be equalized is by grinding a back bevel on the face of the blade, not practical for contoured blades. Relief angle (β) is measured between the tangent to the cutting circle and the ground bevel. This angle also changes as the radius changes, but it can be equalized by honing a land or burnishing the edge on the bevel at and near r_2.

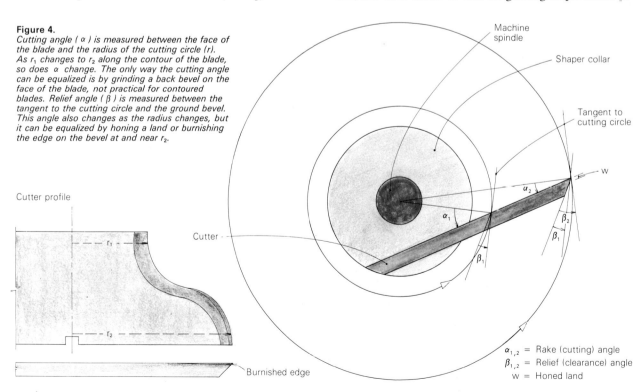

Cutter profile

Cutter

Machine spindle

Shaper collar

Tangent to cutting circle

w

Burnished edge

$\alpha_{1,2}$ = Rake (cutting) angle
$\beta_{1,2}$ = Relief (clearance) angle
w = Honed land

cause they are contoured, so for optimum results you must make an adjustment of another sort: Relieve the extreme edge at and near r_2. Grind initially to the correct angle at r_1 in one pass, then grind a small land, w, at the outer edge of r_2, at the same angle. As an alternative, you could burnish the leading edge of the cutter at the largest radius (as when finishing the edges of hand scrapers), but only if the cutter is not too hard. For a fully hardened cutter, hone the end to produce a land of width w.

The small land on the cutter (which can form through wear as well as by grinding) suppresses tear-out by forcing down the wood fibers just behind the sharp cutting edge. The trade-off, however, is zones that are casehardened. These zones may not be visible, but they are all too apparent during finishing, when they cause the stain to blotch. How casehardening occurs is exaggerated for illustration in figure 5, where both the width of the land and the travel of the workpiece while the cutter is in the cut are much too large for the real world. However, the depth of cut, another variable that influences the finished surface, is pictured in the detail typically. To achieve the best cut with minimal tear-out and casehardening, try a combination of shallow cuts, slow feed and a slight land on the cutter.

The criteria by which a skilled amateur or small-shop professional judges cutter performance are probably quite different from the criteria used in a high-speed mill producing planed, structural lumber. For one thing, softwood lumber is usually planed wet, and it is the after-dry appearance that the customer observes. Casehardening is irrelevant in structural lumber since the wood will not be stained, and may even be preferred for the smooth, slick finish it imparts. On the other hand, the small-shop woodworker generally seeks two types of surfaces—one to be glued and the other to be finished. If you're gluing, precision is all-important in obtaining the best possible fit. Despite some reports to the contrary, I believe roughing up the surface first with sandpaper gives a better glue bond. Now suppose you have a jointer with an optimum cutting edge. The trailing edge of the cutting bevel causes casehardening. Because the wood is kneaded, however slightly, sanding is difficult and in some woods almost impossible. For gluing, it's usually better to accept a little tear-out, which will disappear under clamping pressure.

The more important type of machined surface for most of us is the one that is shaped, sanded and finished. My idea of a good surface is one from which I am able to remove the cutter marks with a pass or two of medium-grit (say, 100) sandpaper. Again, in this case, a bit of tear-out would be preferable to a bit of casehardening. If the shaped surface is to be painted rather than finished with a clear stain, however, I would opt for a bit of casehardening.

To avoid excessive hand-finishing, I keep cutting edges sharp, with a slight burr and no excessive fine honing. This is a good reason for using high-speed steel cutters instead of tungsten carbide—my tests show that even with the greatest care, grinding tungsten carbide leaves little if any burr.

The shaper and its basic tooling — Just why does the shaper work better than the router, where it can be used? First, the shaper has a larger radius of cut, important in a surface to be sanded. The router partly compensates for this with its high speed, but unless its cutter is very sharp, not enough. Second, the shaper cutter can be honed with a rough stone or ground on a medium-grade aluminum-oxide wheel to produce a slightly torn finish, which is optimum. Third, except for certain unfortunate types of cuts—usually a result of poor cutter design—the shaper is safe. Figure 6 (next page) shows what I believe to be an important feature of shaper use—you can submerge the cuts, and the workpiece being machined protects you from flying debris. That the work, if it leaves the table, moves away, rather than toward the cutter, and thus is less easily ruined, is a bonus.

I use a spindle shaper with a ½-in. diameter shaft. These

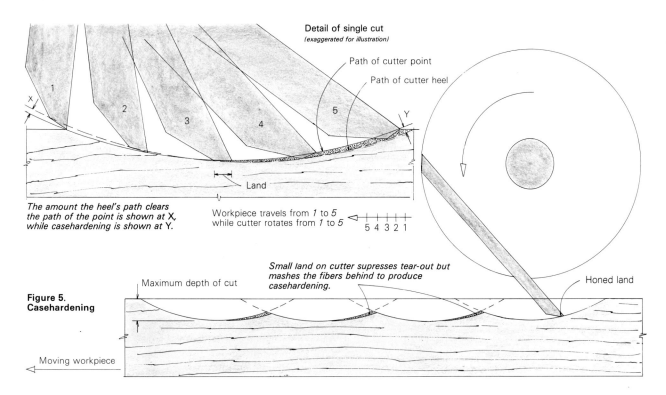

Detail of single cut
(exaggerated for illustration)

Path of cutter point

Path of cutter heel

Land

The amount the heel's path clears the path of the point is shown at X, while casehardening is shown at Y.

Workpiece travels from *1* to *5* while cutter rotates from *1* to *5*

Honed land

Small land on cutter supresses tear-out but mashes the fibers behind to produce casehardening.

Maximum depth of cut

Figure 5. Casehardening

Moving workpiece

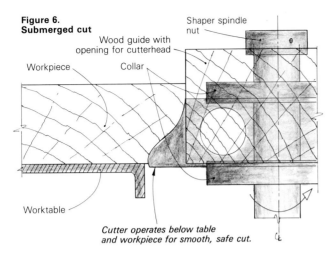

**Figure 6.
Submerged cut**

Shaper spindle nut

Wood guide with opening for cutterhead

Workpiece

Collar

Worktable

Cutter operates below table and workpiece for smooth, safe cut.

machines are usually belt-driven by a motor mounted below the table. Some models have direct-drive motors, but these lack flexibility and I don't recommend them. They're also unduly noisy because of the high speed they must achieve. A good shaper should have a fairly heavy table (I prefer ground cast iron) at a comfortable height, with hold-down-bolt holes, an adjustable bearing carrier to elevate and lower the cutter, and well-made auxiliary components (such as spanner nuts and spacers).

I built my ½-in. spindle shaper; it can be duplicated for about $1,500 (all 1980 prices), using local foundries and machine shops. Low-cost conversion parts for a ½-in. drill press might seem a logical adaptation. Don't do it: The only thing I know of that is more dangerous is the myriad of cut-off items that accumulate on shop floors. If you want a good, nice-looking shaper and don't want to make one, buy Sears' model 2392N (97 lb.) at $209.95. Buy a few cutters, but mostly grind your own. They'll be sharper and work better.

If you're planning to buy a shaper, try to buy it without the fence, at lesser cost—I have a nice factory-built adjustable

fence that I simply never use, preferring instead the wooden work guide shown in figure 7. The guide is fashioned from a piece of scrap wood about ¾ in. thick, with an opening for the cutter. When I want to renew the working edge and know so a day or two in advance, I glue a strip of hardwood to the old edge, leaving a space above the surface of the table for chip clearance.

I also like to use another technique for submerged cuts—especially simple with system *B*, but usually practical in any case with a little trimming of the hardwood strip. I clamp the guide down lightly, with the cutter inside, and then move the guide in while running the machine, to allow the cutter to cut its own opening, a little oversize. I relieve the second edge with a skew chisel to provide good entry without hang-up. For vertical clearance, I place two scraps of thin cardboard under the guide after the cut is made, and run the guide into the cutter again. If I can't use a submerged cut because of cutter design or the nature of the cut, and am going to make a lot of cuts, then I build a guard that completely covers the cutter. In this case it is important to shape the guard so chips can be carried away from the work. Chips that circulate around the cutterhead can cause small but noticeable depressions in the finished surface. Even in the open-topped fence, a chip ramp is a good idea.

I regulate the depth of the cut with a cam adjuster attached to the work guide; it requires minimum (for me) tooling and is ideal. As discussed earlier in this article, tear-out and casehardening can be minimized by making a series of light cuts rather than one heavy cut. The cam adjuster facilitates this by allowing incrementally fine cuts without having to stop the machine or reposition the workpiece. In use, you place the fence over the hold-down bolts through the appropriate holes (there is a choice, allowing gross adjustment) and roughly set the depth of cut, shifting the fence in the hold-down-bolt slot. Set the hold-down knobs loosely and move the cam lever to fine-tune the depth of cut. This care is justified only for finished surfaces; for glue joints only accu-

Figure 7. Adjustable wooden work guide

There are three adjustments possible:
1. *Place guide over hold-down bolt through one of the two holes.*
2. *Swing guide at slot and loosely set hold-down knobs.*
3. *Rotate cam lever for fine adjustment.*

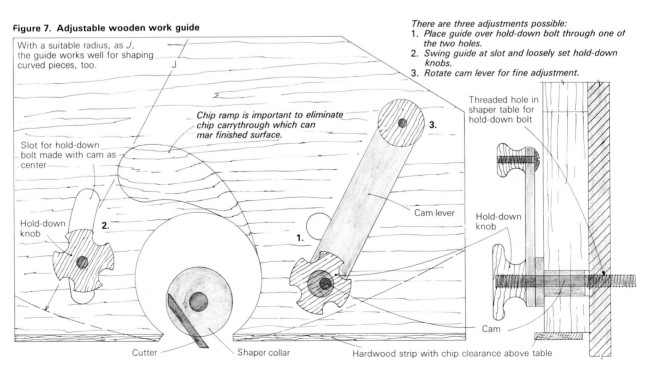

With a suitable radius, as *J*, the guide works well for shaping curved pieces, too.

J

Chip ramp is important to eliminate chip carrythrough which can mar finished surface.

Slot for hold-down bolt made with cam as center

Hold-down knob

Cutter

Shaper collar

Cam lever

Threaded hole in shaper table for hold-down bolt

Hold-down knob

Cam

Hardwood strip with chip clearance above table

Figure 8.
Metal guide for concave cuts can be mounted below the cutter, as shown here, or on spacer blocks above the cutter.

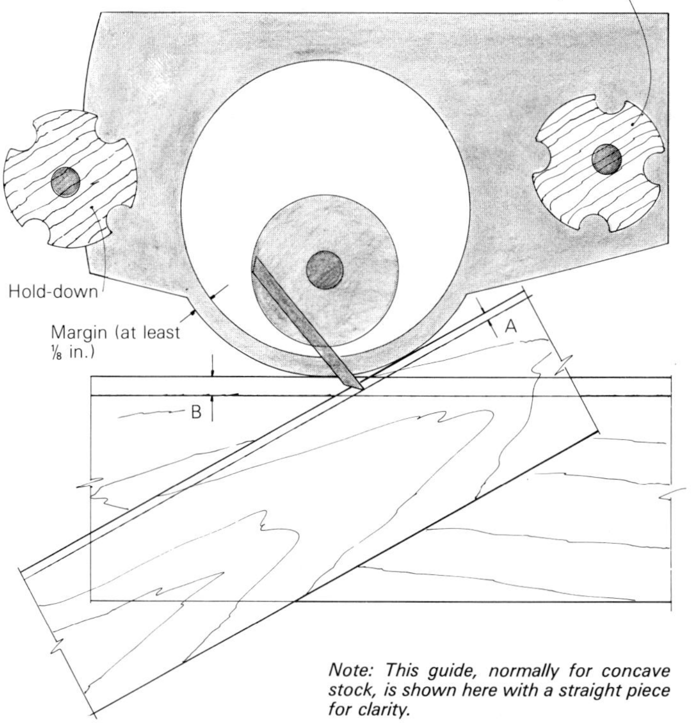

Hold-down may be cam-adjustable

Hold-down

Margin (at least ⅛ in.)

A

B

Note: This guide, normally for concave stock, is shown here with a straight piece for clarity.

Figure 9.
Contour guide

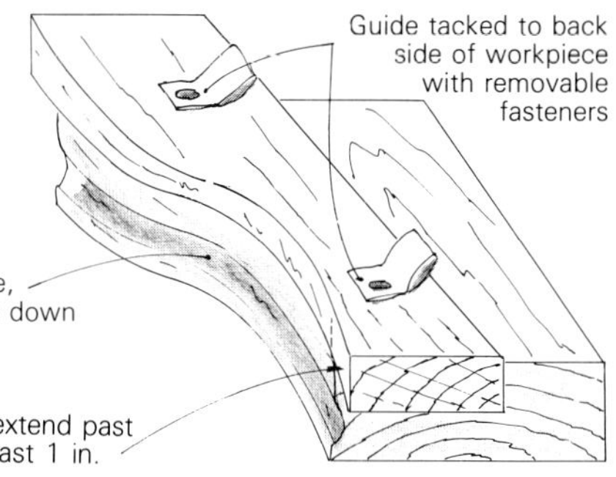

Guide tacked to back side of workpiece with removable fasteners

Workpiece, finish side down

Guide to extend past work at least 1 in.

Figure 10.
Three-sided guide-carriage

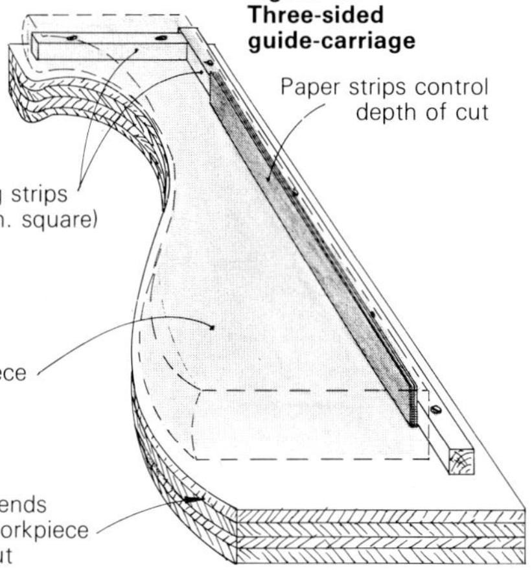

Paper strips control depth of cut

Positioning strips (about ¾ in. square)

Workpiece

Guide extends beyond workpiece to start cut

racy is necessary, and in other cases, say, for tongue-and-groove joints, heavy cuts are usually adequate.

More shaper guides — The straight guide is the safest, most accurate and simplest way to ensure a near-perfect cut in a shaper. Unfortunately, it is useful only for straight or convex work. Where molding of concave stock is desired, it is standard practice to run the work past the cutter, holding it either against a ball-bearing rubbing collar attached to the cutter or a steel rubbing collar inset in a well in the table opening (see the article on "Custom Shapers for Period Moldings," pages 69 to 75). In either case, the cut is started by holding the work against a hold-down stud to avoid having the cutter toss the work back at you—a tricky and dangerous maneuver. There is no quick way to adjust depth of cut in these methods, and the inset collar may interfere with the positioning of the cutter.

The guide shown in figure 8 can be positioned either above the cutter using spacer blocks or bolted to the table and adjusted with the hold-down, cam, or both. It is a useful alternative to the guides discussed above: It provides friction without the rubbing post, a nuisance on certain pieces with small radii, and you can control the depth of cut—change it without turning off the shaper or adjusting the guide—by changing the angle at which the workpiece approaches the cutter. The first shallow cuts, as at *A* in figure 8, are made with the work tangent to the guide at a point to the right or left of center. Final cuts, as at *B*, are made with the work tangent to the center point.

All three types of guides do share certain problems, however. Unless the work is held in a shaped guide that has a surface elevator built in, as in figure 10, you may need a plywood surface elevator. Also, if a template is attached to the workpiece in order to get a precise shape, it's usually

necessary to make the pattern slightly different from the shape of the finished piece because the cutting radius and ball-bearing or insert radius are not the same, as anyone with experience in router control using rubbing collars knows.

You can make the concave-cut guide in figure 8 on a metal or wood lathe of aluminum (⅛ in. to ¼ in. thick) or on a metal lathe of steel (⅛ in. thick)—the size of the opening is irrelevant. You could also cut the guide on a drill press using a fly cutter. In any case, for durability it is best to leave a margin around the hole at least ⅛ in. wide.

Where only one side of a workpiece is to be shaped, you can tack a guide to the back side of the workpiece, as in figure 9. Make sure you carefully cut and sand the guide, as imperfections there will be transferred to the work. The guide should be at least 1 in. longer than the workpiece, in order to enter and leave the cut under full control, with the workpiece held at the correct distance. The workpiece should be sawn about 1/16 in. oversize on the edge to be shaped. Make the guide of any material, depending on the number of times it is to be used—pine for short runs, metal for long runs. I find it useful to keep on hand a supply of pine and hardwood planed to about 5/16 in. I never throw a guide away, although occasionally I get in a hurry and rework one.

Figure 10 shows an alternative to tacking the guide piece to the work. In this case the part to be formed had both faces finished, so I made a three-sided carrier to hold the workpiece. Because I had not developed the cam adjuster at the time, I used paper strips to adjust the depth of cut. □

Earl Beck, of Ventura, Calif., is a semi-retired research engineer and lifelong woodworker who generally builds rather than buys his tools. See page 64 for a followup to this article.

. . . I enjoyed Earl Beck's article (pages 59-63). . . . However, on page 60, he tells about two systems he uses to shape wood on his ½-in. spindle shaper. Since we have been in the business of making shaper cutters, collars and cutterheads since 1926, I must totally disagree with the safety of his system *A*, where he used one knife and a post for balance. Also, to a lesser degree, his system *B*, where he uses a small knife in a disc. The knife is held firm by an allen screw.

On most shapers today, the spindle rotates between 8,000 and 12,000 RPM. I cannot understand how one knife can be balanced safely at that speed. It does not take very much weight to cause an out-of-balance effect at 8,000 RPM. An out-of-balance knife would cause the machine to vibrate, and the knife might be thrown from the cutterhead, which could cause a serious accident.

All manufacturers today must be extremely careful to grind knives to very close tolerances to prevent accidents. Most collars sold today are OSHA approved in either two- or three-knife, safety-type, lock-edged collars, in which the knives are all balanced within one-eighth of an ounce, and are locked into the collars so that there is very little, or no, out of balance on knives. Also, many knives made today are machine-ground in the collars in which they will be used, to ensure that all the cutting edges on all the knives in one pair of collars will cut. . . .

I am speaking from a manufacturer's viewpoint, but whether the shaper is operated by a serious amateur or a worker in a large furniture manufacturing company, the primary concern is safety. I believe it is very difficult, if not impossible, to balance one knife in a cutterhead that rotates 8,000 RPM. It does not cost that much more to buy a good brand-name pair of safety collars and steel, and have the assurance that your shaping job will be done safely, smoothly, and quickly.

—*Richard E. Paul, Charles G.G. Schmidt Co.,*
301 W. Grand Ave., Montvale, N.J.

EARL BECK REPLIES: Richard Paul correctly identifies an important area of concern, balance in high-speed machinery. He is incorrect in thinking that neither of my two systems for supporting a single shaper cutter can easily and carefully be balanced. Generally, I have found it unnecessary to balance system *B*, with its small projection and the very light weight of the tool-steel cutters used. Most of their mass is offset by the milled cut into which they fit and the unfilled portion of the hole for the setscrew. I have fitted some of mine with a hole drilled all the way through in line with the shaft hole. In one end of this fits the allen screw; on the opposite side is placed a similar but longer allen screw with a nylon locking insert. In use, fine adjustment is made by placing the assembly on a pair of level (in my case, metal lathe) ways and running the balancing screw in and out until a nominally perfect static balance is achieved. This takes two minutes or less, with a little practice.

Balancing the more complicated system *A* would be just as simple and direct, but for the variability in cutter sizes, overhangs, etc. In any case, the balancing post combined with other approaches such as drilled holes, and an approach such as that discussed by system *B*, would allow very close balancing. To avoid the nuisance of this, I place and size

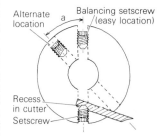

Alternate location · Balancing setscrew (easy location) · *a* · Recess in cutter · Setscrew

Offsetting the balancing setscrew's hole by angle a *brings the setscrew in line with the cutter extension, a slightly better setup.*

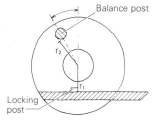

Balance post · r₂ · r₁ · Locking post

my balancing post slightly off a line normal to the cutter. Drilling a hole in the cutter to reduce its mass avoids all the fuss.

As for Paul's value of one-eighth of an ounce, this seems arbitrary, as the unbalancing causes centrifugal forces which must be successfully opposed by a centripetal force within the machine. Unbalanced force = $C N^2 r$, where C is an appropriate constant, N is the RPM and r the radius of unbalance. Based on my experience, I think my system, which I usually operate about 7,000 RPM or less, and for which r would be about 1 in., an unbalance of an eighth of an ounce would be noisy but probably not dangerous. I would neither recommend the use of such an unbalanced machine, even for a short time, nor use it myself. If I did not want to balance the cutter because it was a temporary grind for a single job, not likely to be repeated, I'd slow my machine down temporarily. If the basic spindle assembly is well designed, then bearing noise will be objectionable at unbalance conditions for below those that might cause shaft failure.

There are at least two low-cost shapers on the market with a large overhang; they may be identified as having adjustment by nuts and washers, one of which is kept from rotating by a milled slot in the shaft. The same slot also allows reversal of the spindle, which I can visualize as desirable for some uses, but not critical. One reason that I built my machine was to obtain maximum rigidity with the ½-in. spindle. I adhered to that to use a number of three-wing milled cutters I have had for a long time. If I were making a new machine today, I'd probably make the shaft ⅝ in. or even ¾ in. There's no point in cutting away good metal.

In the drawing below I show an approximate cross section through my spindle assembly's upper end. The two-step pulley at the lower end is threaded on and machined on the shaft. The shaft is

Section through shaper spindle

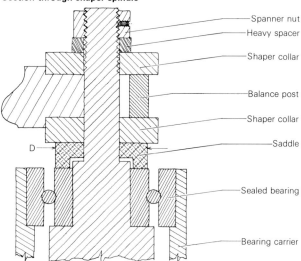

Spanner nut · Heavy spacer · Shaper collar · Balance post · Shaper collar · Saddle · D · Sealed bearing · Bearing carrier

Maximizing D *to make the saddle as large as the exposed part of the inner bearing race yields a very stiff shaper spindle.*

very heavy—unnecessarily so, except that the flexibility for such a long shaft is such that even small unbalance in the portion between the bearings would cause whirl, damaging to both bearings and ears. The bearings, especially dimension *D*, are large by comparison with most small spindle shapers. The bearings are far larger than needed precisely so that the inherent stiffness of the shaft between the bearings and the shaper collar/cutter assembly can be coupled when the nut is tightened. A very stiff assembly results, far stiffer than would occur with a slender, overhung ½-in. shaft.

Let me add a final opinion. If I were for whatever reason driven to buying and using a ground two-blade collar/cutter assembly, I would do what at least three small operators I know have done. The first time they wanted a special shape, they reground one cutter freehand. They then used a dummy blade to balance setups with both the original and the new shape.

Making and Modifying Small Tools
Small-shop methods for those special cuts

by Howard C. Lawrence

There are times, especially when making period furniture and trim, that a woodworker cannot conveniently find a commercial molding cutter, router bit or shaped lathe tool that will produce the exact profile the work calls for. Sometimes we make do with the stock cutter that seems closest to what we want, and then regret it after the piece is finished—a period reproduction just doesn't look right unless its details are authentic. Yet the problem is easily solved. Even a weekend woodworker probably has enough equipment already to be able to make a tool that will do the job right, either by modifying an existing cutter or by starting from scratch.

There are two different approaches to working tool steel, regardless of whether you are reshaping an existing cutter or making a new one. You can choose to work the steel in its hardened state, which requires that you do all your shaping with grindstones (much as you would sharpen a hardened tool's edge), or you can work the steel in a softened state. This second method allows fast, precise shaping with files, and there's no danger of overheating the cutting edge. It does, however, involve some heat-treating to harden and temper the tool for use.

Working hardened steel—For small changes or fine detail, simply touch up the shape with a high-speed hand-held grinder such as the Dremel, using some of the variously shaped stones available. This technique makes it relatively easy to modify router bits such as the ones shown in the photo at right. For larger jobs, you can use your regular bench grinder, or you can use the sort of stones that fit an electric hand drill. These stones are inexpensive and come in a variety of shapes and widths, and you can shape the stones further with a grinding-wheel dresser (available from most stores that sell grinders). Hardened tool-steel stock can be cut to size, and some shaping done, with an abrasive cutoff wheel mounted on a grinder or a tablesaw. Such wheels occasionally shatter, so exercise care—don't stand in line with the wheel, and be sure to wear heavy gloves and goggles.

Basically, for hardened steel, that's it. If you take the same care to avoid overheating that you would when grinding a cutting edge, you won't affect the temper of the steel. As soon as you've honed your edge sharp, you can go put it to work.

Working soft steel—When you have a lot of steel to remove, I think it is much easier to work the steel in its softened state. If you don't want to learn heat-treating, you can buy soft tool steel and file it to the shape you want, then have it hardened and tempered by a local machine shop, which will have special ovens, temperature-measuring equipment, hardness testers, etc. But

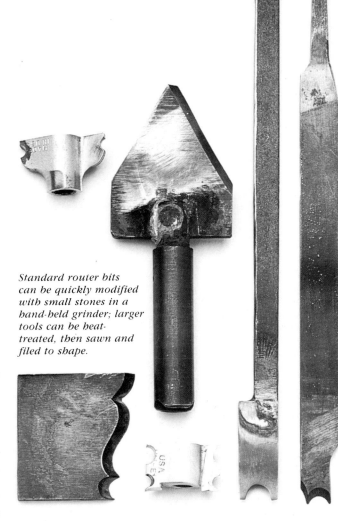

Standard router bits can be quickly modified with small stones in a hand-held grinder; larger tools can be heat-treated, then sawn and filed to shape.

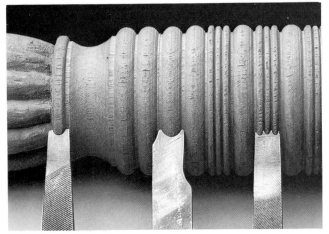

Shopmade scrapers simplify repetitive patterns. The once-brittle file steel was toughened for safety by tempering with a propane torch. Most of the reeding was cut with a reshaped router bit.

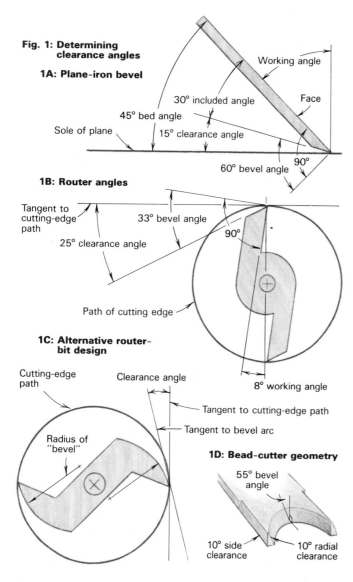

Fig. 1: Determining clearance angles

1A: Plane-iron bevel

Working angle

Face

30° included angle

45° bed angle

15° clearance angle

Sole of plane

60° bevel angle

90°

1B: Router angles

Tangent to cutting-edge path

33° bevel angle

90°

25° clearance angle

Path of cutting edge

8° working angle

1C: Alternative router-bit design

Cutting-edge path

Clearance angle

Radius of "bevel"

Tangent to cutting-edge path

Tangent to bevel arc

1D: Bead-cutter geometry

55° bevel angle

10° side clearance

10° radial clearance

bevel angle represents the material being ground away from the tool. Woodworkers, on the other hand, usually measure the included angle—the amount of steel left in the blade—and call this the bevel angle. The two different viewpoints sometimes cause confusion between woodworkers and machinists, though a good drawing will solve the problems.

To determine the clearance in a rotating tool, first draw it accurately to scale. Around its axis, draw a circle to show the path of the cutting edges, as shown in 1B and 1C. The work will lie on a tangent to this circle, and the working angle of the cutting edge is the angle between the face of the cutter and the radius. In 1B, the face of the cutter is offset 8°, and to get a 25° clearance angle you must grind at 33°. In 1C, the back of the cutter is ground as an arc, and the clearance is the difference between the tangent of this arc and the work surface. This second design has the advantage of allowing a stronger cutter, but if you are modifying such a tool, it is much easier to grind a straight bevel than to try to match the curved one.

Provide a side clearance angle of about 10°. One of my bead molding cutters, for an old molding head, is shown in 1D. Note the clearance angles on the outside edges of the tool and on the nearly radial parts within the bead. Keep in mind that what I've labeled as a 55° bevel angle is from a machinist's viewpoint; most woodworkers would call it a 35° bevel.

Cutter profiles—Shaped lathe tools, such as those shown in the photo of the table leg on p. 65, are used as scrapers: after most waste has been cut away, they are held perpendicular to the work. Thus their cutting edges are essentially the negative of the desired finished shape. Other tools, such as molding heads, router bits and plane irons, cut at an angle to the wood, and it is necessary to first draw a projection of the desired wood shape on the angled tool to determine the profile of the cutter itself. Draw the molding shape as shown in figure 2A, and show the blade in cutting position. This view shows the true cutter width, but since the working blade is not perpendicular to the molding surface, it doesn't show the true edge profile. To determine the true profile, next draw a side view of the cutter, 2B, at its working angle α, which can be determined as shown in figure 1.

View 2B shows the cutter's true thickness. It is possible to use views 2A and 2B to determine the actual shape of the cutter's face, which is shown in 2C. Begin view 2C by drawing the left and right edges of the cutter. The edges should be parallel to the face of the blade in 2B, and at the same width as in 2A. Next draw horizontal lines from 2A to 2B to show the locations of the cutter's corners on the face in 2B. Working perpendicular to the face in 2B, extend these lines over to 2C to show the corners of the blade in this view. For example, point *1* in view 2A has been transferred along the line drawn in red to point *1* in view 2B, and from there over to point *1* in view 2C.

Plot additional reference points along the cutter's profile in view 2A and draw a series of vertical lines from the molding profile up to the top of the cutter. The lines need not be equally spaced, but they should start at points important to defining the shape. Draw the lines on 2C with the same spacings they have in 2A, and transfer each point as you did for the corners. In the illustration, 12 points were used in all. The more reference points, of course, the more accurate the cutter profile will be. After all points have been transferred to view 2C, sketch in the full shape.

When the shape of the tool has been determined, paint the surface of the steel with machinists' layout fluid, a quick-drying

unless such a shop is close by, it is usually more convenient to do the heat-treating yourself, using simple procedures that were once the general practice for all toolmaking. You don't even have to begin with soft steel. You can take a hardened-steel tool, soften it yourself, file it to shape, and then reharden and temper it, all with the low-tech methods and equipment described in this article. Admittedly, a metallurgist or a precision toolmaker could come up with a long list of "buts." Yet for a small shop, the old methods are adequate.

Determining clearance angles—It's best to work out cutter designs on paper before starting to grind or file. The edge of the cutter must have a bevel behind it to provide clearance to the wood surface as the leading edge makes its cut. If you are modifying an existing cutter, it's usually best to keep the original bevel angle. If you are making a new tool, you should aim for a clearance angle to the work surface (not to the tool surface) of somewhere between 15° and 25° (for hardwoods and softwoods, respectively). Figures 1A, 1B and 1C illustrate how to determine the grinding angle. In 1A, for example, a plane iron is set at an angle of 45° to the work surface—this is called the working angle. A 15° clearance angle to the work surface therefore requires a bevel angle of 60°. Notice that I'm using machinists' terminology. Machinists measure bevel angles from a line perpendicular to the face of the tool. To a machinist, the

Drawings: Lee Hov

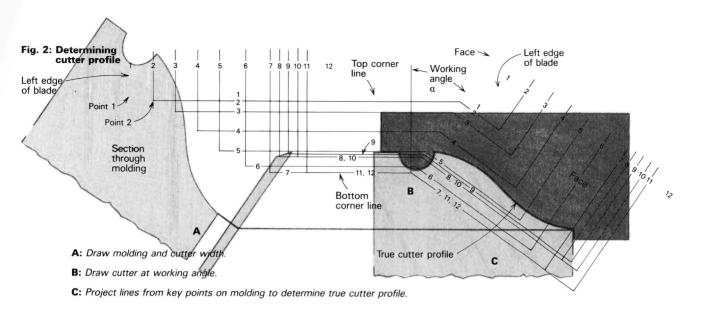

Fig. 2: Determining cutter profile

Left edge of blade

Point 1
Point 2

Section through molding

Top corner line

Face
Working angle α
Left edge of blade

Bottom corner line

True cutter profile

Face

A: Draw molding and cutter width.

B: Draw cutter at working angle.

C: Project lines from key points on molding to determine true cutter profile.

blue or purple paint that can be purchased in an aerosol can from an industrial hardware store, or made by coloring a little alcohol with a piece of carbon paper and adding a small amount of shellac. When the paint is dry, scratch in the pattern with a fine-pointed scriber.

Shaping the cutters—I usually rough in the shape with a saw and bench grinder. If the profile has intricate curves, much of the waste can be removed using metal-cutting blades in a jigsaw, provided that you are working softened steel. To refine the shape, clamp the part in a vise and work with a hand-held grinder or files (depending on whether the steel is hard or soft). I use Swiss pattern needle files to get into tight places, plus whatever other files conform to the shapes. Double-cut files remove metal quickly when roughing out, and single-cut files leave a smooth surface.

Keep in mind that it is not necessary to make the entire cutter from tool steel. The plane blade in the photo on p. 65, for example, consists of a tool-steel cutting edge brazed to a mild-steel tang. The large router bit is similarly brazed, making it much easier to fabricate. But don't plan such brazed joints in a part of a tool that will be under much stress in use.

First shape the profile of the cutting edge square to the face of the tool, then add the bevel. If grinding, keep the metal cool by dipping it in water frequently or by spraying it.

When grinding or filing the final touches, after you've roughed in the bevel, position the cutter in the vise at an angle such that you can see both the back and the face. Work carefully from the back toward the face, holding a piece of white paper against the face periodically as an aid to seeing the edge. When you've almost reached the face, position a light to give a reflection from the unfinished edge, and carefully file until the reflection just disappears.

Keeping cutters uniform—If you have to make more than one identical cutter blade (for a molding head, for example), first make a template out of thin brass or aluminum and scribe around it onto the blanks. Shape all the profiles square, then bevel each one in turn. Repeating the steps this way helps ensure uniformity. A single bit with matched cutters, such as the average router bit, is an exception. I find it best to grind one blade to shape, bevel and sharpen it, then scribe its shape on a piece of thin brass or aluminum cut to fit so it bears against both the

face of the cutter and the shank at the same time. You can then use the template as a gauge to check the length and profile of the other cutter.

It is not always necessary to have matched blades. If you plan to run only a small amount of wood, you can shape just one blade to cut, and grind back any other blades so they don't cut. Be careful to maintain balance in the cutter by leaving enough steel in the short blade or blades so that each weighs about the same as the blade that is cutting. With only one blade cutting, of course, the work must be fed to the cutter more slowly. Don't use the cutter if it is so out of balance that it vibrates.

Heat-treating—If you heat tool steel hot enough, it glows, and the color gives a rough idea of its temperature. Once the steel is heated above a certain critical temperature and then cooled very slowly (a process called annealing), it is left in a relatively soft state and can be worked with saws and files. If cooled quickly, the steel is hardened. It will be too brittle to make a good cutting edge, but if it is then reheated to just the right temperature (a step called tempering), it is slightly softened again to arrive at a balance that gives a good, tough tool edge. You can gauge tempering by colors, too: if steel is polished and heated, colored oxides that form on its surface indicate the temperature.

You can judge the hardness after any of the heat-treating steps by trying to file an edge with a sharp smooth file. The file will easily cut soft steel, will slide over very hard steel, and will just barely cut tool steel tempered to the desired hardness.

Keep in mind that we are talking about tool steel. You can't harden and temper mild steel such as I-beams and angle irons in this way. But if you start with a tool-steel blank or with an existing tool, regardless of which particular tool-steel alloy it is made from, you should succeed using the following procedures.

Flat-ground tool steel, sometimes called die steel, can be purchased soft in various sizes from an industrial-hardware or other machine-shop supplier. Its chemical analysis and heat-treatment requirements are shown on the wrapper or can be supplied by the seller. A typical temperature for both hardening and annealing is 1450°F to 1500°F. At this temperature, the steel glows a light red color, a little brighter than full cherry.

You can heat-treat small tools with a propane torch. Larger tools require more heat, but a MAPP gas torch, sold by Sears and others, will handle most small woodworking tools. In borderline cases, reduce air drafts by placing fire brick, pieces of asbestos shingle or other high-temperature insulating material around the tool as it is heated. Large tools may require an acetylene torch with a large tip.

Figure 3 lists two color spectrums: one for hardening steel, the other for tempering. Nobody would claim to be able to tell exact temperatures by observing colors, but the range is close enough for most small tools. Experience helps. The chart lists the glowing colors as seen in moderate light. In bright light or in very dim light, different temperature/color relationships apply. Higher-than-necessary temperatures may distort thin sections, so be sure to direct the flame at broad surfaces, not at sharp edges. While heating brazed cutters, like the two shown on p. 65, hold them at the brazed point with pliers to lower the temperature there so that the braze will not melt.

Annealing—If you want to modify an existing tool by filing or sawing, the steel must first be softened by annealing. Heat the steel with the torch, hold it at a temperature of about 1450°F for a minute or so and then cool it slowly. If the steel is cooled too rapidly, it will not be softened. Test it with a file, and if the file won't cut easily, try again.

For most complete softening, the steel should be held at the elevated temperature for as much as an hour and then cooled in a container filled with ground soapstone, fine sand, ashes from which all carbon has been removed, or a similar insulating material that will keep air away and cause the steel to cool over a long period of time, perhaps 10 hours. Large tool shops have special ovens for this. For softening small tools, it is usually adequate to heat the steel to a light red for a minute or so, and then slowly reduce the heat by gradually withdrawing the flame. When no color can be seen in dim light, the temperature is below 1000°F and the tool can be set aside until cool enough to test with a file. You can now shape the tool.

Hardening—Hardening is accomplished by heating the steel to above its critical temperature (the same temperature as for annealing) and then quickly cooling it, usually by plunging it into a liquid. This is called quenching. The rate of cooling affects the hardness, the depth of penetration of the hardness, and, especially in large tools, the possibility of cracks forming. The most

common quenching liquids are water and oil. Water cools the steel faster than oil, but because of this faster cooling, water is more likely to cause cracks and distortion. Cracking isn't often a problem with small tools, though. Oil-quenching gives a softer core to the tool, and thus a tougher tool. Any kind of oil can be used for quenching, as long as it is thin and does not become gummy. Kerosene was often used in the past. Common salt (NaCl) added to water, making brine, also reduces cracking.

The quenching solution should be warm, 125°F, although for small parts the temperature is not critical. Just make sure there is enough solution to allow you to completely immerse the part without appreciably raising the liquid's temperature. When the steel glows at the desired temperature, plunge the part into the quenching solution, cutting edge first, aiming to wet both sides of the tool at the same time. Agitate the tool and keep it in the solution until the bubbling stops.

The cutter will now be so hard and brittle that a smooth file won't cut it. In use, such an edge would soon chip.

Tempering—When a hardened tool is reheated to a particular temperature, it is softened to a predictable degree, toughening it. You can control the temperature by heating the tool in a household oven, or you can estimate the temperature by observing the oxide colors. The degree of tempering is partially a preference of the person doing the tempering. If the tool is too hard, it will chip easily; too soft, and it will dull too soon. Tools are usually drawn to between a light straw color (quite hard) and a dark blue (softer). A sharp file will just barely cut steel drawn to a light straw. I prefer a light straw for shaper blades, and have never had one chip.

Polish the face of the tool with fine sandpaper or emery cloth. Holding the tool with pliers as far back from the cutting edge as possible, apply low heat from the propane torch well back from the cutting edge. The polished metal will show a sequence of colors as the flame heats it, starting with a light yellow. As this color moves toward the cutting edge, it will be followed by darker shades of yellow, straw colors, purple, blue, etc. When the desired color reaches the cutting edge, plunge the blade in water to prevent the edge from absorbing any more heat from the body of the blade. The plane iron in the photo on p. 65 shows what a typical tool will look like at this stage.

When tempering, heat the steel slowly to ensure even penetration into the tool and to prevent the color progression from moving to the cutting edge so fast that it would be difficult to stop it at the proper time. The desired final temperature is only about 450°F for straw, 560°F for blue. When the edge is properly tempered, a smooth file will be just barely able to cut it.

Fig. 3: Colors observed in heat-treating

Glowing colors:

Lowest red visible in light 890°F	Dull red 1020–1160°	Full cherry 1300°	Light red 1550°	Full yellow 1750–1830°	Light yellow 1900°

Oxide colors:

Faint yellow 420°F	Light straw 440°	Medium straw 460°	Dark straw 490°	Purple 530°	Blue 560°	Pale blue 600°

Approximate hardness, Rockwell C scale						
60	59.5	59	58	57.5	57	56

Steel glows in the temperature range required for annealing and hardening, and the colors progress as in the top table, providing a built-in approximate temperature gauge. The temperatures required for tempering are much lower, and can be judged by observing the colored oxides that form on polished steel when it's heated. Colors are listed as they appear in moderate light—bright or dim light will change the relationships, and you may find that other authorities have their own names for the colors. No matter, hardness is easy to test, and experience brings consistency.

Further reading—For more about modern toolmaking as done in industry, consult the *Tool Engineers Handbook* (American Society of Tool Engineers, published by McGraw-Hill). Some of the older tool engineering books, such as *High-Speed Steel* by O.M. Becker (published by McGraw-Hill in 1910), discuss in greater detail the simpler, then more often used methods. These and other useful and interesting books can be found in the industrial-arts reference section of a large public library, or in the reference section of an engineering college library. □

Howard Lawrence is a retired aerospace engineer whose avocation was house and small-boat building and who now makes period-style furniture. He is a member of the Society of Philadelphia Woodworkers.

Custom Shapers for Period Moldings
When copying furniture, don't settle for standard cutters

by Lelon Traylor

Early American furniture represents a substantial contribution to an artistic period. American craftsmen took the best designs of European styles and adapted them to meet American tastes and needs. From this came a style superior to anything Europe ever produced. The Goddard block-fronts, with their subtle gracefulness, the so-called Chippendale highboys, and Duncan Phyfe's chairs, tables and sofas are all works of art and craftsmanship at its finest.

To reproduce one of these masterpieces is a challenge of the highest order, requiring a full understanding of all phases of design and craftsmanship. One advantage the amateur craftsman has is that time usually is not pressing, and he can determine to do the job perfectly; if a mistake is made, he does it over. Only by working in this manner can one hope to obtain the results achieved by our ancestors.

In this article I will examine how a museum-quality piece may be reproduced from the limited exposure to such pieces most of us have, which necessitates taking dimensions and detailing from photographs. The oftentimes large and intricate moldings called for in reproductions of period furniture make building your own shaper and grinding your own knives an integral part of building the piece. Directions for accomplishing these tasks are therefore included herein.

Scaling from photographs — The first step is to select the piece to copy or design. Access to a number of the best volumes on antiques is important, and the bibliography found on page 75 should help. Overall dimensions of early pieces,

often given in books, vary in height, especially for highboys. Tables are more or less standard: 29 in. to 31 in. for dining and writing, 25 in. to 26 in. for lamp and bedside tables. If the piece you are copying lists the overall dimensions you may not need to alter them, but you will need to determine all the other dimensions. This necessitates scaling.

If we take a photograph of a bedpost, for instance, and wish to make the post 82 in. high, regardless of its original height, the post must be scaled. First see if you can locate 82 divisions on a draftsman's scale that equal the height of the post in the photo. If so, you can start measuring the post. If not, and this is usually the case, slant the scale and drop perpendicular lines from the post to it. This will do the job.

A method to use on a piece photographed at an angle is to extend lines from the piece until they converge or diverge

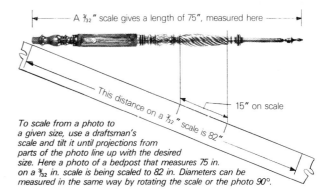

A ³⁄₃₂″ scale gives a length of 75″, measured here

This distance on a ³⁄₃₂″ scale is 82″

15″ on scale

To scale from a photo to a given size, use a draftsman's scale and tilt it until projections from parts of the photo line up with the desired size. Here a photo of a bedpost that measures 75 in. on a ³⁄₃₂ in. scale is being scaled to 82 in. Diameters can be measured in the same way by rotating the scale or the photo 90°.

Reproduction of a Goddard secretary in cherry, 44 x 22 x 94, displayed by John S. Walton, Inc., N.Y. The broken pediment, including the Chinese fretwork, was taken from a photograph in Nutting's Furniture Treasury *(fig. 717). Finials and a carved head at top with flames have yet to be mounted. The drawer-pull bails were made commercially by Ball Brass in West Chester, Pa.; the posts, plates and hinges were blanked from dies made at the School of Technical Careers, Southern Illinois University. The writing compartment was assembled first, then slipped into place. Locks, keys and round drawer pulls were machined from solid brass.*

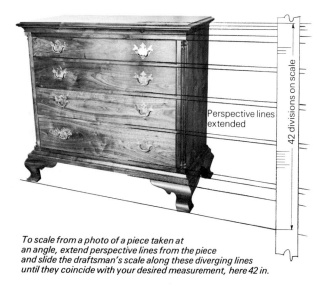

To scale from a photo of a piece taken at
an angle, extend perspective lines from the piece
and slide the draftsman's scale along these diverging lines
until they coincide with your desired measurement, here 42 in.

Perspective lines
extended

42 divisions on scale

enough to match the scale you are using. The value of the
scale does not matter. If a chest is to be 42 in. high, move the
scale right and left until 42 divisions fit exactly between the
top and bottom extension lines. Draw a vertical line at this
point and pick off such dimensions as drawer heights.

Sometimes none of these methods works and you have to
make your own scale. Let us take for example the block-front
secretary with raised-panel doors and broken pediment, on
page 69. The amount of detail, especially in the writing
compartment, makes the use of a scale custom-made for this
photograph attractive. A word of caution: When scaling a
slant-top secretary, or any piece with detailing in more than one plane, keep in mind that a perspective photo has more than one vanishing point. Measurements on the drawer fronts will therefore be out of proportion to measurements on parts farther away from you, as in the case of the inside drawers of the writing compartment. You will have to extend the lines either backward or forward to get everything in the same plane.

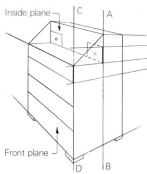

Take into account the two vanishing points when scaling from perspective photos of pieces like secretaries with details in more than one plane. To measure drawers on the front and inside planes, for example, scale along line AB, which is on a plane common to both, or project inside plane to front plane and scale there, along line CD.

To construct the scale, measure the height of the piece as it appears in the photograph, say 6½ in., and divide that number by the height you desire to make the piece, say 89 in. The resulting .073 in. is the size of each division on your scale. The problem now is accurately laying out 89 lines .073 in. apart. It can be done by stepping with a divider, which is trial and mostly error, or you can use a vernier caliper with fine points for inside measurements. Set the points at .073 in., transfer the divisions to a piece of stiff paper, and you are ready to take dimensions directly from the photograph.

An opaque projector is useful for details such as broken pediments, as well as for overall dimensions. Cover a section of a wall with paper (white, brown or tracing), and mark the desired height of the piece, top and bottom, on the paper.

Project the image of the piece onto the paper, and move the projector forward or backward until the image fits exactly between top and bottom lines on the paper. Focus and take dimensions, or outline the piece directly. You can project quarter, half or full size, and adjust your dimensions accordingly.

If the piece has been photographed from an angle, the image will be foreshortened and compensations will have to be made before you can take dimensions. One way is to estimate the camera angle used to photograph the piece, and shift the projector to a similar angle. When you have it right, the front of the piece will appear about head-on and square. Again move the projector in and out until the overall height matches your top and bottom lines. Now measure overall widths only. Take vertical measurements on the centerline or on a single vertical line. Don't skip around. I reproduced the VanPelt Highboy (opposite page) using the projector in this way to pick up carving details as well as dimensions.

Recently, while attempting to establish dimensions from the picture of a block-front secretary, nothing would come out right. Scaling, projecting from every angle, researching every old piece and cross-checking dimensions, nothing checked out. I would quit, study about it some more and come back determined to get it this time—no luck. Our daughter came by and said, "Why don't you write to them for the dimensions." My reply: "Never." This went on for some time, and I got to thinking about her solution. I finally wrote the letter, and learned that the writing surface was 34 in. from the floor, not 30 in. or 32 in. as was standard. The piece must have been built for a tall person. It didn't appear amusing at the time, but it points out what can happen when you are copying old pieces. This is what makes it interesting.

A second approach to the problem of reproducing antiques is to work up your own design from photographs of several pieces, choosing the best points of each piece where applicable. For instance, a block-front secretary may be perfect with the exception of its pediment or finials. Combining features from several pieces is fine, so long as the features fit the rest of the design and so long as you don't switch periods. This can be abominable.

Make the first drawing about 14 in. to 16 in. high. From 36 in. to 48 in. away, the eye can take in all the details of a drawing this size without shifting about, allowing the uninterrupted studying and sensing of proportion that is essential to good design. I have used this technique for years with excellent results, having tossed aside my books on design and proportion years ago. Books cannot substitute for what your own eyes can tell you.

One quick study of a drawing in this manner will not do the job. Tape the drawing to a wall at eye level and leave it there for four to six weeks. Study it daily but do not change it unless some point really starts to stand out. Drawings can be reduced or expanded by cutting and sliding the two pieces together or apart. Make sketches of any point in question, such as a foot or a pediment. Tape these sketches over the first drawing. Continue until you are satisfied, one way or another, and then redraw your composite to the same scale. This sounds like a lot of time and trouble, but compared to making a mistake on a major piece it is of small concern.

Sometimes it is best to make a full-size drawing of a piece from the small-scale drawing, or it may be sufficient to make full-size drawings of only the highly detailed areas such as corners, moldings or pediments. Naturally it depends on

Photos: Robert K. Raben; Illustrations: B. Mastelli

Reproduction of the VanPelt highboy, 96⅜ by 48 by 22, in cherry. The bases of highboys present special problems of strength in relation to weight, which can amount to several hundred pounds with the drawers full. Cracked sides are not uncommon. A strong lower frame cannot be used because usually the lower center drawer cuts the frame in two. Frame-and-panel construction of the sides of the piece would not be in keeping with the single-board style. Traylor's solution was to use solid wood, 2 in. thick before carving, reinforced by a steel rod embedded on the inside. No problems have developed in the 25 years since it was put together. All carvings are from the solid, not applied. Moldings were cut on home-built shaper.

An exact copy of the Goddard chest, 42 by 21 by 38, on p. 94 of John T. Kirk's Early American Furniture. A special spoon-shaped tool was forged to cut the groove around the concave shell. The beaded molding around the drawers was cut with a scraper ground from a power-hacksaw blade. Wallace Nutting states that the bracket foot on a block-front is more difficult to execute than a ball and claw. Traylor agrees.

whether the piece is simple, like some chests of drawers, or complex, as highboys, secretaries and the like.

Draw interior construction details full size. A cutaway drawing of a corner section is of great help. Many times it will reveal what could cause problems later if not worked into the design from the beginning. Do all planning, designing and detailing before starting construction. It is much less trouble to correct mistakes on paper than on the piece itself.

Making a shaper — Moldings either make or break a design. They must be well done and appropriate for the piece being built. Don't feel restricted to available cutters. If you design around your in-stock cutters or from catalog cutters, the result will suffer. Sketch ideas for moldings full size, and let your eye be the judge. A molding that is the wrong size or shape can ruin an otherwise fine piece of furniture. A good molding will tie the piece together, smoothing out what would otherwise be an abrupt transition between sections.

To exercise full choice and execution of design you need some basic equipment, most of which you can make yourself. A heavy-duty shaper with a spindle diameter no less than 1 in. is the first piece. You may feel a ¾-in. diameter spindle is okay, but I wouldn't want to be in the same room as a shaper with cutters extending 2½ in. from the head, running at 5,200 RPM. Weight and rigidity are important in damping vibration. A frame built of 4x4 or 4x6 stock with 2x6 rails is fine; 3-in. angle iron or 2-in. iron pipe will work too. The top may be laminated and draw-bolted as workbenches are, or made of two thicknesses of ¾-in. plywood covered with Formica, or of ¼-in. steel plate. Whatever the thickness of the rest of the top, a ¼-in. steel throat plate is necessary so the spindle can be raised close to the work surface.

Commercial shaper housings that come complete with ball bearings and elevating screw are available from Woodworkers Tool Works, 2420 East Oakton Street, Arlington Heights, Ill. 60005. If you decide that you want to make the spindle and elevator yourself, you will find that ball-bearing pillow blocks of industrial medium-duty capacity are adequate. Pillow blocks are designed to run at 3,600 RPM under load, but a shaper sustains very light loads and by using the proper grease the pillow blocks can be run at 5,200 RPM for years, eight hours a day. Use what is commonly called cup or axle grease, an inexpensive, low-heat grease which thins when it gets hot. Don't use chassis lube (it will overheat in minutes), and don't use wheel-bearing grease (it is for low speed and greater load). I have designed and built high-speed oscillating mortisers to run at 5,200 RPM in industrial situations; they haven't had a bearing failure in more than 20 years.

If you are not equipped to machine the spindle and fit the bearings yourself, take a plan of your shaper to a competent machinist who will lathe-turn the spindle using in the headstock a soft center that has been trued with a light cut. Have him turn the spindle from oversize bar stock to include a section about ½ in. long by at least 1¼ in. in diameter to tighten the cutterhead against. This cutterhead stop should not be built up by pressing, threading or welding a collar in place; it should be part of the original stock. Spindle runout should not be more than .0005 in. when the spindle is rotated by hand between centers and checked with a dial indicator. The bearing fit you want is close—the spindle's final diameter should be only .0001 in. smaller than the inside diameter of the bearings, so the bearings will slide on with no play at all. To get this close a fit, turn the spindle .001 in. to .0015 in. oversize, slip the bearing over the tailstock center, and lightly

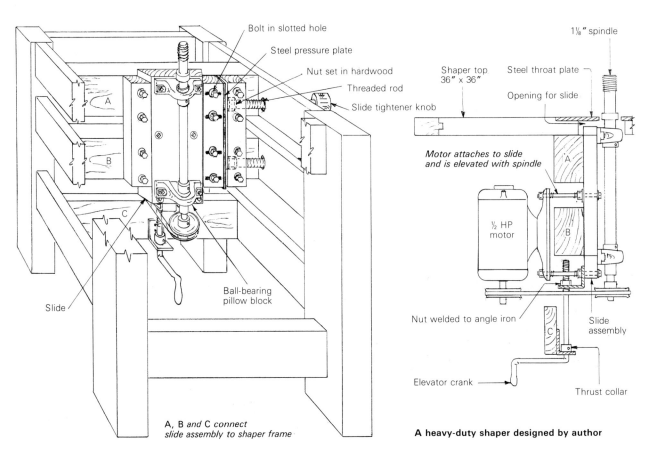

A, B and C connect
slide assembly to shaper frame

A heavy-duty shaper designed by author

file the spindle until the bearing just goes on. Continue filing toward the headstock, sliding the bearing along as you bring the spindle down to size. The bearing is in effect its own gauge, producing a perfect fit.

The spindle may be threaded with square threads, acme threads, national fine V-threads or national coarse V-threads. I have used all kinds. On the last shaper I built I used a 1-in. national coarse, 8-threads-per-inch, commercial nut. The face on a commercial nut isn't very true as to wobble or runout and should be faced off while screwed on the spindle, using a second nut as a jam. Cut the spindle threads on a lathe—a hand-held threading die is not accurate enough. The knives and collars will wobble and be dangerous to operate if the threads aren't true. Commercial nuts give a no. 2 fit. Ask for a no. 3 fit, which has no play.

The bearing slide may be made from hardwood, or from two pieces of ¾-in. plywood glued together. The assembly is a sliding dovetail. Face the contact areas with metal strips or plastic, or leave them as is. If you use plywood, treat the edges with hot paraffin. The elevator crank is made of ¾-in. threaded steel rod, heated and bent to form the handle. It is mounted to a 2x6 in the frame through a thrust collar attached to an angle iron. A nut fixed to another piece of angle iron mounted on the spindle slide receives the thread in the elevator crank. Rotating the crank moves the spindle slide up and down. The slide is released to move and locked in position by two bolts through nuts set in wood mounted to the frame. These bolts are adjusted to press or release a beveled block against the beveled slide. The motor is mounted directly to the slide and moves up and down with the spindle.

It is best to have cutterheads 1¾ in. and 2½ in. in diameter. The smaller one allows stock of a tighter radius to be shaped, and the larger one gives the "beef" necessary to hold the long, heavy knives necessary for moldings commonly found on highboys, secretaries and clocks. You won't be able to switch cutters back and forth, though, because on the small heads the distance from the center of the cutter out to the knife groove is less than on the larger heads. The knives require a different grind to produce the same molding. I would suggest, as the easiest solution to this problem, that you lay out two diameters and check it out.

Shaper knife collars and knife-steel blanks with notches to prevent slipping of the cutters are available from Woodworkers Tool Works. This equipment is more expensive than plain knife steel and smooth 60° V-groove collars, but safer.

Shaper knives — Before you make the cutter knives, it is important to understand that because they are mounted in the cutterhead along a chord of the cutter circle, and not along a radius, the knife profile will not be identical to the molding profile it cuts. Instead, the knife profile will be an elongated version of the molding profile, the amount of elongation depending on the depth of the cut. There are several ways to lay out knife profiles; the method I find most convenient relies upon a strip of paper as the principal measuring tool. This procedure is detailed in the panel at right. Note that the deepest cut (A′ on the diagram) plus the length of the blade inside the cutterhead is the length of the whole blade. Once you have drawn the correct profile on stiff paper, carefully cut it out for use as a pattern.

Now apply layout ink (Dykem Steel Blue is available from industrial suppliers) to the knife blank and let it dry. A con-

Designing shaper knives

Because a molding knife is set on a chord across the cutterhead, and not on a radius, its profile is not quite the same as the cross section of the molding it will produce. To find the knife shape that will make a given molding:

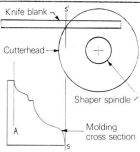

1. Draw full size a molding cross section and a plan of the shaper head. Extend vertical line S from the shallowest part of the profile, and vertical S′ where the knife enters the cutterhead. S and S′ are base lines for subsequent measurements. Label also A, the profile's deepest point.

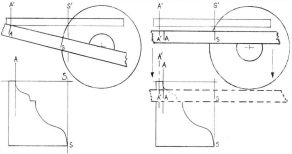

2. Mark distance AS on a strip of paper and transfer this distance to the cutterhead plan, placing the edge of the strip across the spindle center with point S on the cutterhead circumference. Mark A′ where A intersects the knife, left.
3. Align the paper strip with the knife so that S coincides with S′. Transfer distance A′ to the strip, then to the molding profile, right.

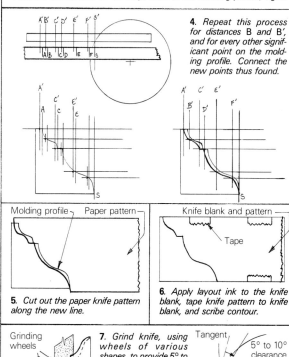

4. Repeat this process for distances B and B′, and for every other significant point on the molding profile. Connect the new points thus found.

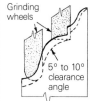

5. Cut out the paper knife pattern along the new line.

6. Apply layout ink to the knife blank, tape knife pattern to knife blank, and scribe contour.

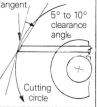

7. Grind knife, using wheels of various shapes, to provide 5° to 10° clearance angle. This angle is measured between the bevel and the tangent to the cutting circle, and will vary with the radius of the cutting circle.

centrated solution of copper sulfate (bluestone, available from swimming-pool suppliers) makes an excellent layout dye. Tape the pattern to the knife blank and scribe around it.

To grind molding cutters you need grinding wheels of various shapes. Grinding wheels should therefore be dressed with a diamond nib, a short rod with an industrial diamond set in the end by brazing, available from mill suppliers. It is important to proceed properly because the diamond can be dislodged. First pre-dress the wheel with a conventional dresser. Then, holding the nib in your hand (don't rest it on the tool rest) point it slightly downward and swing it in an arc around the edge of the wheel. Keep the nib pointed downward to prevent it from digging into the wheel and jarring the diamond loose. A diamond can be reset by holding it down with a small steel welding rod, while brazing it in place. Completely cover the diamond, let cool and carefully grind the rod to barely expose the diamond.

When grinding the cutter, don't overheat the blank or you will lose your layout line. I find it easier to control the grinding process if the tool rest is removed from the grinder. Try it both ways and use the method that is easier. More clearance is necessary in some places than in others. The side clearance doesn't need to be as great as the clearance on the periphery of the cutter. To prevent the heel of the cutter from dragging, more metal must be removed from small-diameter cutters than from larger ones. This makes the included angle of the knife steel less on the smaller cutters. Always turn the spindle by hand after mounting cutters to see if the heel clears a piece of stock held against the table. When tightening the main spindle nut to lock the knives in, I run it up as tight as it will go and give it another quarter-turn. I place on edge a 3-ft. piece of 2x8 on the table, which is about buckle height, before I turn on the machine. If the knives are going to come out, the 2x8 should stop them.

Several types of guides are used to make shaper cuts on contoured pieces, the most common being a depth collar mounted directly on the spindle. If the cut does not span the entire thickness of the stock, the unmolded portion can run directly on the depth collar. Apply paraffin to the edge that will be in contact with the collar, and after the cut, scrape the paraffin off with a pocket knife. Ball-bearing collars are also available, but they can seize and paraffin is easier to clean off than a burned edge. Whatever the collar, be sure to use a starting pin mounted in the tabletop to rest the stock against while feeding it into the cutter.

If the entire thickness of the stock is to be molded, a

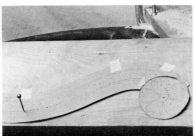

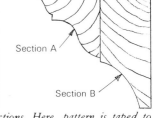

The finished molding forms the pediment of the Goddard secretary shown on page 69.

Large moldings are best made in two sections. Here, pattern is taped to molding stock with scriber marking dividing line between sections A and B into which blank will be bandsawn. Piercing the pattern and connecting the points in this way saves cutting the pattern apart. Second row of pinpoints (½ in. back) is line used to cut jig that will run against ring collar. Because collar follows jig rather than work, only edge of jig need be smoothed.

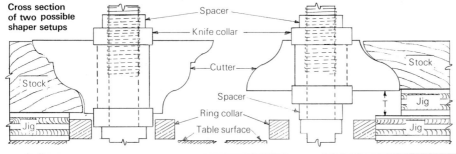

Cross section of two possible shaper setups

Spacer — Knife collar — Cutter — Spacer — Ring collar — Table surface — Stock — Jig

Cutters can be mounted to cut from the top or from the bottom of stock. Cutting from the bottom is safer because blades will not dig in if stock is lifted from table, especially important for long pieces. It's a good idea on large cuts to make more than one pass, raising or lowering the cutter into the stock between passes. Cutting from the bottom requires a thicker fixture because in its lowest position blades must turn clear of most of the stock. T is available travel to allow for shallow starting cuts.

First and final cuts, as cutter is lowered into work over several passes. Notice that the jig contour is set back from stock contour because

ring collar extends past shallowest part of cut. The guard has been removed for photograph.

spindle-mounted depth collar cannot be used: the stock will have to be mounted on a jig to be run against a fixed ring collar mounted concentric to the cutterhead, but not attached to it. The contour of the jig can be taken directly from the original molding pattern, except that the ring collar is usually larger than the smallest diameter of the cutter. The jig must therefore be cut down to allow the whole molding profile to reach the knife.

To do this, tape the pattern of the molding to the blank from which the jig is to be cut. Say the ring collar extends ½ in. beyond the smallest diameter of the cutter. Measure back ½ in. on the paper pattern and draw a contour parallel to the edge of the full length of the pattern. With the point of a compass or scriber, pierce the paper at intervals along this contour, and connect the points made on the jig, free-hand or with a French curve. Bandsaw outside this line and carefully work down to the line using a curved sanding block or a drum sander on a drill press. Remember that this surface determines the finished contour of your molding. A careless job here will be transferred by the jig to your finished piece. Use paraffin on the edge of the jig to facilitate feeding.

Heavy cuts are impossible to make in one pass. To get around this and to allow the molding to be produced in several passes, the cutter can be mounted to cut from the bottom side of the stock, and the cutter raised at each pass. You may need to use a jig with a fixture made from a second piece of ¾-in. plywood to raise the work adequately for shallow first cuts. When cutting against the grain, several light cuts with freshly honed cutters are in order.

As you are about to shape your stock, ask yourself if the material being machined were suddenly and at any time removed from your grasp, would your hand or fingers go into the cutter. If the answer is maybe, you are not 100% safe, which means that on a lot of work you are going to have to mount your stock on a fixture. The fixture may be nothing more than a 2x4 attached to the stock by glue, screws or clamps. If the stock is large and can be safely held, a fixture isn't necessary—shape first and with a band saw remove the extra stock afterward. Either way, safety first and caution always is the motto when operating a shaper.

Building your own shaper assures you of having a machine that fits your own needs at a vastly reduced price. A shaper is an important part of any complete shop. It is a satisfying experience to build your own furniture with machines and knives that you have designed and built. □

Lelon Traylor has been reproducing museum pieces for 30 years. He teaches tool and manufacturing technology at Southern Illinois University, Carbondale.

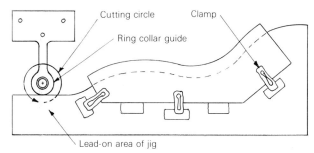
Use a jig with lead-on area to guide contoured stock past cutter that spans entire thickness of stock.

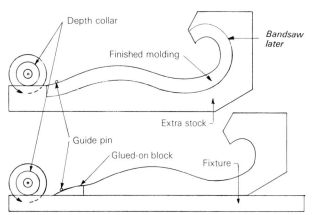
Fixture is 2x4 glued, screwed or clamped onto stock.

Extra stock or a fixture added on—either way be sure you have enough to hold on to to keep your fingers away from the cutter. If stock is squared off at the end, glue a block in place to lead cutter into stock.

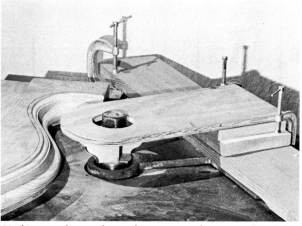
Machine guards must do two things: protect the operator from injury and stay out of his way. The shaper guard shown is constructed from plywood rather than metal for two reasons: It is quick and easy to make, and it is safe; if the cutter grabs and the guard touches the knives, shavings rather than knife pieces are thrown about.

Further reading
These excellent guides to furniture design contain pieces completely dimensioned. Check libraries for out-of-print sources.
Construction of American Furniture Treasures, Lester Margon, Dover (NY; paper); Peter Smith Pub. (NY; hardcover).
How to Design Period Furniture, Franklin Gottshall; presently OP but in my opinion the best book on furniture design ever published.
Masterpieces of American Furniture, Lester Margon, Architectural Book Pub. (NY); OP.

These books have overall dimensions only:
American Furniture: Queen Anne and Chippendale Periods, a Winterthur Museum book, Bonanza (NY), Crown (NY); OP.

Furniture Treasury, Wallace Nutting, Macmillan (NY). 3 vols. in 2: vols. I and II in 1; vol. III.

These sources contain no dimensions but contain excellent examples of period furniture and rooms of furniture.
Antiques Magazine, Straight Enterprises (NY).
Early American Furniture, John T. Kirk, Alfred Knopf (NY).
Fine Points of Furniture—Early America, Albert Sack, intro. by J. Graham II, Colonial Williamsburg curator; Crown Pub. (NY).
The Golden Treasury of Early American Houses, Richard Pratt, Harrison House (NY). (Completely in color, 279 pp. Excellent for rooms of furniture and close-ups of individual pieces.)
Living with Antiques: A Treasury of Private Houses in America, Alice Winchester and *Antiques* magazine, E.P. Dutton (NY); OP.

Horizontal Boring Machine
A translating mechanism with many uses

by Michael G. Rekoff, Jr.

A horizontal boring machine is really nothing more than a drill press on its side. But unlike the drill press, the boring machine can bore into the edges of boards of any length and width while the work is supported on its widest dimension. This makes the boring machine a good tool for fast, accurate doweling. The horizontal borer is often considered standard equipment only in high-volume shops, but the one I designed can be shop-built cheaply by anyone with moderate metalworking skills.

My boring machine uses a simple horizontal translating mechanism that smoothly moves the bit, spindle and motor, to bore work clamped to an adjustable table. This mechanism can be adapted to other uses: a router mounted horizontally or vertically, for example, could become a slot mortiser.

The translating mechanism consists of a mandrel mounted on a carriage that slides back and forth on a pair of steel rods. A steel cable connected to a foot pedal delivers the force to pull the bit into the work. I made a sleeve for attaching the bit to the mandrel, but a chuck could be substituted. Although most of the parts are readily available, some could be

made by a machine shop. Since my machine isn't in constant use, I designed the motor mount so the motor can be easily removed for use on other machines. The dimensions given can be altered to suit your needs, and I suggest that you round up all the parts—particularly the mandrel—before you start.

Making the base—Begin construction with the base, on which the spindle/motor carriage slides back and forth. It's made of two pieces of angle iron connected by two ¾-in. separator rods and spanned by two ⅝-in. guide rods, on which the channel-iron carriage slides. Make sure the holes in the base ends line up, or these rods won't be parallel and the carriage won't slide smoothly (detail A). After you've bored the holes, assemble the base on a flat surface, and test-fit the guide rods. Incidentally, separator rods can also be made with ⅜-in. ID gas pipe sleeves over a threaded rod.

Making the carriage—The guide-rod holes in the carriage will be fitted with Oilite bearings—oil-impregnated brass sleeves in which the guide rods run. Drill them to final size, and drill and tap holes for the tension bolts that connect the carriage flanges (detail B). These bolts keep the channel iron from distorting when the mandrel is snugged. I had to fiddle with their tightness to get the carriage to move smoothly.

Any mandrel should work, although it should have a collar to prevent longitudinal shaft motion in the bearings. Use a straight output shaft if you plan to use a sleeve to hold the drill, or a threaded shaft for a chuck. Make sure the mandrel axis is perpendicular to the edges of the carriage.

Next install the Oilite bearings, and assemble the carriage and base. Put a light coat of oil on the rods and, holding the bearings in place with your fingers, slide the carriage back and forth. It should move smoothly and freely through its entire travel. If it doesn't, you may have to ream out the bearing holes a little or dress the rods with emery cloth. This will relieve any binding in the guide rods and allow the bearings to self-align for the smoothest operation. Then fix the bearings in place with a slow-drying epoxy.

A ½-HP 1,750-RPM motor is adequate. I made up a motor-mounting system that pivots the motor so the drive belt can be installed and tensioned. The support brackets suit the motor I had on hand; you'll have to modify the dimensions to fit your motor. Before screwing the brackets to the carriage, make sure that the position you select will result in good alignment between the motor drive pulley and the mandrel pulley. Put an adjustable collar on one guide rod between the carriage and the front end of the base, to serve as a depth stop when boring. The belt tightener is a block of steel screwed to the carriage, with a bolt threaded into it so the head bears against a plate attached to the motor. Unscrewing the bolt tightens the belt.

To complete the spindle, make the sleeve by boring

This shop-made horizontal boring machine can simplify doweling and other drilling operations. It can be made from readily available materials with simple tools. You may need the services of a machine shop, however, to make some of the parts.

From *Fine Woodworking* magazine (November 1982) 37:98-100

Horizontal boring mechanism

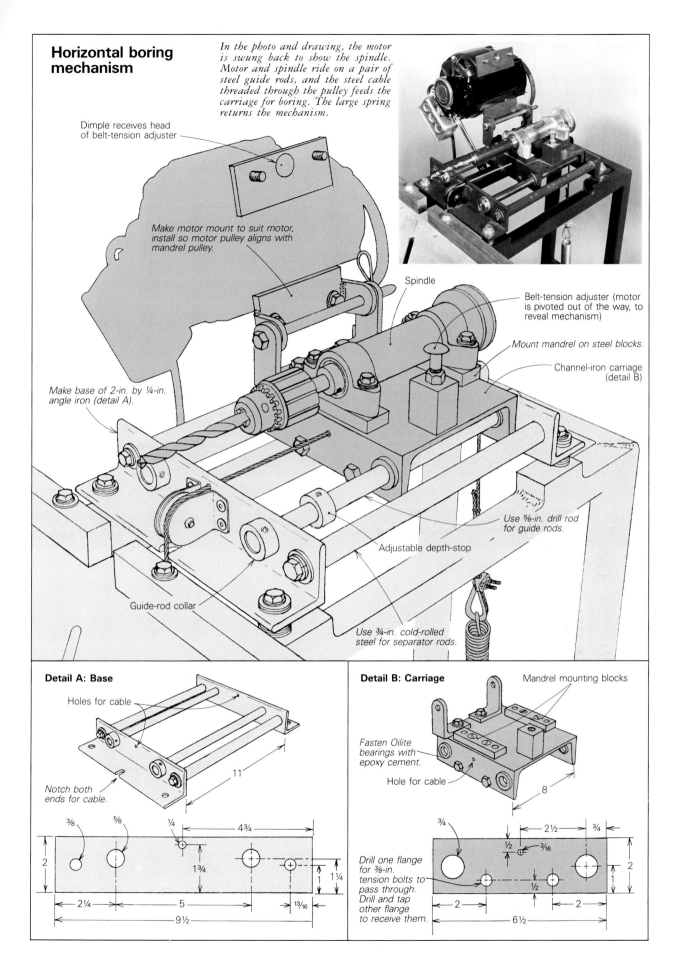

In the photo and drawing, the motor is swung back to show the spindle. Motor and spindle ride on a pair of steel guide rods, and the steel cable threaded through the pulley feeds the carriage for boring. The large spring returns the mechanism.

Dimple receives head of belt-tension adjuster

Make motor mount to suit motor, install so motor pulley aligns with mandrel pulley.

Spindle

Belt-tension adjuster (motor is pivoted out of the way, to reveal mechanism)

Mount mandrel on steel blocks.

Channel-iron carriage (detail B)

Make base of 2-in. by ¼-in. angle iron (detail A).

Use ⅝-in. drill rod for guide rods.

Adjustable depth-stop

Guide-rod collar

Use ¾-in. cold-rolled steel for separator rods.

Detail A: Base

Holes for cable

Notch both ends for cable.

11

⅜   ⅝   ¼   4¾
1¾
2   1   1¼
2¼   5   13/16
9½

Detail B: Carriage

Mandrel mounting blocks

Fasten Oilite bearings with epoxy cement.

Hole for cable

8

Drill one flange for ⅜-in. tension bolts to pass through. Drill and tap other flange to receive them.

¾   2½   ¾
½   3/16
2
2   ½   1
6½

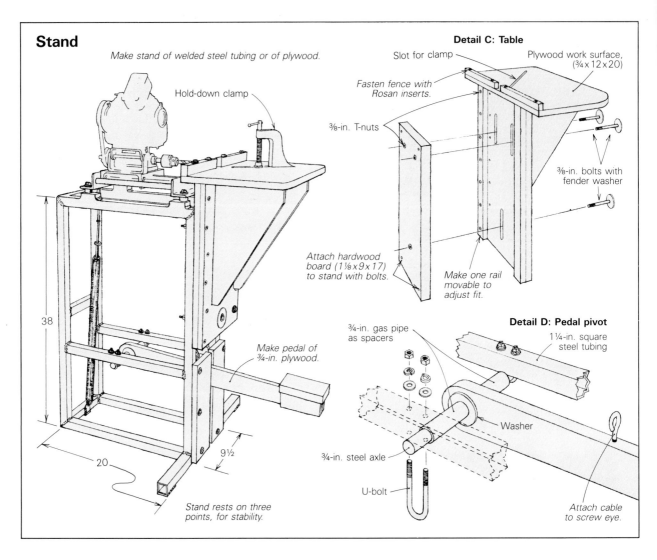

Stand

Make stand of welded steel tubing or of plywood.

Hold-down clamp

38

Make pedal of ¾-in. plywood.

20

9½

Stand rests on three points, for stability.

Detail C: Table

Slot for clamp

Plywood work surface, (¾ x 12 x 20)

Fasten fence with Rosan inserts.

⅜-in. T-nuts

⅜-in. bolts with fender washer

Attach hardwood board (1⅛ x 9 x 17) to stand with bolts.

Make one rail movable to adjust fit.

Detail D: Pedal pivot

¾-in. gas pipe as spacers

1¼-in. square steel tubing

Washer

¾-in. steel axle

U-bolt

Attach cable to screw eye.

---

through a length of 1-in. rod stock and tapping for setscrews, or have it made by a machine shop. If you are using a chuck, thread it onto the mandrel.

Making the stand—I made my stand in two pieces—a frame and a platform—using square steel tubing welded together. The platform has three-point contact with the floor, making it easier to level the machine. The machine can be mounted on a bench top, in which case a feed lever could replace the pedal. The actual dimensions of the stand depend upon your particular needs. I made the machine's adjustable table and fence out of plywood, as in detail C. It slides up and down on the front uprights, aligned by a pair of hardwood rails, one of which is adjustable. I milled slots in the table and fitted them with bolts and T-nuts to lock the table in position. A clamp that also rides in a slot holds the stock down.

The critical requirement of the table is that it must hold the work parallel and at right angles to the travel of the drill bit, and this alignment must be adjustable. The table's maximum upward travel should go no higher than the lower edge of the drill bit, and its downward travel shouldn't be lower than the feed pedal in its released position.

Make and fit the feed pedal, install the steel feed cable and use a heavy-duty door spring to return the carriage. I ran the cable through thimbles before attaching it with cable clamps

to the spring and to the pedal eyebolt. Another cable clamp, this one inside the carriage flange, transfers the cable movement to the carriage. Experiment with the length of the cable and the tension of the spring to achieve full carriage travel and comfortable pedal movement.

Aligning the machine—You'll need a dial indicator with clamping fixtures for this job. With the machine on a flat, level surface and drill rod in the chuck, clamp the indicator to one of the guide rods. Check vertical alignment first by placing the sensing tip on the top edge of the drill rod. Move the carriage back and forth to check runout, and correct it by putting shims under the mandrel mounting blocks. Then check horizontal alignment by putting the sensing tip against the side of the rod. Correct runout here by loosening the mandrel mounting bolts and repositioning the mandrel slightly. This is a trial-and-error process that should be continued until no runout is indicated. Mount the table and clamp the indicator to the drill rod to test the table for vertical alignment. Finally, install the fence so it's at right angles to the spindle's horizontal travel. □

Michael Rekoff, Jr., is a professor of electrical engineering at the University of Tennessee at Chattanooga. Photos by the author.

Q & A

Low-tech sander revisited

Re T.R. Warbey's sander (see page 38), the following suggestions: Replace the pillow blocks with self-aligning ball bearings. Replace the hex-nuts of the left-side hold-down bolts with wing nuts, and replace, if possible, the wooden drum with a steel one that has the same outside diameter as the inside diameter of standard PVC 6-in. gas or drainage or sewer pipe with walls about ¼ in. thick. Cut three or four slots about ½  in. long and ⅜ in. wide in the right-hand end of the tube, so they will fit over keys mounted on the drum; for example, two wood screws side by side in a wooden drum, or some ¼-in. key bar welded or bolted to a steel drum. Various sleeves of PVC tube can be kept with different grits glued to them.

I might add that I don't use wood in machine tools. The pillow blocks in the low-tech thickness sander are presumably fixed with wood screws in end grain. As the drum is not dynamically balanced, sooner or later Warbey will have a close encounter of the unpleasant kind with it. The cost of a small electric welder and the little effort necessary to acquire some skills are quickly repaid by the tools and structures that can be made for a song out of scrap iron and discarded machine parts. —*Harry J. Coffey, Lewisburg, W. Va.*

Larger wooden jointer?

I was very impressed by the way Galen Winchip built his wooden jointer (see pages 30 to 36). I once saw a jointer that was built almost the same way Winchip's is, by the grandfather of one of my friends, about 35 years ago. It was still working fine after all those years, although it seemed to me slightly out of true. Anyway, it still does a fine job. Before I saw it, I didn't believe such a precise machine could be homemade. I would like to ask Winchip if it's safe to build a larger jointer, the same way he did (let's say 10 in. or 12 in. or even 16 in.). —*Michel Chevannelle, Quebec, Canada*
EDITOR'S NOTE: Winchip doesn't advise building a wooden jointer wider than 8 in. Larger tables would be too difficult to keep true.

Meat saw does double duty

My solution to the bandsaw problem is two saws. One is a cheap, older 12-in. Craftsman, with modified blade guides. It is fine for light scrollwork and most small jobs. I picked it up for $100 with a ½-HP motor at a used-tool shop a few years ago. The other is a heavy cast-iron 14-in. meat-cutting saw. It weighs around 300 lb. The depth of cut is 14½ in., and with its 1-HP motor it doesn't even slow down when resawing 12 in. of walnut. It has a stainless-steel sliding table (which can be covered when the sliding feature isn't wanted) and a sturdy, accurate rip guide. I found it for $200, and again I had to rebuild the blade guides. It's too much saw for most of the bandsawing I do, and the table doesn't tilt, but for resawing it works fine. There are many of these old saws around because thousands of small butcher shops have closed in the past 10 years. I also bought a meat-cutting blade, and find it works fine for its original purpose, too.
—*George Pilling, Springville, Calif.*

High-speed steel

I've heard that a tool made from high-speed steel holds an edge much longer than a high-carbon-steel tool. Is this true? —*Allen B. Carstensen, Alfred Station, N.Y.*
JERRY GLASER REPLIES: High-speed steel will keep its temper and hold an edge longer than high-carbon tool steel. That's why it's used to make cutters for power woodworking machines. But there's a tradeoff: It won't take as keen an edge as high-carbon tool steel. About 30 high-carbon steels alloyed with tungsten, molybdenum or cobalt have been developed to help cutters for power machines resist the abrasion and high edge temperatures that would quickly soften and dull high-carbon-steel tools.

Lathe tools are the only hand tools that are subject to high abrasion and high temperature at the same time. Cutting an abrasive wood at high speed concentrates a lot of wear at one small spot on the tool's cutting edge and the edge can get very hot. A lathe tool made from high-speed steel will therefore stand up to this punishment better than one made from high-carbon tool steel. This means that you won't have to regrind as often.

Since plane irons, chisels and carving tools are never subjected to this kind of wear and heat, there's no need to make them from high-speed steel. High-carbon tool steel is the better choice because it takes the very keen edge that these cutting tools require.
[Jerry Glaser is a manufacturing engineer who lives in Playa del Rey, Calif.]

Belt-tracking solutions

EDITOR'S NOTE: Reader Brian De Marcus asked for advice about how to keep his belt sander's belt on track. Readers responded with solutions that had worked on their particular machines. Some of the advice is contradictory, so if your belt sander is troublesome, you'll have to experiment.

For a flat belt to track right, the pulleys must be barrel-shaped, not cylindrical. Bevel the sides of the drive roller—so that the edges of the belt don't touch—leaving a 1/16-in. ridge in the middle. This can easily be done by running the sander without a belt and using coarse sandpaper on the roller as it turns. Or you could, instead, build up the middle of the rollers by wrapping them with electricians' tape.
—*Hugh Blogg, Kent, England*

My machine wouldn't track because vibration kept loosening the adjusting knob. I removed the nut and hacksawed a horizontal slot through the side of the nut to the center, then compressed the nut in my vise, so that it would bind on its threads. It's a little too tight now to turn by hand, but once I've set it with pliers it holds its adjustment. I go through many belts without having to touch the knob.
—*Harvey Freeman, Halifax, N.S.*

I tried the usual trick of making the rollers convex, with no success. I finally tried just the opposite—I applied one or two thicknesses of black plastic tape to the outside edges of the rollers, and it worked. —*K.E. Bloom, Oakland, Calif.*

I had the same problem and cured it by adding a small wooden wedge between the yoke and its pressure spring to increase the tension.
—*Kenneth Schumacher, Clearwater, Fla.*

Try storing the machine with no tension on the belt, and if your shop is damp, store your belts in a plastic bag.
—*Lou Buda, Syracuse, N.Y.*

I had the same trouble because I once dropped my sander and bent the yoke that holds the idler pulley. By eye, nothing seemed wrong, but after replacing the yoke, I had no more trouble. —*S.C. Edwards, St. Simons Island, Ga.*

Making a Router Table
Poor man's shaper is a handy beginners' tool

by Donald C. Bjorkman

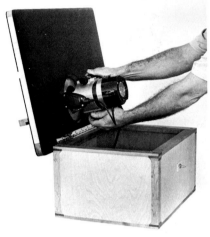

For both novice and experienced woodworkers, Bjorkman's router table is a versatile, easy-to-make tool that will perform many operations, including grooving, molding, and mortise-and-tenoning. It's constructed from the plywood and solid wood components pictured below, and the tabletop pivots on a continuous hinge, allowing access to the router for quick bit changes.

A router table is indispensable for shaping, molding and cutting joints, but the utility of many of the tables I've seen suffers for want of simple improvements, such as accurate, easy-to-adjust fences and a groove for a miter gauge. And the routers always seem tucked so far beneath the table surface that you have to be a contortionist to change bits or to make depth adjustments.

Using scraps left over from other projects, I designed and built this table to remedy those shortcomings. For rigidity and so it can be clamped to a convenient work surface, the table cabinet is of stress-panel construction—simple mortise-and-tenon frames with plywood solidly glued into a rabbet routed in the frames. I hinged the tabletop so that the router can be mounted with little fuss and the bits changed quickly. The router is positioned near the hinge so that its weight counterbalances the tabletop when the top is open, keeping undue stress from damaging the hinge.

As the drawing shows, the table consists of upper and lower frames, joined at the corners by doweled vertical posts. I made the frame parts out of maple, then used a ⅜-in. rabbeting bit in a router to mill the rabbets for the stress panels after the frames were glued up. To make the panels, I scribed the rabbet outline directly onto pieces of ⅜-in. Baltic birch, cut them to size and rounded the corners on my disc sander. If you prefer, you could sidestep the stress-panel construction and make the table base out of plywood panels joined at the corners by a rabbet-and-groove joint or by screws.

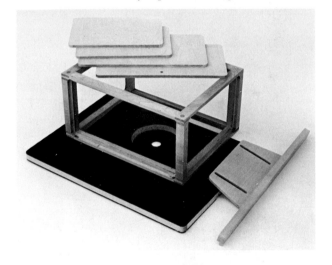

The top is a piece of ¾-in. particleboard edge-banded with hard maple. For a longer-wearing miter gauge groove, I let a strip of maple into the particleboard where the groove is dadoed. I sized the groove to fit my tablesaw miter gauge, but you could just as easily make your own wooden gauge. For a smoother, more attractive working surface than particleboard, I glued ⅛-in. tempered Masonite to the top. It's important to cover the back side of the top, too; otherwise, differential moisture absorption will warp the particleboard.

The Sears router I used is constructed in such a way that

From *Fine Woodworking* magazine (September 1983) 42:50-51

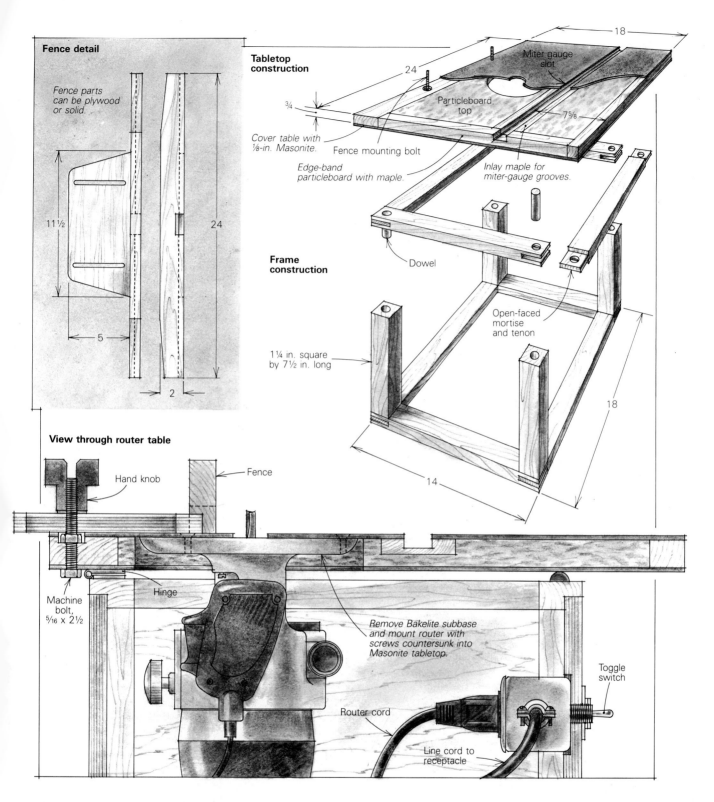

Fence detail

Fence parts can be plywood or solid.

11½

24

5

2

Tabletop construction

18

24

Miter gauge slot

Particleboard top

¾

7⅝

Cover table with ⅛-in. Masonite.

Fence mounting bolt

Edge-band particleboard with maple.

Inlay maple for miter-gauge grooves.

Frame construction

Dowel

Open-faced mortise and tenon

1¼ in. square by 7½ in. long

18

14

View through router table

Hand knob

Fence

Machine bolt, 5/16 x 2½

Hinge

Remove Bakelite subbase and mount router with screws countersunk into Masonite tabletop.

Toggle switch

Router cord

Line cord to receptacle

the motor can't be easily removed from the base. If you have only one router and it's of this type, you'll have to remove the tool's Bakelite base and fish the three mounting screws through the hardboard top each time you use the table. A router with a removable base (such as a Milwaukee or a Porter Cable) is more convenient: you can just buy an extra base and leave it permanently mounted in the table.

The router's power cord can be snaked out through the bottom of the table to be plugged in for each use, but I think it's safer to connect it to a switched receptacle mounted inside the cabinet. I wired mine to a toggle switch passed through one of the knockout plugs in the electric box and out the front of the cabinet.

To use the router table, clamp the lower-frame ledge to a pair of sawhorses. With a good selection of sharp bits, this machine does nearly as much as a shaper, but a lot cheaper. □

Donald Bjorkman teaches interior design at Northern Arizona State University in Flagstaff. Photos by the author.
See page 93 for readers' modifications for the router table.

The Router Rail
Using a router to surface large panels

by Giles Gilson

How often have you needed to plane a large surface such as a tabletop? The usual choices are to use a very expensive 2-ft. to 3-ft. planer or to use hand-controlled tools such as a plane or belt sander. Having faced this problem, I looked for a router accessory that would hold a router at a set elevation while allowing it to travel over a large area. I couldn't find such a device for sale anywhere, so I built an inexpensive one.

The router rail is fairly easy to build, and there are several designs possible. The principle is simple: A carriage just large enough to hold the router runs on rollers in two rails that form the long sides of a narrow frame, thus providing lateral motion. The frame itself has rollers at its narrow ends, and these ride in two rails that form the sides of a larger frame, thus providing longitudinal movement. Bars attached to end plates support the stock to be planed, and elevation wheels raise and lower the larger frame and the stock-support bars independently of one another. The dimensions of my system are 72 in. by 48 in. by 12 in., excluding the sawhorses.

The materials can be obtained from a well-stocked hardware store or by scrounging in the scrap barrels of a metal distributor. The carriage is made from a piece of aluminum plate and has two rollers on each side. The rollers on my system are from a conveyor belt that happened to be living in a friend's junk-shop. A wiper, made from felt cut to the shape of the inside of the track, should be mounted next to each roller so that the track is kept clean ahead of the rollers. The rails can be made of garage-door track. Stiffeners (angle iron or plywood gussets) may be necessary on rails over 5 ft. long if the system feels bouncy. The ends of the large rail frame and the stock-support bars can be made of aluminum or wood. The stock-support bars should hold the work without flexing; the stock is clamped to these bars. The pieces are fastened together with corner brackets, bolts, and hex nuts or wing nuts, as shown in the drawing.

Eight elevation wheels allow for independent adjustment of the rail system and the stock-support bars. I use a 4-ft. level to level the rails first, then the stock. The elevation wheels can easily be turned from a piece of wood or composite board with a nut captured in the center, and the jackscrews on which the wheels run are threaded rod. To capture the nut I first counterbore a hole in the wheel blank the diameter of the distance across the nut's flats. Then I bore a clearance hole through the wheel for the threaded rod and use a bolt with a washer to draw the nut into the counterbore. The nut will cut its way into the wood and remain there when the bolt is removed.

The end plates and stock-support brackets are made of wood: 2x6s for the end plate, and birch plywood for the stock-support brackets. These brackets have cutouts in the

A router becomes a planer, using garage-door track and conveyor-belt rollers to control its movement on two axes. Small work can be surfaced if it is mounted on boards spanning the stock-support bars.

Four wing nuts disassemble the whole system for storage.

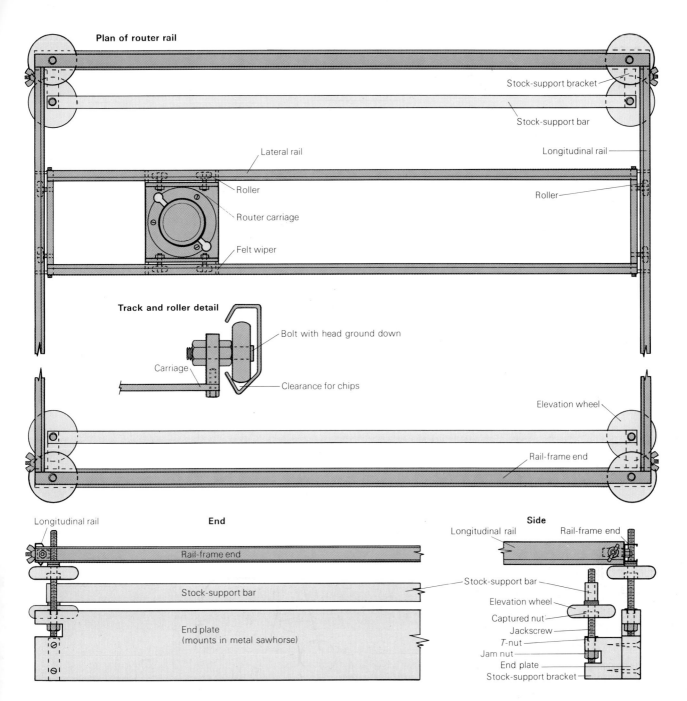

Plan of router rail

Stock-support bracket

Stock-support bar

Lateral rail

Longitudinal rail

Roller

Router carriage

Roller

Felt wiper

Track and roller detail

Bolt with head ground down

Carriage

Clearance for chips

Elevation wheel

Rail-frame end

Longitudinal rail

End

Rail-frame end

Stock-support bar

End plate
(mounts in metal sawhorse)

Side

Longitudinal rail

Rail-frame end

Stock-support bar

Elevation wheel

Captured nut

Jackscrew

T-nut

Jam nut

End plate

Stock-support bracket

ends and a clearance hole drilled from the top through to the cutout. Fit a *T*-nut in the top of the clearance hole, screw the jackscrew in and secure it with a jam nut at the bottom in the cutout. The stock-support brackets can be fastened to the end plates by long wood screws and glue, or by through-mortising the end plate and cutting a tenon on the bracket long enough to be wedged crossways. The end plates mount in metal folding sawhorse legs that clamp to it when opened.

Bolts with wing nuts hold the larger rail frame together. Removing these breaks down the system into the endplate assemblies, including the stock-support bars and elevation screws, the two longitudinal rails, and the lateral rail assembly, including the carriage. The disassembled parts can be hung on a wall for storage.

The router rail is particularly well suited for planing end-grain panels, like butcher block. Although the largest bit I

feel safe with in a router is a 1¼-in. carbide-tipped straight-faced bit, still I can surface a 6-ft. by 3-ft. tabletop in less than a half hour, including setup time, and that's significantly faster than I can do it by hand. Someday I'll build a heavy-duty version rigid enough to support a 2-HP motor that will take a 3-in. diameter cutterhead.

The router rail has possibilities for other routing operations besides planing. Stops can be placed on the long rails to allow the router to move only crossways. The carriage can be clamped, allowing only lengthwise movement, or stops can be placed to allow only a certain length of cut, for making stopped dadoes and slots. A sharp individual can get pretty inventive with one of these gadgets—so get to work. □

Giles Gilson, of Schenectady, N.Y., is a woodworker and sculptor who makes many of his own machines.

Photos: Giles Gilson and Rick Siciliano; drawing: Robert Croston

Miniatures by Machine
Three router-powered setups for precision cuts

by Herbert Consor

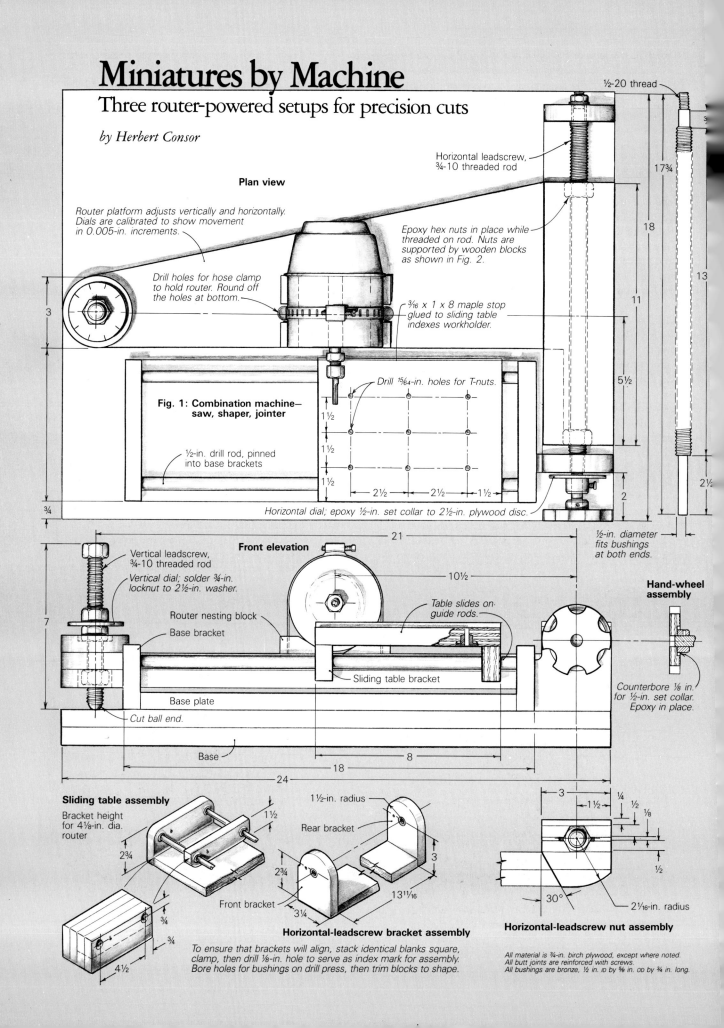

½-20 thread

Horizontal leadscrew, ¾-10 threaded rod

Plan view

Router platform adjusts vertically and horizontally. Dials are calibrated to show movement in 0.005-in. increments.

Epoxy hex nuts in place while threaded on rod. Nuts are supported by wooden blocks as shown in Fig. 2.

Drill holes for hose clamp to hold router. Round off the holes at bottom.

³⁄₁₆ x 1 x 8 maple stop glued to sliding table indexes workholder.

3

17¾

18

13

11

Fig. 1: Combination machine— saw, shaper, jointer

Drill ¹⁵⁄₆₄-in. holes for T-nuts.

5½

½-in. drill rod, pinned into base brackets

1½

1½

1½

2½ 2½ 1½

2

¾

Horizontal dial; epoxy ½-in. set collar to 2½-in. plywood disc.

2½

½-in. diameter fits bushings at both ends.

Front elevation

21

Vertical leadscrew, ¾-10 threaded rod

Vertical dial; solder ¾-in. locknut to 2½-in. washer.

Router nesting block

Base bracket

10½

Table slides on guide rods.

Hand-wheel assembly

7

Sliding table bracket

Base plate

Counterbore ⅛ in. for ½-in. set collar. Epoxy in place.

Cut ball end.

Base

8

18

24

Sliding table assembly

Bracket height for 4⅛-in. dia. router

1½

1½-in. radius

Rear bracket

3

1½

¼

½

⅛

2¾

2¾

½

Front bracket

3¼

13¹¹⁄₁₆

30°

2¹⁄₁₆-in. radius

¾

¾

4½

Horizontal-leadscrew bracket assembly

Horizontal-leadscrew nut assembly

To ensure that brackets will align, stack identical blanks square, clamp, then drill ⅛-in. hole to serve as index mark for assembly. Bore holes for bushings on drill press, then trim blocks to shape.

All material is ¾-in. birch plywood, except where noted.
All butt joints are reinforced with screws.
All bushings are bronze, ½ in. ɪᴅ by ⅝ in. ᴏᴅ by ¾ in. long.

Despite having made a lot of full-scale and half-scale furniture, I found I was totally unprepared when I was first bitten by the ¹⁄₁₂-size miniature bug. The techniques, equipment and measuring tools that had worked so well in the past just wouldn't cut the mustard. So I designed three router-powered machines for precision work: a combination machine (saw, shaper and jointer), a duplicating lathe, and a miniature pin router. Any one of them might prove just as useful for a woodworker making small, precise, full-scale parts.

Close cutting—A miniaturist has to work to precise dimensions or the piece just won't look right. So that I don't have to deal with unwieldy fractions, I convert measurements down to the nearest thousandth of an inch. In general, dimensions don't have to be machined *exactly,* but they should all be close. I usually work to the nearest 0.005 in., but sometimes closer. If each of the dimensions on the face of a typical cornice molding is enlarged by 0.005 in., for example, the equivalent full-scale error amounts to almost ½ in. This is considerable, and just as such an error would ruin the looks of a full-scale piece, so will it ruin a miniature.

In designing the machines, I started out with some clear ideas about the problems they would have to cope with. Miniature parts, for instance, are too small to be safely held by hand. So as one of my first decisions, I borrowed the workholder idea from metalworking practices—the work would be rigidly clamped, and the cutter-to-workpiece relationship controlled by ways, leadscrews, cams, templates and stops.

I knew that normal cutting-tool forces could deflect, split or break the fragile parts. Supporting the work in the holder would partly prevent this, but I also wanted to minimize cutting forces. I accomplished this by allowing for very precise travel, and by using extremely high cutter speeds with controlled feed and depth-of-cut adjustments for taking light cuts. Despite my strong prejudice in favor of heavy cast-iron

machinery, the tool forces are so low that the wooden construction of my machines hasn't led to problems.

In addition, I tried to design machines that required little precision metalworking to build. I don't have the equipment these days to do metal turning and milling, so I wanted to job out that work without spending a fortune. In the end, the total cost of outside work—machining the leadscrews and spindles—came to $40 (1983).

My three machines take care of all normal operations except drilling, rough-cutting and thicknessing. For the latter, a thickness sander is a must. Mine is an old belt sander rigged up with a sliding table. For the first two operations, I use conventional equipment.

Combination saw, shaper, jointer—The drawing on the facing page and the photo, below, will show you how this machine works. Its table, with various workholders attached, slides by hand on drill-rod support rods, and will carry a variety of workholders past the horizontally mounted router motor. Drill rod, instead of cold-rolled steel, offers greater stiffness, and its accurately ground surface makes a better fit and smoother movement in the bearings. The router's position can be accurately adjusted by means of the two leadscrews, one of which raises the platform the router is attached to, while the other moves the platform forward and back.

The two leadscrews are ³⁄₄-10 threaded rod with rolled thread instead of cut thread. You'll probably have to get them at an industrial supply house, but it's worth the trouble—the action is much smoother. Brass nuts make the action smoother still. One turn of the screws will move the embedded nuts ¹⁄₁₀ in. (0.100 in.). Thus, on the horizontal leadscrew, an indicator dial with 20 divisions shows back-and-forth cutter movement in increments of 0.005 in. To allow vertical movement, the router platform pivots up and down on the horizontal leadscrew as the vertical leadscrew is

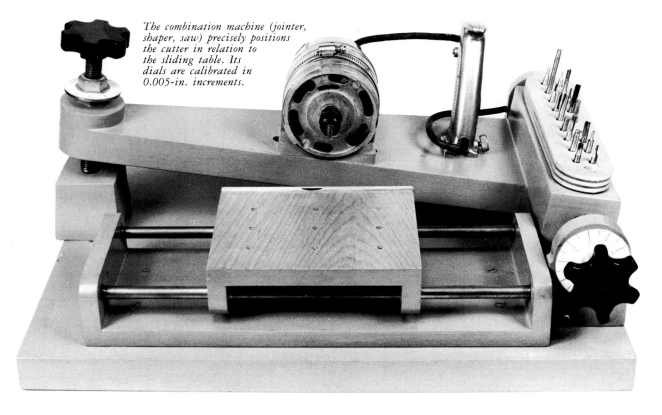

The combination machine (jointer, shaper, saw) precisely positions the cutter in relation to the sliding table. Its dials are calibrated in 0.005-in. increments.

The combination machine's router wears many hats, depending on which appliance is attached to its sliding table. Clockwise from above left, it performs as a shaper, making miniature moldings element by element in a series of passes; as a surface planer, tapering the sides of a pair of pedestal-table legs held in a workholder that maintains the correct taper angle; as a curved-molding shaper, with a pivoting workholder; and, below, as a tablesaw, with rip fence in place.

The tablesaw attachment, like the workholders, bolts to the sliding table's embedded T-nuts. Clamps, visible on the front guide rod, can either lock the table in place or restrict its movement for safety. In order not to extend the vertical leadscrew beyond the point of stability, Consor made various support blocks that raise the router platform higher than its normal operating range. When ripping, he pushes the work along the fence with the sliding table stationary. When crosscutting, he slides the table while the work is held against a stop block. For mitering, he sets up a stop block that holds the work at 45° to the blade.

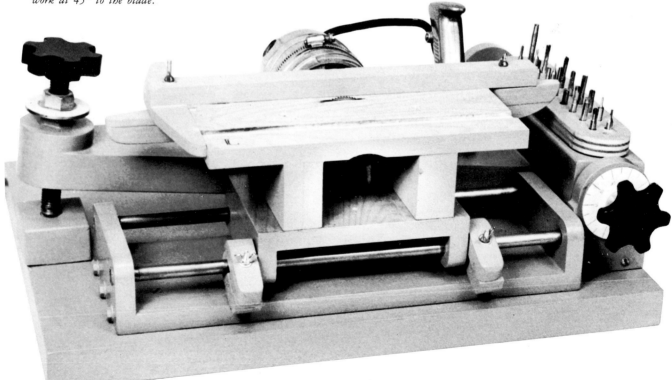

turned. Because the axis of the router is midway between the leadscrews, each full turn of the vertical leadscrew will move the router 0.050 in. up or down. Thus 10 divisions on the vertical leadscrew dial indicate increments of 0.005 in. Theoretically, the differing angles of the router platform introduce an error in the vertical dial reading, but the effect is inconsequential with the small angles involved.

As with most machine tools, different-size cutters preclude a fixed zero point. I bring the tool to a reference point on the workpiece, then shift to the exact cutting point by reading the dials. When I'm using the machine as a shaper (top left photo, facing page), this locating accuracy allows me to cut moldings one step at a time with straight and veining cutters. I round convex shapes by sanding them, or by grinding special cutters. You can freehand-grind one flute of a ¼-in. bit to shape, then grind clearance on the other flute (see pages 59 to 63). As in full-scale work, moldings are best cut on wide stock that is stiff and can be clamped. They are sawn off when finished. A tapered workholder allows me to duplicate tapered legs for one piece or for a production run. Circular moldings can be cut on a rotating jig, with the sliding table fixed so that the pivot point is at the centerline of the router.

To use the machine as a jointer, clamp the work to an attachment on the sliding table, and use the end of a ¼-in. bit to mill the edge of the work straight and smooth. It's similar to making a molding, but you make just one straight cut.

The tablesaw fixture, like most of the workholders, bolts to T-nuts in the sliding table, and it covers all but a few of the blade's teeth. After the ripping fence or cutoff gauges have been set for sawing, very exact final adjustments can be made within the width of the table slot by turning the dials.

Brackets ensure accuracy—Aside from the leadscrew adjustments, the accuracy of the machine depends on the table's traveling perpendicular to the router axis. In addition, the top face of the sliding table must be parallel to the router axis, and must not rise or fall as it moves from end to end. This alignment depends on the four brackets—two on the table itself and two on the base—that align the guide rods and the sliding table, as well as on the brackets that hold the horizontal leadscrew (figure 1). By carefully making and installing these brackets, you will achieve all the accuracy you can use.

To make the brackets, cut four identical plywood blocks, stack them flush and clamp them for drilling. Mark the stack (I drilled a small hole through it) so that you can align the blocks in the correct relationship when you set up the sliding-table assembly, then drill the holes on a drill press with a brad-point bit that will ensure a straight hole. I had planned to epoxy bronze bushings into the sliding brackets only where they are necessary to avoid wear, but I bought enough bushings from a local bearing-supply house for all the bracket holes. That way I could drill all the holes the same size and I didn't risk losing the centerline by changing bits. With this method, the spacing and relative heights of the holes will be the same in each set of blocks.

Trim the bottom of the two sliding-table brackets so they will clear the base, then mount them to the sliding table with the bushings, rods and base brackets assembled. Be sure that the table can slide freely. Epoxy the bushings to the brackets, then glue and screw the base brackets to the base, with the table and rods in place.

Use similar procedures for the horizontal leadscrew, but

mount it so that its centerline is perpendicular to the guide rods. This alignment doesn't have to be absolutely accurate; you can rely on a carpenters' square to check it. Figure 2 shows details of some ways I mounted nuts on these machines.

After you have installed the router platform, mount the router nesting blocks so that the router axis is perpendicular to the front face of the sliding table. When this is done, use the machine itself to make a light cut on the edge of the sliding table; this will true it exactly to the line of travel of the table. I glued a thin maple strip to the trued face so that its edge projects slightly above the surface of the table. When I mount the workholders and fixtures shown in the photos, I just push them up against the strip to locate them in relation to the cutting line. This saves a lot of measuring time.

Duplicating lathe—Despite very fine cuts and a variety of tool shapes, I encountered problems in turning slender table legs and bedposts with a small metalworking lathe. Deflec-

Fig. 2: Mounting nuts

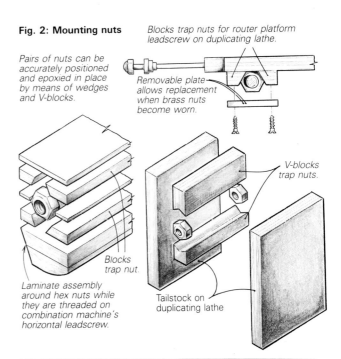

Pairs of nuts can be accurately positioned and epoxied in place by means of wedges and V-blocks.

Blocks trap nuts for router platform leadscrew on duplicating lathe.

Removable plate allows replacement when brass nuts become worn.

V-blocks trap nuts.

Blocks trap nut.

Laminate assembly around hex nuts while they are threaded on combination machine's horizontal leadscrew.

Tailstock on duplicating lathe

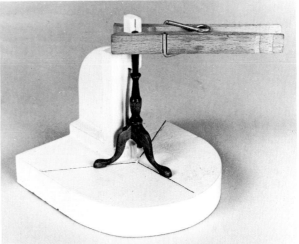

Miniatures not only need precision cutting, they call for special assembly fixtures for glue-up. The parts for this pedestal table are visible in mid-manufacture in some of the other photos.

tion of the workpiece caused out-of-round parts with non-uniform tapers and chewed-up surfaces. The template lathe, shown at right and below, cured these problems because it turns slowly, makes a light cut, and cuts mostly with the grain of the wood. In fact, the tool forces are so low that I don't usually need a steady rest or the tailstock support, and I routinely turn short parts down to as small as 1/32 in. in diameter.

With this machine, the router platform is carried from end to end on a hand-cranked leadscrew. You can vary the speed of travel to suit the cut. The router pivots until the template follower meets the template.

Figure 3 shows a method for quickly producing templates. Once the sliding wedges are adjusted, duplicate parts can be turned without any measuring or tool adjusting. A stepped spool on the template follower can be shifted on successive passes to cut the work down in small increments. I hold the spool against the template with one hand while I advance the router with the other. The router cannot cut sharp inside corners, or recesses that are smaller than the cutter diameter, but you can easily add these details later with needle files as the work rotates.

In construction of the lathe, no unusual precision is required. I mounted the pillow blocks for the headstock on a wood platform atop a block that I made from five vertical

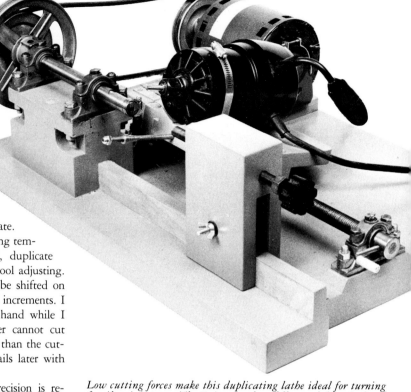

Low cutting forces make this duplicating lathe ideal for turning fragile miniatures. The 1/4-in. template follower, below, is fitted with a stepped spool that allows depth-of-cut to be gradually increased as the blank is cut down to final form.

Fig. 3: Lathe-template construction

The template is a series of 1/8-in. wide blocks glued to the top wedge. The height of each block can be figured from the table, below right.

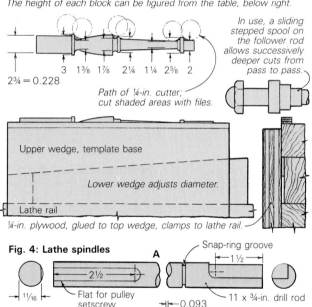

3   1 3/8   1 7/8   2 1/4   1 1/4   2 3/8   2

2 3/4 = 0.228

In use, a sliding stepped spool on the follower rod allows successively deeper cuts from pass to pass.

Path of 1/4-in. cutter; cut shaded areas with files.

Upper wedge, template base

Lower wedge adjusts diameter.

Lathe rail

1/4-in. plywood, glued to top wedge, clamps to lathe rail.

Fig. 4: Lathe spindles

A

Snap-ring groove
1 1/2

2 1/2

11/16   Flat for pulley setscrew

11 x 3/4-in. drill rod

0.093

Lathe spindle A forms a 1/4-in.-square recess when the two parts are joined by a hose clamp.

0.125   1 1/2

1/2-20 thread fits chucks.

11/16   Setscrew flat   B   0.093   Chamfer first thread.

1/2   1/2   3   9 7/8 x 3/4-in. rod

3/4

Wrench flats for chuck removal   Snap-ring groove, 1/8 in.

Template Heights			
Diameter full-size	Radius full-size	Radius at 1/12 scale	Height above smallest radius
1 1/4	5/8	0.052	0
1 3/8	11/16	0.057	0.005
1 7/8	15/16	0.078	0.026
2	1	0.083	0.031
2 1/4	1 1/8	0.093	0.041
2 3/8	1 3/16	0.099	0.047
2 3/4	1 3/8	0.114	0.062
3	1 1/2	0.125	0.073

¾-in. thick pieces of wood laminated together. I left the center piece of the stack long to form the rail on which the tailstock rides, which is also the resting surface for the templates. To ensure that the template is parallel to the spindle, cut the top surface of the rail parallel to the top surface of the block.

First glue the headstock block and rail to the base. Then line up the pillow blocks: Take a 36-in. long, ¾-in. diameter drill rod (from which you will later make the spindles), insert it through the pillow blocks and sandwich it between two boards clamped to the sides of the rail. This ensures that the spindle is parallel to the rail. When everything lines up, epoxy the pillow blocks to the headstock block. Wait until the epoxy has set before you drill and bolt the pillow blocks.

The tailstock spindle is ½-20 threaded rod (which fits a standard ½-in. Jacobs chuck) running through two nuts epoxied into the tailstock (figure 2). The ¾-in. spindle in the headstock and the ½-in. threaded rod in the tailstock must line up exactly. Rather than attempting to line them up by measuring, I used the pillow blocks to register the height of the tailstock spindle. To do this, I supported a length of ½-in. threaded rod in the pillow blocks by means of two shopmade wood bushings. Centered by the pillow blocks, the threaded rod was thus in the correct position for the tailstock. I then threaded two nuts on the far end of the rod, and built up and epoxied the tailstock around the nuts.

The double-pulley drive provides speeds for low-speed turning as well as for high-speed sanding and filing. A simple, hinged motor mount provides quick belt-shifting.

The specific dimensions of the machine depend on the diameter of your router. In a horizontal position, the centerline of the router should be about ³⁄₁₆ in. above the spindle's centerline. The leadscrew should be at the router's center of gravity, so that the router's own weight will cause it to remain tilted up and out of the way when it isn't being controlled by hand.

The first spindle shown in figure 4 holds ¼-in. square stock. For smaller stock, use four shims for centering. For larger stock, cut down the surfaces to fit the chuck.

For offset turning, such as when making a cabriole leg, offset the end away from the chuck by inserting shims in the chuck. Brass shim stock or brass sheets obtained in auto supply stores will do nicely. Shim thickness may be determined by proportions or by trial.

A second headstock spindle is a ¾-in. rod threaded to receive a standard ½-in. drill chuck. This will handle dowels up to ½ in., which in full scale corresponds to 6-in. diameter work. This thread holds many small 3-jaw and 4-jaw chucks as well. For boring, use a chuck on the tailstock spindle.

Pin router—The photo, above right, shows my pin router, which cuts small-scale, complex shapes of the sort that you would bandsaw in full-scale work. The machine is an inverted form of the normal pin router, which has the pin in the table and the router suspended overhead on an arm. Inverting the design simplifies construction and improves visibility.

On any pin router, a pin and a bit, usually the same size, are aligned on the same axis. In use, the pin contacts the edge of a template (to which the work is clamped), and the bit cuts the work to the template's exact size and contour as you move it around the pin. In small-scale work, the template acts as a workholder as well, helping to support fragile stock. A typical template is shown in figure 5.

This inverted pin router allows better visibility for small-scale work. Bit and pin can be varied according to the work.

Fig. 5: Pin-router workholder

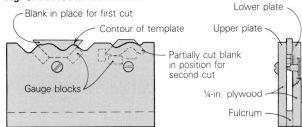

The upper plate is the template that bears against the pin; the bottom plate serves only to clamp the work to the upper plate. Gauge blocks, mounted to the bottom of the upper plate, locate the work in the sandwich. To concentrate clamping pressure at the cut and to minimize tearout or splitting, put clamp screws and recessed T-nuts as close as practical to the cut, and make the fulcrum slightly thicker than the work.

Once you have carefully laid out and cut a template, you can make any number of duplicate shapes. This is a great timesaver for the preliminary cutting of Queen Anne legs, pedestal table legs (such as the ones in the photos on pages 86 and 87) and other repeat patterns. Make the base and table, then install the router. The pin's height must be adjustable, to suit stock and template variations, and the pin must be removable, so that you can change router bits. I drilled a ¼-in. hole through a cap nut so that the pin would be a snug sliding fit, then installed a setscrew that would lock the pin's height. To support the pin above the router, I cut a sheet-metal holder and locked the cap nut to it with a jam nut beneath. With the pin through the cap nut and its end chucked in the router—to align it—I epoxied and screwed the sheet-metal holder to its base.

These three machines can help you overcome some of the wasted hours and frustrations I experienced in making the transition from full-scale to miniature work. Accept what you like, ignore what you will, find better ways, but do try your hand at miniatures. Even the most competent woodworker will find them a challenging and rewarding change of pace, and possibly a lifelong fascination. □

Herbert Consor, from Chagrin Falls, Ohio, is a retired engineer and manufacturing manager.

Shop-Built Sharpener
Salvaged garbage disposal grinds a keen edge

by Tom Dewey

Jeffrey C. Carts

Author photo

Salvaged parts keep the cost of this water-cooled sharpener below that of similar store-bought machines. Above, after honing the bevel on a plane blade, Dewey opens the machine's hinged port and removes the burr from the back of the blade. A steady stream of water keeps the edge from overheating. The nut in the foreground locks the tool rest at the desired angle.

Nearly everyone agrees that the best cutting edge comes from hand-sharpening on water or oil stones, but it takes time and practice to get a perfect edge. I'm not very fast at hand-sharpening, and in my shop, where time equals food on the table, I can't justify the luxury of hand-honing. Instead, I wanted to build an inexpensive machine that would speed both jobs—something with a water-cooled horizontal wheel, a wide selection of abrasive grits, and a solid, adjustable tool rest. My first two versions had problems, but the one shown here works fine.

The grinder took me a little more than a day to build, using a salvaged garbage-disposal unit, a few parts and some scrapwood. I use a 60-grit stone and/or 7-in. abrasive discs, either store-bought or homemade, ranging from 36-grit to 600-grit. The grinder can sharpen blades as wide as 2½ in.

A garbage-disposal motor (usually ⅓ HP or ½ HP, and 1725 RPM) is ideal for a water-cooled grinder because it is designed to run in a vertical position, has a waterproof seal on the shaft to keep the motor dry and has built-in overload protection. When a disposal stops working properly, usually it's because the food choppers have worn out—often the motor is still in good shape. Few people bother to have broken disposals repaired, opting for replacement instead. Check with a local plumber and you probably won't have much trouble finding a unit with a good motor. (New disposals from Sears are as cheap as $50.) You can use almost any brand, but try to avoid models labeled "automatic self-reversing" or "auto-grind," because they'll re-

quire some rewiring. You'll have to make some mechanical modifications to any unit.

The food-grinding chamber must be cut away to expose the chopper plate on the end of the motor shaft, as shown in the drawing. If your unit has a stainless-steel liner in the grinding chamber, pry it out before cutting the case. Anything goes in this removal operation—sawing, chiseling with a cold chisel—but be careful not to crack the casting. It may take plenty of penetrating oil before you can loosen the retaining nut and unscrew the plate from the shaft. If the plate has a recessed nut, the shaft won't be long enough to mount the stone and discs. You'll have to make another plate from ¼-in. thick acrylic, a worn-out circular-saw blade with the teeth ground off, or exterior plywood.

Most of the other modifications should be clear from the drawing, and I'd suggest that you do them in this order: Plug the drain opening in the side of the disposal case with a piece of wood and file the wood flush with the outside of the housing. Epoxy the laminated-plywood ring that supports the table to the case, and drill a hole through both the ring and the wooden plug for a new copper-tubing drainpipe.

The table can be any convenient shape and size. Mine is round because I happened to have a small sink cutout handy. Glue and screw the table to the plywood ring, level with the top of the case, then cement plastic laminate on the table, overlapping the edge of the disposal unit.

Add the splash guard (mine is a section of heavy PVC plastic

From *Fine Woodworking* magazine (September 1984) 48:52-53

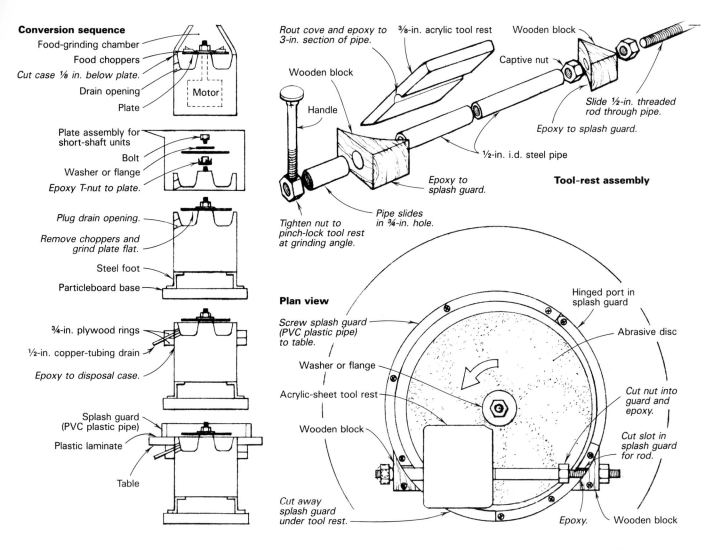

Conversion sequence

Food-grinding chamber
Food choppers
Cut case ⅛ in. below plate.
Drain opening
Plate

Plate assembly for short-shaft units
Bolt
Washer or flange
Epoxy T-nut to plate.

Plug drain opening.

Remove choppers and grind plate flat.

Steel foot
Particleboard base

¾-in. plywood rings
½-in. copper-tubing drain
Epoxy to disposal case.

Splash guard (PVC plastic pipe)
Plastic laminate
Table

Rout cove and epoxy to 3-in. section of pipe.
⅜-in. acrylic tool rest
Wooden block
Captive nut
Wooden block
Handle
Slide ½-in. threaded rod through pipe.
Epoxy to splash guard.
½-in. i.d. steel pipe
Epoxy to splash guard.
Tool-rest assembly
Pipe slides in ¾-in. hole.
Tighten nut to pinch-lock tool rest at grinding angle.

Plan view
Screw splash guard (PVC plastic pipe) to table.
Washer or flange
Acrylic-sheet tool rest
Wooden block
Cut away splash guard under tool rest.
Hinged port in splash guard
Abrasive disc
Cut nut into guard and epoxy.
Cut slot in splash guard for rod.
Epoxy.
Wooden block

---

pipe that I picked up from a construction site—wooden rings epoxied together would work as well). Seal the joint with silicone caulk. Note that the splash guard is positioned slightly to the left of center to make room for wide blades on the tool-rest side. For deburring the backs of plane blades, I cut a hinged port in the side of the splash guard.

Next cut two slots in the splash guard for the tool-rest pivot rod. Mark off a 25° line on the side of the guard as shown in the photo on the facing page. I cut two shallow slots, then gradually deepened them until the top of the tool rest lined up with the 25° line. When fitting this assembly, make sure that the rod is high enough off the plate for abrasive discs to slip underneath. I cut away a section of the splash guard under the rear of the tool rest so the rest can be tipped up for changing discs.

To provide a continuous flow of water to the disc, I use a plant-watering gadget called Water Whiz (available from Edmund Scientific, 101 E. Gloucester Pike, Barrington, N.J. 08007). It comes with a 50-ft. hose which attaches to a faucet and provides any flow from a spray to a stream. I heated the plastic wand of the Whiz and bent it into shape. The Whiz is fastened to the grinder with two metal broom-hanging clips from the hardware store. To get rid of waste water, run a length of garden hose from the copper drain tube to a sink or a catch bucket.

I added a light, then mounted my grinder/honer on a 30-gal. drum filled with about 100 lb. of sand for stability. Casters on the bottom allow the setup to be rolled about the shop.

The workhorse of the grinder is a 6-in. dia., ³⁄₁₆-in. thick, 60-grit resin-bond stone (available from Foley-Belsaw Co., 90472 Field Bldg., Kansas City, Mo. 64111). This stone gives a very good edge and cuts quickly. You'll need to make a plastic or aluminum bushing to reduce the center hole of the stone to fit the garbage-disposal shaft.

For occasional coarser work, I use 36- to 80-grit, cloth-backed auto-body grinding discs fastened with contact cement to ⅛-in. thick acrylic discs (Brodhead-Garrett Co., 4560 E. 71st St., Cleveland, Ohio 44105, sells ⅛-in. acrylic sheet). For honing, I cut my own discs from silicon carbide paper and cement them to acrylic discs. The finer grits—400 and 600—produce a beautiful sheen. Abrasives can be mounted on both sides of the acrylic discs—coarse on one side, fine on the other—to cut down on storage and handling. You can sharpen blades by sliding them back and forth on the tool rest, or by holding them in one place—it doesn't seem to make much difference. By rolling gouges on the rest, several different profiles are possible and the bevels will be consistent from corner to corner.

I normally grind with the stone, then hone with 180-grit or 320-grit, or both, for a really fine edge. A buffing wheel whisks off the wire edge. It's hard to resist "going all the way" with the polishing grades. It's easy to get hooked on seeing such nicely polished edges come off a shop-built machine. □

Tom Dewey is a cabinetmaker in Coudersport, Pa.

Q & A

Machines from Gilliom kits

EDITOR'S NOTE: Over the years readers have shared their experiences, problems and solutions in making band saws and combination drill-press/lathes from kits manufactured by Gilliom. For more information on these and other kits, write Gilliom Mfg., Inc., 1700 Scherer Pkwy., St. Charles, Mo. 63303. See also Andrew Maier's treadle-powered band-saw adaptation on page 27.

. . . I bought and built a Gilliom 18-in. band-saw kit and have been using it for about six months. It is the first band saw I have used, so I don't have much to compare it with. However, for what they're worth, here are some comments:

The saw is reliable. The blade tracks well, and things like blade tension and wheel alignment don't have to be constantly fiddled with. I have sawn woods ranging in hardness from basswood to oak and maple, and it does reasonably well on all of them up to a thickness of perhaps 3 in. I saw tenon cheeks with it, for example. However, I was disappointed to find that it will not resaw anything much deeper without the blade curving badly to one side. . . . Also, it takes forever. The feed rate for even a soft wood 6 in. or so thick is excruciatingly slow (the motor is ¾ HP, the larger of two recommended). I gather this blade curvature is what is called bellying, sometimes ascribed to inadequate chip clearance. I intend to try using a coarser blade, but am skeptical about whether it will make much difference. The blade that I've been using is ½ in., four teeth per in., supplied by Gilliom.

I would not buy this saw again because a resawing capacity is too important to me. However, Gilliom gives fair warning of the saw's limitations, advertising it as a light-to-medium-duty saw primarily for home workshop use. I think that the saw lives up to this. —Ted Sittler, New York, N.Y.

The first band saw I ever owned was, like Ted Sittler's, an 18-in. model I built from the Gilliom kit. I had some of the same problems . . . and I have gained a good deal of experience since, so here are my suggestions.

Gilliom's design can be beefed up a bit in several ways. I added an extra 2x4 to the left support column and used glue blocks in strategic places throughout the body of the saw. I also used nails and glue, and extra screws and bolts. I built my saw from ⅝-in. construction plywood and yellow pine. If I were to build another, I would use rock maple and veneer-core birch plywood. Perhaps some angle iron, too.

There are several possible causes for the blade to belly out on thicker cuts. The main reason I found was that the upper frame, being wood, did not have the necessary rigidity. Therefore the blade could not maintain its tension. My solution was to add a detachable support column at the right of the blade—from the upper frame to the lower body of the machine. For most resawing it did not get in the way, and for curve and panel cutting it could be removed. I had to modify the table, however, making a part of the right-hand section removable to allow for the extra piece. Most important, I had to add a strong spring to the blade tensioning mechanism to keep the blade from breaking. An old automotive valve spring worked very nicely. . . .

If the saw is built fairly well, the speed can safely be increased. I ran mine at 3600 blade feet per minute instead of the 2000 specified. Three thousand would be optimum and probably easier on the wood frame, especially if the tires or wheels haven't been dressed true. I simply substituted a slightly smaller motor pulley. . . .

Resawing takes a bit of patience and skill. Use a slow, firm, even feed speed. Let the machine do the work. Make sure the fence and the blade guides are adjusted properly and that the tires are in good shape and clean. Use enough tension. It doesn't go as fast as you might think, but it's still faster than a 10-in. table saw and infinitely less nerve-wracking. —James L. Wheeler, Houston, Tex.

. . . Many of the machines built for the home workshop are quite small, which limits their usefulness. Also, the price of a band saw dampens the desire of the prospective buyer. After thorough checking, I decided to build a 24-in. three-wheel band saw of my own design.

In order to accomplish my goal I checked out the band-saw castings for a 12-in. saw, made by Gilliom, and found them to be satisfactory for my purpose. Obviously I had to purchase an extra wheel and its bearing and a shaft in order to design and build the saw to my own specifications. Also, the 12-in. band-saw kit contained some items that could not be used on the 24-in. saw, and likewise it was necessary to add an item or two. Gilliom was very cooperative in deleting from and adding to the 12-in. kit. . . .

The saw is a floor model with a 3-ft.-by-3-ft. table, which tilts to 45°. The upper blade guide can be raised to a maximum height of 13 in. above the table. Since my shop is in the basement it was necessary to construct the base so that the saw could be raised easily and quickly onto casters for moving when necessary. The entire construction, with the exception of the castings, is ¾-in. plywood and No. 1 yellow pine. For sturdiness, in critical areas I doubled the plywood using contact cement, and used a good woodworking glue on the frame members. Lag screws were used except where the size of the components dictated otherwise. The fact that the saw is a three-wheeler gives ample room beneath the table for a cabinet to store extra blades. Painting is extremely important so the wood's dimensions will not change because of moisture absorption. —Harlan D. Price, Eureka Springs, Ark.

. . . I bought, about three years ago, the 18-in. band-saw kit from Gilliom. I found the instructions adequate and had no particular difficulty constructing the machine. The parts generally were of acceptable quality, with one very important exception. The upper guide support arm that holds the upper blade guides and roller and has the very important function of supporting the sawblade was in rough-cast form and in no way capable of being raised and lowered with any assurance of stability or alignment. Fortunately, I have a swell machine shop so I was able to mill the part myself and make it work properly. —George H. Rathmell, Los Osos, Calif.

. . . I'm an amateur woodworker who does not make his living from his hobby. The Gilliom kit appealed to me as a way to have both a drill press and a lathe at low cost, as well as to have the fun of building my own machine. Certainly these are not tools of industrial or production quality, but I'm happy to improvise jigs and methods that extend and refine my tools.

Having used both the drill press and lathe regularly for several months, I am quite pleased with the results. The kit was enjoyable to build and seems sensibly designed. I used heavier lumber than called for and added glued joints to the bolt-together construction. The castings seem durable enough but not well finished so I had to dress them myself to render the headstock, which also serves as the carrier for the drill spindle, square to the lathe bed. The drill-press table, which travels on a rack-and-pinion mechanism, required some shimming to reduce play and to bring it square to the spindle. I'm not complaining, as I view these problems as opportunities for creativity on my part. Also, "close enough" is good enough. —Steve Bien, Battle Creek, Mich.

I built a 12-in. band saw from a Gilliom kit and I used oak plywood for the wheels. The machine runs and cuts well, but there is a slight vibration which I think comes from the tires' being of uneven thickness. How can I grind the tires flat and even? —T.T. Ormiston, Outlook, Sask.

RICH PREISS REPLIES: Bumps or bulges in the tire could be caused by the wrong size tire, crud that got under the tire during installation, or a joint that isn't smooth. To find the high spots, rotate the wheel by hand and read the runout with a dial indicator, or clamp a block in a fixed position on the saw frame and see if the rotating wheel contacts it evenly.

Try spot-sanding with coarse sandpaper to knock down the high spots. If this doesn't work, use the belt-sander jig shown in the drawing to bring the tire into round. Recrown the tire

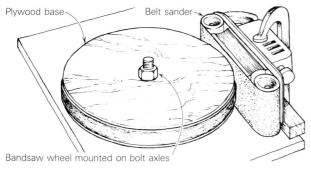

Plywood base   Belt sander

Bandsaw wheel mounted on bolt axles

by hand-sanding or by mounting the belt sander on a beveled block; otherwise the blade won't track correctly.

If the vibration persists, the wheels themselves may be out of round or twisted. Remove the tires and true the wheels on a lathe large enough to accommodate the wheel diameter. Since the wheels are of wood, you can plane or sand out any twist, using winding sticks to check the results. Finally, check that the wheels are aligned and in the same plane when you mount them back on the saw. Hold a long straightedge across the face of the wheels—the straightedge should contact the rim and hub of both wheels evenly.

[Rich Preiss supervises the architectural woodworking shop at the University of North Carolina at Charlotte.]

Router-table modifications

I read Donald Bjorkman's router-table article (see pages 80 and 81) just after completing my own router table (see photo), which offers several advantages. I purchased a double-sink cutout of Formica-covered ¾-in. particleboard from a

Bretz's router table shares his tablesaw's fence.

local cabinet shop for $5. The top was 19 in. by 27 in., the same size as my 10-in. tablesaw. I had gotten a fence slide gear rack from the manufacturer of my saw, and I mounted

this to a length of angle iron rabbeted into the front of the table and flush with its surface. I then screwed a wooden auxiliary fence to the saw's regular fence so that the router bit could work through it. . . . The miter gauge rides in a piece of aluminum channel contact-cemented into the table. The table is hinged to heavy sawhorses so that I can tilt it up for router and bit removal. The dust pick-up system is made from a dog-food can that fits very nicely to my dry vacuum. It gets 80% to 90% of the dust. The switch turns on both vacuum and router.

As I had to buy a fence gear rack at $14, I may have a little more in my table, but Bjorkman's fence is frustrating to set accurately. The biggest design fault is the enclosed base for the router. After a period of use, a router will get quite warm. With no air circulation, you risk cremating a good router.
—Robert C. Bretz, Decatur, Ill.

Donald Bjorkman's router table is a handsome variation on a tried-and-true design. Ours is quite similar, but a bit cruder in the finish. An easy addition to Bjorkman's jig is a hole cut in the back for a vacuum hose. With a closed box such as this, the vac really pulls the chips away from the cutter. I suspect that the airstream serves to cool the motor also.
—Bill Lego, Springfield, Va.

Sturdy router table

Take a Rockwell Unisaw table extension to a machine shop; have a hole bored between the ribs and three flats milled on the underside for stand-off bushings. Attach a router base underneath; *voila!* router table with an adjustable fence.
—Bob Laughton, San Francisco, Calif.

Homemade tires for bandsaw

I have a 9-in. Montgomery Ward band saw, circa 1949, that parts are no longer available for. I need to replace the rubber bands on the wheels but have been unable to locate any. All the catalogs list sizes down to 12 in., but no lower. —R. McKenzie, Grand Junction, Colo.

LELON TRAYLOR REPLIES: You will probably have to make the tires. I have used Eastman's 910 adhesive to glue O-rings for hydraulic cylinders. It works very well. Cut the rubber with a new razor blade, apply the adhesive and bring the ends together quickly and accurately, as the adhesive seizes instantly. Use a fixture to help align the ends to be joined.

[Lelon Traylor teaches tool and manufacturing technology at Southern Illinois University, Carbondale.]

EDITOR'S NOTE: Contact Eastman Kodak headquarters at 343 State St., Rochester, N.Y. 14650 for distributors.

. . . I had the same problem with my old band saw. So I cut two cross-sections from an old truck inner tube and stretched them evenly around the band-saw wheels. This made a continuous rubber band with no ends to join. I then neatly trimmed the edges of rubber with a razor blade. The tension of the rubber is enough to keep the tires in place with no adhesive. My saw now runs smoothly and the rubber holds up well. —Stephen A. Dean, Welch Creek, Ky.

Source for mini-parts

I am fascinated by Herbert Consor's ingenious lathe machines (see pages 84 to 89). Other readers might like to know that there is a company that sells drill rod, gears, pulleys and bearings by mail: Small Parts, Inc., 6901 N.E. Third Ave., Miami, Fla. 33138. They would make a good source for the bearings, etc., in Mr. Consor's machines, and they are pleasant people to deal with. —C.A. Smith, Lake Wales, Fla.

Treadle Lathe
Build your own

by Jim Richey

W hen Chester Knight of Conroe, Tex., built his wooden treadle lathe, he had several goals in mind. He wanted it to be lightweight and portable, easily knocked down to its components. He wanted something pleasing to look at, clean and balanced with subtle curves. But most of all, he wanted a functional, mechanically sound tool capable of producing, on a smaller scale, the same high-quality turned goods as a modern power lathe.

The design is Knight's own, but he readily admits borrowing a few ideas from early treadle lathes. Heinrich Scholl's Texas-German treadle lathe, built in the 1870s, was especially influential. That 9-ft. monster has a heavy, solid wood flywheel that can be worked from the treadle or belted to a motor. The lathe is pictured in *Texas Furniture*, by Lonn Taylor and David B. Warren (University of Texas Press, Box 7819, University Sta., Austin, Tex. 78711), and is occasionally displayed in Scholl's hometown, New Braunfels, Tex. Knight also borrowed from the treadle lathe in the cabinet shop at Old Sturbridge (Mass.) Village. The large, spoked flywheel on this reproduction is fastened above and behind the lathe bed. Like Knight's, both of these lathes have mortise and tenon construction (with tusk tenon locks), double beam bed and solid wood, wedge-locked headstock and tailstock, but both are more massive and awkward-looking.

Except for a few templates and overall rough measurements, Knight didn't make or use plans. He explains, "I feel better about the end result—there's more a feeling of creativity and accomplishment." Knight roughs out the main dimensions of a project, and the remaining parts are "cut to fit." He urges other woodworkers to use this approach if they decide to make a treadle lathe—many non-critical measurements have been left off these drawings, in hopes that the woodworker will rely on his own sense of scale.

Knight used ash throughout the lathe. It's tough and springy, and has a flashy grain. It's also available in the 3½- in. squares necessary for the tailstock and headstock. Curiously, the bed ways are yellow pine. Knight wanted to experiment with the bed length, so he designed the leg notches to take a garden-variety 2x4 bed way. After he found the right length he just never substituted ash for the pine. For consistency and bed "spring" (a reputedly important attribute of wood-bed lathes) ash would be marginally better

than yellow pine. But consider the flexibility of a 2x4 bed. A few bucks buys a new bed of virtually any length.

The only metal parts are the headstock and tailstock spindles and the flywheel shaft and crank. Knight owns a small metal lathe and he has 40 years of metalworking experience—all the metal parts (with the exception of the spur center he bought from Sears) were custom-machined. Each woodworker should choose metal parts on the basis of his preferences, projected uses of the lathe and access to metalworking machines. The choices range from simple solid shafts running in wood bearings to more advanced hollow shafts with Morse taper sockets running in bushings or ball bearings. You'll also need access to a wood lathe to turn the hub and spokes of the flywheel, and the spindle pulley.

Frame — The first step in making a treadle lathe is building the frame—legs and bed. Start by bandsawing the legs

From *Fine Woodworking* magazine (March 1979) 15:60-64

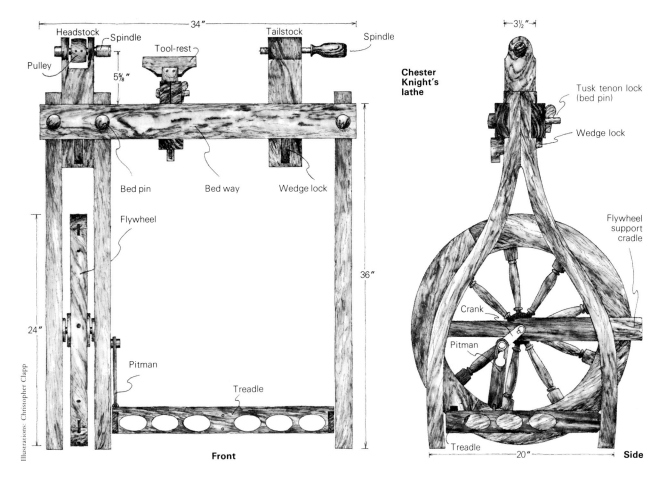

Illustrations: Christopher Clapp

Chester Knight's lathe

Labels on front view: Headstock, Spindle, Pulley, Tool-rest, Tailstock, Spindle, Bed pin, Bed way, Wedge lock, Flywheel, Pitman, Treadle

Dimensions: 34", 5⅝", 24", 36"

Front

Labels on side view: Tusk tenon lock (bed pin), Wedge lock, Flywheel support cradle, Crank, Pitman, Treadle

Dimensions: 3½", 20"

Side

from 1¾-in. thick by 8-in. wide ash planks. The wishbone profile causes a lot of waste, but most of it will be used later for flywheel spokes and smaller parts. Cut the notch in each leg a little small so that it can be trimmed to a snug fit with the ways. Leg pairs are not permanently joined to each other, but dowel pins are glued in one leg and mated to corresponding holes in the other leg to keep the leg halves from shifting.

After the leg pairs are ready, trim the notches to accept the bed ways. This operation is more important than it seems. The depth of the notches will determine the spread of the bed ways (2½ in.), which should be exact and consistent from head to tail. Also, any slop in the fit of the bed in the notches will translate to side-to-side racking later on.

With the bed ways installed in the notches, drill the 1-in. bed pin holes through both ways and the leg pairs. Position the outside legs about ½ in. from each bed end. Position the middle leg so that the gap between the two left legs will fit the headstock (3½ in.).

Turn the bed pins for a slip fit in the 1-in. pin holes. Leave a shoulder (or cap) on the front of each pin and about 1½ in. of extra length on the back. Mark and cut the ¼-in. tusk mortises on

Lathe legs are joined with dowel pins glued in one leg and mated to the other. Bed pins, which hold the ways to the frame, are mortised on back ends. Tapered tusk tenons are wedged in for a tight fit.

the back end of the three pins and fit a tapered tusk tenon (wedge) to each. With the pins home and the tusk tenons tapped tight, the frame should be solid and wobble-free.

Flywheel — The flywheel is the most challenging aspect of the lathe. The goal is to end up with a perfectly round, true-running wheel of sufficient size and weight to operate the lathe easily. Knight departed from tradition here in both design and construction. He used three rim sections (not the traditional four) and nine spokes (rather than an even number). He says "an odd number of spokes is more interesting, balanced and pleasing to the eye." He also used dowel joints, driven through the rim into the outboard end of each spoke, to fasten the spokes to the rim, replacing the usual dowel-tenoned spoke end. This allows the rim and the spoke-hub units to be glued up separately and fitted at final assembly.

The first step of flywheel construction is jointing and rough-cutting the three rim sections. For a 24-in. wheel you'll need three ash planks 1¾ in. by 8 in. by 24 in. Make and use a template of a rim section to get the angles right. Joint the three sections to a perfect fit where they meet, but leave the outside and inside curves about ½ in. wide. Knight recommends a simple jig (next page), basically a circle of plywood with a pivot hole at its center, for cutting both the outside and inside of the rim. Tack the three sections in place on the jig. The jig is center-pivoted on an extension to the band-saw table (band-saw outrigger). Then the jig with attached rim sections is rotated against the blade, cutting a perfect circle on the outside of the wheel.

Before cutting the inside curve (which destroys the jig),

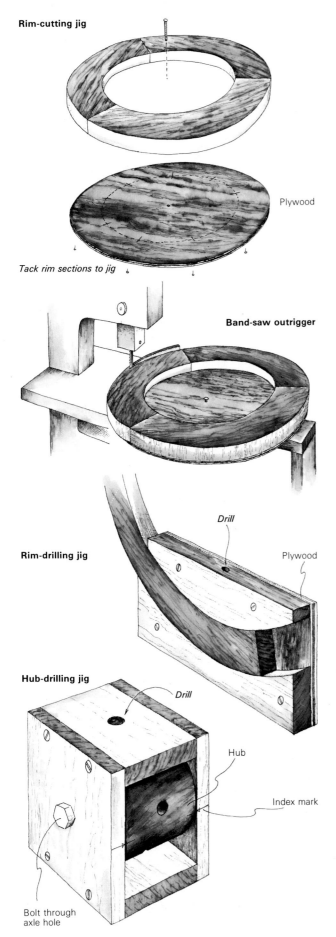

Rim-cutting jig

Plywood

Tack rim sections to jig

Band-saw outrigger

Rim-drilling jig

Drill

Plywood

Hub-drilling jig

Drill

Hub

Index mark

Bolt through
axle hole

mark the nine spoke locations on the rim using a protractor for the 40° spacing. Cut the inside circumference by moving the pivot point toward the blade. Temporarily remove one rim section to enter the blade and rotate the jig against the blade as before. After that's done, remove the rim sections and drill ⅜-in. dowel holes where marked. It's a good idea to construct and use a drilling jig, as shown in the diagram, so that the holes are at the correct angle. Drill these holes all the way through the rim. To complete the rim, cut and fit splines at the joints of the three rim sections. Glue up the rim on a flat surface using a strap clamp to tighten the sections.

Hub and spokes — For the hub, select a good chunk of 3½-in. square ash about 4 in. long. Predrill the shaft hole before the hub is turned. Drive a dowel through the shaft hole, trim the dowel flush with the block, and pin the hub to the dowel at one end to prevent the hub from slipping. Mount the block on the lathe with the spindles dead center on the dowel, so the shaft hole is true with the hub. Turn the hub to a 3¼-in. diameter. Score the centerline of the hub for easier spoke-hole drilling later. Hub length depends on the spread of the legs and the thickness of wood to be used in the yet-to-be-constructed flywheel cradle: Knight's hub is 2¼ in. long. Turn the hub a little short in length so it won't rub the cradle. You can later add fiber or leather spacers to center the wheel in the cradle. Remember not to part the hub through to the shaft until all turning and sanding is completed.

Next, remove the hub, mark and drill the nine ½-in. spoke holes on the centerline. Again, make and use a drilling jig so the holes will be at the correct angle and the same depth. Turn the nine spokes using 1¼-in. ash. Allow a little extra length on the outboard end to be trimmed later. Knight left the last couple of inches of the outboard end of the spokes square. This puts more weight on the rim of the wheel and leaves more wood for the dowel joint. Drill the outboard end of each spoke to accept a ⅜-in. dowel.

Finish-sand the hub and spokes, then glue the spokes in the hub carefully, maintaining a flat plane perpendicular to the hub. After the glue is dry, trim the spoke ends with the same band-saw table outrigger setup used to cut the rim. Pivot the hub at its shaft and rotate the spokes into the blade, trimming each one to length. Be careful not to cut the spokes short. If everything goes right, the spokes should be trimmed to length with their ends rounded to match the inside curvature of the rim.

Before final assembly, finish-sand the rim, especially the inside circumference where the installed spokes will frustrate further sanding. The last step is to drive home a ⅜-in. dowel through the rim into each spoke end. Taper the dowel ends, cut a *V*-groove and apply glue to the dowel (not the hole). Trim the dowels flush with the rim. The result of all this careful cutting and drilling should be a round, true flywheel.

Knight successfully used a flat rim, but he suggests that a slightly crowned rim would help keep the drive belt centered. Crowning could be done on the outboard end of a power lathe or with a router setup.

Shaft, crank and flywheel — The next step is fitting a shaft to the flywheel. The flywheel exerts a lot of torque on the shaft, and it is important to lock the shaft and hub into a solid unit. Knight used a ⁹⁄₁₆ drill-rod shaft keyed to the hub. This approach is difficult to duplicate without metal-working equipment, but there are alternatives. The most direct is the approach used by early builders—a square shaft (with rounded ends) fitted to a snug, square hole in the hub. A wedge driven into the hub contacting a flat spot on the shaft is another possibility. Or make a flanged shaft, as spinning-wheel maker Bud Kronenberg suggests: Drill four holes for brads in a washer, then weld the washer to the steel-rod axle. Brad the washer to the hub. These methods make it possible to take the wheel apart later if necessary.

On the outboard side, the shaft should extend slightly more than the thickness of the support cradle. On the inboard side the shaft should extend beyond the cradle so the crank arm can be attached. If the crank is to be bent right from the shaft (as suggested by Knight) an extra 4 in. or 5 in. of shaft extension is needed.

Knight made a separate crank arm from aluminum, keyed it to the inboard shaft end and locked it in place with a set screw. As an alternative, he suggests bending the crank directly from the shaft material. This is direct, requires no metal-working tools and is as effective, if not as elegant. Knight's crank arm is about 2½ in. from the center of the shaft to the center of the pitman keeper.

The wooden pitman transfers power from the treadle to the crank. The pitman is fitted to the crank by a keyhole slot and is tied to the treadle with a leather thong. You'll have to experiment a bit to find the right pitman length and tie point on the

Shaft, crank and pitman assembly connect to hub through flywheel support cradle.

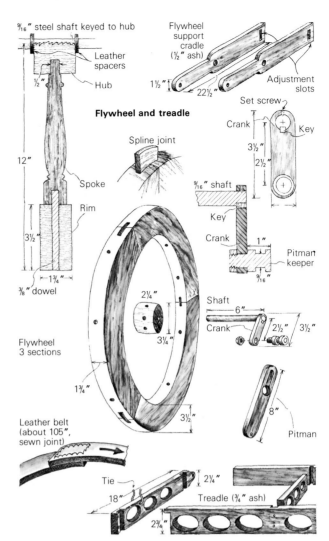

Flywheel and treadle

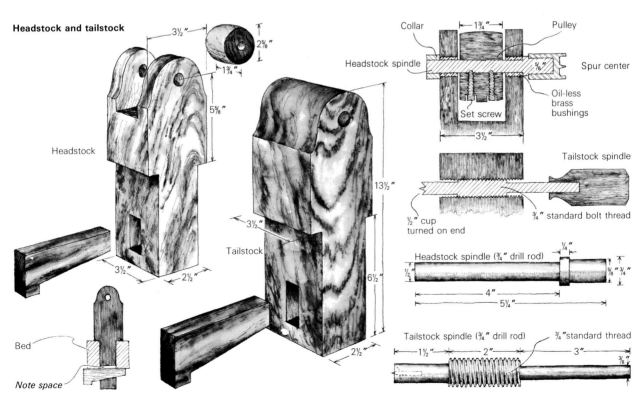

Headstock and tailstock

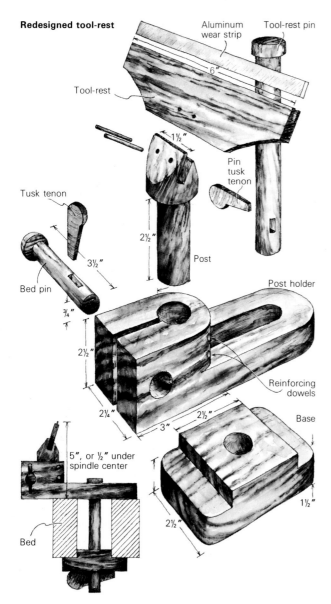

Redesigned tool-rest

Aluminum wear strip

Tool-rest pin

Tool-rest

6"

1½"

Pin tusk tenon

Tusk tenon

2½"

Post

3½"

Bed pin

Post holder

¾"

2½"

Reinforcing dowels

2¼"

2½"

3"

Base

5", or ½" under spindle center

2½"

1½"

Bed

treadle side—both of these can be varied to give the treadle different actions. As the tie point is moved to the back, the treadle throw increases. Knight used an 8-in. pitman tied about a third of the way back from the treadle's front edge. Combined with a 2½-in. crank, this gives about a 6-in. throw to the front of the treadle. To position the pitman, Knight turned and threaded an aluminum keeper that screws to the crank. The middle ⅜ in. of the button was turned to a smaller diameter. If a bent crank is used, machine or grind the pitman keeper groove near the shaft end before the crank is bent. Grinding could be done by rotating the shaft against a cut-off wheel mounted in a table saw. A simple jig should be constructed so the grind will be consistent.

Knight first tried a "floating" flywheel cradle pivoted on wooden pins at the front and left free at the rear. He found it difficult to get the necessary stiffness in the U-shaped cradle: His solution was to cut slots in the cradle arms where they cross the back legs. He installed screws through the slots into the legs to allow adjustment of the cradle sides for proper belt tension and flywheel axis alignment.

The treadle is simply a box frame pivoted on wooden pins

set into the legs at the rear. The treadle should fit comfortably between the legs, with the front edge just inside the legs at the front. Knight used a template-guided router to cut elliptical holes in the treadle frame. Although the holes aren't necessary, they reduce weight and add a nice design touch.

Headstock and tailstock — The headstock and tailstock (diagram on previous page), or puppets (as they were called on early lathes), are bandsawn from solid 3½-in. square stock. The bottom of each is cut thinner (to 2½ in.) so that the lower parts fit snugly between the ways. Cut a tapered mortise in the bottom of each puppet so that a wedge can be driven in, locking the unit in position. The wedge should exert equal pressure on both front and back bed ways and should extend slightly at the back so it can be loosened easily.

Knight machined the headstock spindle from drill rod. Dimensions are given in the drawings. The inboard end was turned to ⅝ in. to accept an inexpensive spur center available through the Sears tool catalog. The original lathe used oil-less brass bushings for the spindle bearings. These were later replaced by small ball bearings let into the headstock and capped by wood. Knight feels the slight reduction in friction (because of the ball bearings) makes a difference.

Drill the headstock for the bushings or bearings and cut the notch on the headstock top for the spindle pulley. Select a turning block for the pulley and predrill the pulley shaft hole (as before in the wheel hub). Turn the pulley with a crowned rim profile. Install the shaft in the headstock through the pulley. Lock the pulley to the shaft with long hex-head set screws threaded through the pulley and mated with drill-point dimples in the shaft. To save set-up time at craft shows, Knight uses a threaded headstock spindle and predrilled turning blanks that screw right on the spindle, eliminating use of the tailstock.

Knight machined the tailstock spindle from drill rod. To adjust the spindle, he threaded the middle portion of the rod and tapped the wooden spindle hole with a standard metal tap. Metal taps don't cut particularly clean threads in wood but this seems to have worked well. Knight turned the cup center right on the inboard end of the spindle, but an inexpensive cup center is available from Sears. He fitted a wood handle to the other end. For those lacking access to a metal lathe, a large bolt or lag bolt could be effectively adapted for use as a tailstock spindle. The power drive is provided by a 1¾-in. wide leather (latigo) belt stitched together at its ends. The belt on Knight's lathe is about 105 in. long.

The tool-rest requires some nifty engineering. It must move from side to side on the bed, in and out, and ideally, up and down for different cutting angles. Knight's original tool-rest is excellent in most respects, but he is not satisfied because of two small design flaws: The rest is set vertically (it should have been canted slightly toward the work) and the height is not adjustable. The drawings show a slightly redesigned tool-rest that eliminates these drawbacks.

Knight used a router with a ⅜-in. rounding-over bit to shape the legs and outside bed way edges. Since the lathe is a throw-it-in-the-trunk tool, he kept the finish-sanding to a minimum. He used a synthetic oil finish (Minwax) with a light stain base to seal the wood and bring out the grain. □

Jim Richey, of Katy, Texas, is Methods of Work editor for Fine Woodworking *magazine.*

Freewheel Lathe Drive
Bicycle parts convert muscle power

by Richard Starr

Photos: Richard Starr

A foot-powered lathe must somehow convert the downward motion of the turner's foot to rotary motion of the workpiece. The crank and flywheel (pages 94 to 98) have been used for this at least since Leonardo's time. The problem with this system is that power transmission is not linear. The treadle turns the flywheel farther in midstroke than it does at the top and bottom of the stroke—as the treadle descends, it becomes easier and then more difficult to push. Thus, the system can accept a strong power impulse only in midstroke, while our legs can efficiently apply a heavy, constant push throughout the motion of the treadle.

A freewheel lathe drive can more efficiently harness muscle energy since it can use all the power we can supply during the treadle stroke. It can be built from bicycle parts and inexpensive hardware. Two lathes based on this drive system have been in use for several years in our shop at the Richmond Middle School, Hanover, N.H. (the children use no power tools); the lathes have proven sturdy and reliable in a very demanding situation. Freewheel lathe drive has other advantages over the crank and flywheel. The lathe starts in the right direction as soon as the treadle is pressed, with no need to nudge the flywheel into motion by hand. The turner is free to stop pumping without fear of being thrown over backwards by a treadle that keeps moving while the lathe coasts. It is easy to learn to use, because the turner needn't develop the rhythmic pumping skill required by the crank and flywheel. Most important, the freewheel lathe is simpler and easier to build than other continuously rotating foot-powered lathes.

The freewheel lathe is a direct descendant of the springpole lathe. On these ancient lathes, the treadle is attached by a rope or thong to a flexible pole or bow hung from the ceiling of the shop. The midsection of the rope is wrapped several times around the turning stock, which is set between dead centers on the lathe. As the treadle is pressed, the work spins toward the turner; when it is released, the bent pole tugs the treadle upwards, spinning the work backwards. Turning on such a lathe is a series of interrupted cuts.

The freewheel system substitutes a bicycle chain for the rope and a long spring for the pole or bow. The idea came from Berny Butcher, of Alstead, N.H., who converted a springpole lathe to continuous rotation by adding a ratchet mechanism. I replaced his clever homemade ratchet with an ordinary bicycle sprocket commonly known as a freewheel, mounted on a shaft. The chain runs on this sprocket. As the treadle is depressed, the chain rotates the sprocket and shaft toward the turner. But as the spring pulls the treadle and chain back to the starting point, the ratchet in the freewheel disengages, allowing the shaft to continue turning in the same direction. A flywheel on the shaft keeps the work mov-

Richard Starr, of Thetford Center, Vt., is a teacher and the author of Woodworking with Kids *(The Taunton Press).*

Seventh-grader Mike Kelly turns a bongo-board roller on freewheel lathe. The lathe, which is about 5 ft. long and can swing 12 in., is the second Starr has built. He says, 'The first was kind of crude, but it allowed me to work most of the bugs out of the drive mechanism. The newer one is solid and easy to use but not a thing of beauty. I consider it a prototype subject to modification and improvement. If I were to build a third lathe, I would retain the same basic structure but I would make it much heavier and more rigid than this one.'

ing between power strokes. The bicycle freewheel is a rugged, though inexpensive, piece of 20th-century machinery. I found I needed one with the smallest high gear available: 13 teeth. Five-speed clusters with this sprocket are available at good bike shops and can be equipped with low gears of 21, 24 or more teeth. The larger sprockets offer lower lathe speeds and a higher mechanical advantage, useful for large work and for powering a drill bit in the lathe.

The freewheel is fixed to a ⅝-in. threaded shaft by locking a couple of nuts against it from either side. The shaft rides in ball bearings, which are set into wooden puppets and held in place by nuts pressing outwards against them. The threaded shaft is slightly undersized for standard ⅝-in. I.D. ball bearings and must be fitted with shims to make up the difference.

The speed of the lathe is affected by the size of the sprocket and by the point at which the chain is joined to the treadle. Mounting the chain farther from the treadle pivot magnifies the motion of the foot—the longer the extension, the faster the lathe will run for a given pumping speed. On our more recent lathe the chain is fixed 23 in. from the pivot, while the front edge of the footrest is 15 in. from the pivot. With the chain on the 13-tooth sprocket the lathe makes about 450 revolutions per minute at a relaxed pumping speed. It can be pushed to about 600 rpm by rapid treadling. Extremely low speeds are easy to maintain.

The treadle must be lightweight because part of the turner's effort is used to tension the spring for returning the treadle to its upper position. To keep lifted weight to a minimum, I used a ½-in. cherry plank for a footrest, mortised into

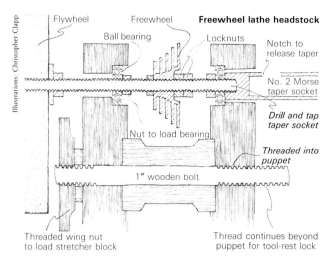

Freewheel lathe headstock

Flywheel · Freewheel · Ball bearing · Locknuts · Notch to release taper · No. 2 Morse taper socket · Drill and tap taper socket · Nut to load bearing · Threaded into puppet · 1" wooden bolt · Threaded wing nut to load stretcher block · Thread continues beyond puppet for tool-rest lock

Illustrations: Christopher Clapp

Freewheel lathe headstock. The socket accepts standard No. 2 Morse taper centers and chucks. Below the spindle shaft is a stretcher that locks the headstock puppets tightly together. The stretcher is mortised into both puppets, which are pulled against it by a wooden bolt passing through the center of the stretcher. The bolt is threaded into the right-hand puppet and is tensioned by a wing nut located between the flywheel and the left-hand puppet. The compression on the stretcher resists the outward pressure of the loaded bearings on the puppets. The right end of the wooden bolt extends beyond the right-hand puppet and serves as a threaded stud for the tool-rest extension lock.

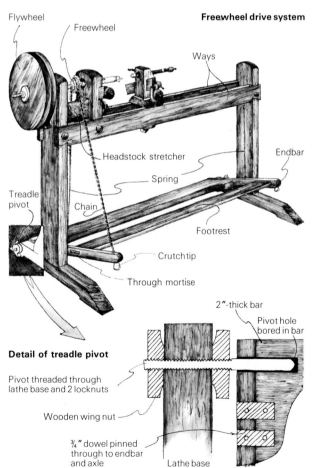

Freewheel drive system

Flywheel · Freewheel · Ways · Headstock stretcher · Endbar · Spring · Treadle pivot · Chain · Footrest · Crutch tip · Through mortise

Detail of treadle pivot

Pivot threaded through lathe base and 2 locknuts · Wooden wing nut · ¾" dowel pinned through to endbar and axle · 2"-thick bar · Pivot hole bored in bar · Lathe base

¾-in. endbars. The endbars are locked together by a heavy 2-in. square axle that adds no lifted weight because it is located along the axis of the pivot. The treadle is returned by the drive-system spring and by a second spring on the right end of the lathe. Without the helper spring, all the work of lifting the treadle would be transmitted through the drive chain, straining the lathe shaft and bearings and resulting in a sluggish return. My springs resemble those sold as screen-door closers but are limper. They are about 18 in. long and ¾ in. in diameter, from the local hardware store. The impact of the treadle hitting the floor is softened by mounting rubber crutch tips on wooden studs under the endbars.

Because the flywheel on a freewheel lathe runs at full spindle speed, it can be much smaller than one on a crank-and-flywheel lathe, but due to its speed it must be well balanced or the lathe will shake. I've found that wooden discs are seldom uniform in density and make poorly balanced flywheels. I solved the problem by cutting two discs from the same knot-free board and rotating them 180° to each other on the shaft, i.e., 12 o'clock to 6 o'clock. Discs cut from the same board tend to have similar distribution of density (if knot-free) and the opposed orientation cancels out most of the imbalance. The flywheel on our new lathe is 11 in. in diameter and almost 4 in. thick. Our older lathe runs with a 17-in. diameter wheel that is about 1½ in. thick and stores up more momentum. A much bigger flywheel, possibly a bicycle wheel, would not strain the mechanism and would make it easier to maintain high speeds and a longer coasting time. But I prefer lighter flywheels because they accumulate less power, making them safer for kids to use.

The headstock socket is made from a No. 2 Morse taper extension (available from hardware specialty houses), with the male end sawn off. The end is drilled and tapped to screw to the end of the shaft of the lathe. If the socket does not run true, the high point is marked and whacked with a wooden mallet until centered. Though the business end of the spur center in this socket extends more than 5 in. from its bearing, the structure is rigid and stays true.

Threaded wood fittings hold the lathe together and make all the tailstock and tool-rest adjustments. (I use a handmade tap and screwbox to make large-diameter fittings.) The tailstock quill is a hornbeam screw drilled to accept a center made from a threaded rod. With the metal center removed, a hollow conical fixture can be screwed on for boring lamps and musical instruments. A ½-in. shell auger will pass through the bore of the quill.

The drawback of freewheel drive is that it's a little noisy. While the treadle is coming up the ball bearings in the freewheel clatter and the ratchet pawls click. I found that the noise was reduced considerably by packing the bearing races with axle grease.

One could think of other applications for this efficient foot-powered drive system. It could be adapted to grinders, sanders, jigsaws and band saws. Woodworkers who prefer to rely on their own muscle power rather than on the electric company might put it to good use. □

AUTHOR'S NOTE: A "chain and freewheel" lathe was manufactured in Norfolk, England, in 1922 by Hobbies, Inc. There is a reference to their instruction book in *A Bibliography of the Art of Turning*, published by the Society of Ornamental Turners, 2 Parry Dr., Rustington, Littlehampton, Sussex, England BN16 2QY. It goes to show that good and simple ideas are seldom really new.

A Shop-Made Bowl Lathe
You can add ways for spindle turning

by Donald C. Bjorkman

After building my disc sander (see pages 42 to 43) and getting so much use out of it, I decided to build a lathe I've wanted for a long time but have been unable to afford. As most of my turnings are bowls and I do not have room in my shop to keep a full lathe, I designed a large bowl lathe that can be expanded into a bed lathe. It has a 17-in. swing inboard, a 74-in. swing outboard and a 48-in. span between centers. As with the disc sander, the motor is positioned low, contributing to the stability of the machine, and it is enclosed in a cabinet to protect it from shavings and dust. A door allows access for easy speed changes, and the cabinet can be used to store tools or hold sandbags for ballast. The motor platform slides back and forth on the shaft that supports it, so that by using two four-step pulleys, 16 speeds are possible. For this system to work, the machine must be level, or the motor will creep on the support shaft. With the size pulleys

chosen, the speeds range from approximately 500 RPM to 2,300 RPM. Although I have turned a piece containing 50 bd. ft. on a pattern lathe, I doubt that I will ever gamble with a 74-in. dia. item, as the outer edge at 500 RPM will be traveling at almost 10,000 FPM. Maybe I'll work up to it.

The frame is hard maple; all the joints are open mortise and tenon. The stress panels are ⅜-in. Baltic birch plywood; the shaft and pulley cover is vacuum-formed plywood. (My vacuum press is a tough sheet-vinyl bag attached to a frame clamped to a platform; a converted shop compressor provides vacuum.) The stress panels are glued into rabbets in the frame, except the front panel, which is screwed in place to allow complete access to the interior. The floor of the machine can also be removed so the corner braces can be bolted to the floor.

The sloping sides and perpendicular base of the machine require that the slot mortises in the base be cut on an angle. I

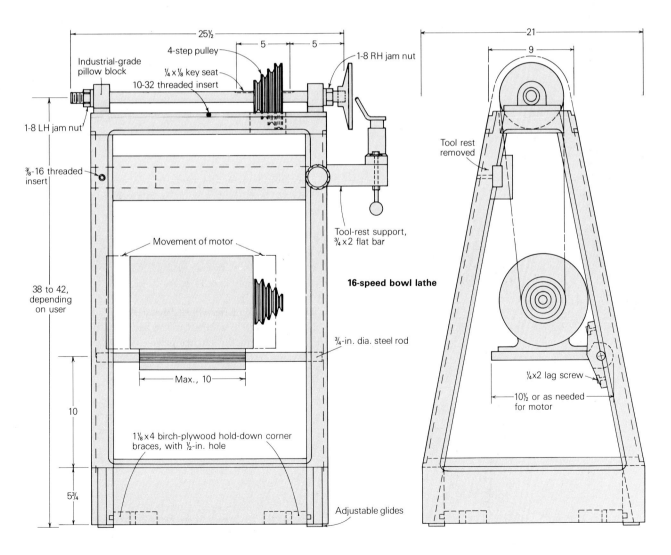

16-speed bowl lathe

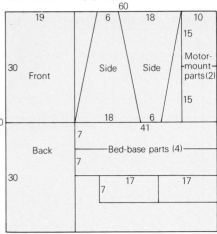

Layout of parts from sheet of ⅜-in. Baltic birch plywood

```
                    60
   19          6        18        10
                                      15
30                                  Motor-
   Front     Side     Side         mount
                                   parts(2)
                                      15
               18        6
          7          41
60
   Back           Bed-base parts (4)
          7
30             17        17
          7
```

Parts for tailstock base not included

Bjorkman's 16-speed bowl lathe.

Materials List

Quantity	Purchased parts	Approx. cost (Fall, 1980)
	Lumberyard	
17 bd. ft.	8/4 maple, 5 in. by 20 ft.	$ 35.00
1 sheet	⅜-in. by 60-in. by 60-in. Baltic birch plywood	28.00
	Machinery supplier	
1	Motor-shaft pulley, 1¾-in., 2⅝-in., 3⅜-in., 4-in. dia.	9.50
1	1-in. shaft pulley, 3-in., 4-in., 5-in., 6-in. dia.	16.00
2	Medium-duty self-aligning pillow blocks	45.50
4	Heavy-duty adjustable nut glides	4.00
1	Motor switch	9.00
1	2¼-in. locking knob	1.50
	Tool rest and faceplates as needed	
	Steel supplier	
25½ in.	1-in. dia. cold-rolled rod	2.50
20½ in.	¾-in. dia. hot-rolled rod	1.00
2	¾-in. by 2-in. hot-rolled flat bar, 8 in. & 24 in.	4.00
4 in.	Tubing sized to tool rest	.50
1	1-8 RH jam nut	1.00
1	1-8 LH jam nut	1.50
	Welding of tool rest	5.00
	Machining of shaft	15.00
	Hardware store	
2	10-32 threaded inserts	
2	⅜-16 threaded inserts	
8 ft.	14/3 SJ electric cord	
1	220 V electric plug	
1	⁵⁄₁₆-18 by 4-in. hex bolt	
1	⅜-16 by 6-in. hex bolt	
4	⁵⁄₁₆-18 by 1¼-in. hex bolts	
4	⁵⁄₁₆-in. hex nuts	
4	⁵⁄₁₆-in. lock washers	
8	⁵⁄₁₆-in. flat washers	
4	¼-in. by 2-in. lag screws	
1	⅜-16 by 3½-in. hex bolt	
4	½-13 by 3-in. hex bolt for pillow blocks	
4	½-13 hex nut	
4	½-in. flat washers	
3	Ball-shaped wooden drawer pulls	
1	1¹⁄₁₆-in. by 24-in. continuous hinge	
1	¼-in. by ¼-in. by 2-in. key for pulley	
1	½-in. by 50-in. V-belt	
2	10-32 by ¾-in. knurled finger bolts	
6	1¼ x 8 FH wood screws (Phillips)	
18	¾ x 6 FH wood screws (Phillips)	
1	Cabinet door catch	
	Total, miscellaneous hardware	24.50
	Total cost	$203.50

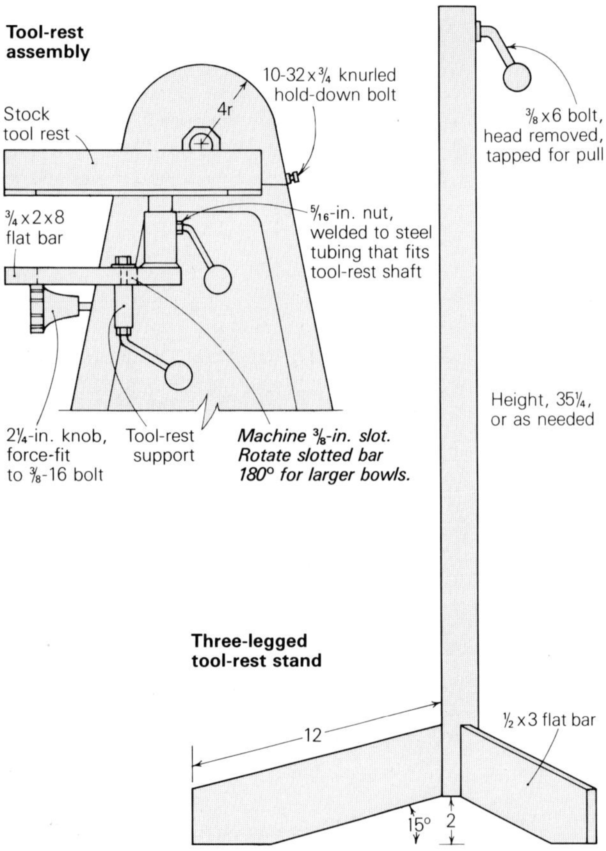

Tool-rest assembly

Stock tool rest
10-32 x ¾ knurled hold-down bolt
4r
¾ x 2 x 8 flat bar
⁵⁄₁₆-in. nut, welded to steel tubing that fits tool-rest shaft
2¼-in. knob, force-fit to ⅜-16 bolt
Tool-rest support
Machine ⅜-in. slot. Rotate slotted bar 180° for larger bowls.

⅜ x 6 bolt, head removed, tapped for pull

Height, 35¼, or as needed

Three-legged tool-rest stand

12
½ x 3 flat bar
15° 2

From *Fine Woodworking* magazine (November 1981) 31:78-80

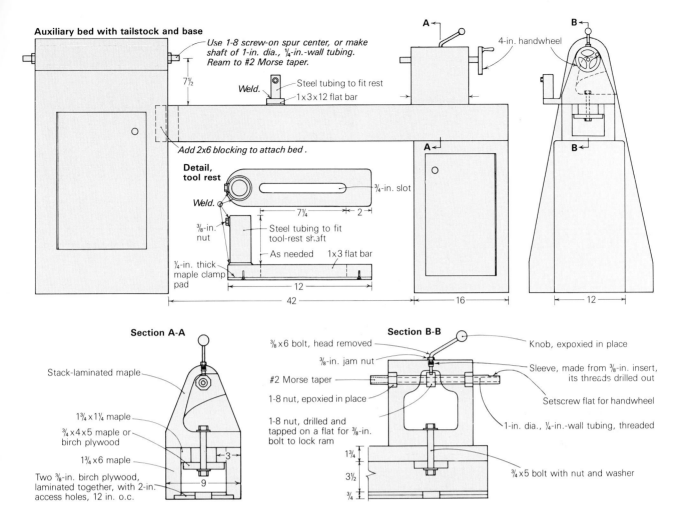

Auxiliary bed with tailstock and base

Use 1-8 screw-on spur center, or make shaft of 1-in. dia., ¼-in.-wall tubing. Ream to #2 Morse taper.

7½

Weld.

Steel tubing to fit rest

1 x 3 x 12 flat bar

Add 2x6 blocking to attach bed .

Detail, tool rest

Weld.

⅜-in. nut

¾-in. slot

7¼   2

Steel tubing to fit tool-rest shaft

As needed   1x3 flat bar

¼-in. thick maple clamp pad

12

42

16

12

4-in. handwheel

A   A

B   B

Section A-A

Stack-laminated maple

1¾ x 1¼ maple

¾ x 4 x 5 maple or birch plywood

1¾ x 6 maple

3

9

Two ⅜-in. birch plywood, laminated together, with 2-in. access holes, 12 in. o.c.

Section B-B

⅜ x 6 bolt, head removed

⅜-in. jam nut

#2 Morse taper

1-8 nut, epoxied in place

1-8 nut, drilled and tapped on a flat for ⅜-in. bolt to lock ram

1¾

3½

¾

Knob, expoxied in place

Sleeve, made from ⅜-in. insert, its threads drilled out

Setscrew flat for handwheel

1-in. dia., ¼-in.-wall tubing, threaded

¾ x 5 bolt with nut and washer

used the table saw and a simple tapered jig. When the frame is fully assembled, a ⅜-in. rabbeting bit and router cut the rabbets for the plywood panels to fit into.

The guide through which the tool-rest support slides consists of two 1½-in. by 4-in. pieces of maple that span the uprights of the frame. To form the ¾-in. by 2-in. channel in the guide, I grooved each piece and glued them together. To align the groove I wrapped the steel bar in wax paper and positioned it in the groove during glue-up. Then I cut the angle on the guide's face to match the slope of the sides of the machine. A 2¼-in. knob on a ⅜-in. bolt through a threaded insert in the machine frame locks the sliding section of the tool-rest support in place. The pivoting section of the support consists of an 8-in. length of flat bar steel welded to a 4-in. length of steel tubing. A ⅜-in. slot is machined in the flat bar for the ⅜-in. hold-down bolt to slide in.

You can make ways for spindle turning on this lathe from two pieces of 1¾-in. by 6-in. maple, 58 in. or however long you desire. Laminate a 1¾-in. by 1¼-in. piece of maple along the length of the top edge of each way to create the lip that the tailstock and tool rest clamp to. Reinforce the bed along its lower side with a double thickness of ⅜-in. birch plywood, rabbeted into the inside edge of each way. As you will not have plywood pieces long enough to extend the length of the ways, stagger the joints for strength. Drill 2-in. holes on 12-in. centers along the length of this plywood for access to the hold-down bolts on the tailstock and tool-rest support. By epoxying and/or flush-screwing a thin piece of maple to the bottom surface of the tool rest, you can prevent a metal-to-

wood sliding contact, thus forestalling damage to the wooden ways. Secure the tail end of the bed to the tailstock pedestal by bolting through the plywood along the bottom of the bed. The tailstock itself is stack-laminated maple. When the 1-8 nuts that hold the ram are epoxied into the tailstock, be sure to have the ram screwed in place so that the nuts are indexed to each other. The same is true when drilling the hole into the flat of the nut that locks the ram. With the tailstock in place bolt the ways to the headstock through two maple attaching blocks, one between the ways, the other between the frames under the spindle. It is important that both the longitudinal and horizontal planes of the bed are parallel to the centerline of the spindle; if not, you could end up with tapered turnings. Sight through the headstock spindle and move the tailstock until it is aligned. Shim where the headstock attaches to the bed as needed. You can also adjust the mounting of the pillow blocks.

The dimensions given are for my lathe and may be modified, but if the machine is built much larger, one piece of plywood will not be enough for all the stress panels. Also note that the spindle size and tool-rest holder were chosen to accept manufacturer's stock units. When buying steel, consider purchasing enough to build an outboard tool-rest stand. The materials list includes parts for the bowl lathe only. As motor prices vary considerably, I have not figured the price of one in the costs, but a ¾-HP to 1-HP motor is recommended.   □

Donald Bjorkman is professor of interior design at Northern Arizona University in Flagstaff.

Index

Fine WoodWorking

To subscribe

If you enjoyed this book, you'll enjoy *Fine Woodworking* magazine.
Use this card to subscribe.

1 year (6 issues) for just $18—$4.50 off the newsstand price.

Outside the U.S. $21/year (U.S. funds, please)

Name _____

Address _____

City _____ State _____ Zip _____

☐ My payment is enclosed. ☐ Please bill me.

☐ Please send me more information about Taunton Press Books.

☐ Please send me information about *Fine Woodworking* videotapes.

FPCT

Fine WoodWorking

To subscribe

If you enjoyed this book, you'll enjoy *Fine Woodworking* magazine.
Use this card to subscribe.

1 year (6 issues) for just $18—$4.50 off the newsstand price.

Outside the U.S. $21/year (U.S. funds, please)

Name _____

Address _____

City _____ State _____ Zip _____

☐ My payment is enclosed. ☐ Please bill me.

☐ Please send me more information about Taunton Press Books.

☐ Please send me information about *Fine Woodworking* videotapes.

NO POSTAGE
NECESSARY
IF MAILED
IN THE
UNITED STATES

BUSINESS REPLY CARD
FIRST CLASS PERMIT No. 19 NEWTOWN, CT

POSTAGE WILL BE PAID BY ADDRESSEE

The Taunton Press

63 South Main Street
Box 355
Newtown, CT 06470

NO POSTAGE
NECESSARY
IF MAILED
IN THE
UNITED STATES

BUSINESS REPLY CARD
FIRST CLASS PERMIT No. 19 NEWTOWN, CT

POSTAGE WILL BE PAID BY ADDRESSEE

The Taunton Press

63 South Main Street
Box 355
Newtown, CT 06470

M L

3/24/87